The Wed-Locked Agunot

# The Wed-Locked Agunot
*Orthodox Jewish Women
Chained to Dead Marriages*

SUSAN ARANOFF *and*
RIVKA HAUT

McFarland & Company, Inc., Publishers
*Jefferson, North Carolina*

LIBRARY OF CONGRESS CATALOGUING-IN-PUBLICATION DATA

Aranoff, Susan B., author.
 The wed-locked agunot : Orthodox Jewish women chained to dead marriages / Susan Aranoff and Rivka Haut.
   p.    cm.
 Includes bibliographical references and index.

 **ISBN 978-0-7864-7967-2** (softcover : acid free paper) ∞
 **ISBN 978-1-4766-2031-2** (ebook)

 1. Agunahs.  2. Jewish women—Legal status, laws, etc.—United States.  3. Divorce—Law and legislation—United States.  4. Divorce (Jewish law)  I. Haut, Rivka, 1942–2014, author.  II. Title.
 KBM550.5.A73  2015
 296.4'444—dc23                                    2015013133

BRITISH LIBRARY CATALOGUING DATA ARE AVAILABLE

© 2015 Susan Aranoff and Rivka Haut. All rights reserved

*No part of this book may be reproduced or transmitted in any form or by any means, electronic or mechanical, including photocopying or recording, or by any information storage and retrieval system, without permission in writing from the publisher.*

Front cover images © 2015 iStock/Thinkstock

Printed in the United States of America

*McFarland & Company, Inc., Publishers*
 *Box 611, Jefferson, North Carolina 28640*
  *www.mcfarlandpub.com*

תפארת בנים אבותם
To my Parents
Max and Lila Bernstein
Who taught me by word and deed
to love the Jewish people and Judaism,
to act with kindness and to pursue justice.

עטרת זקנים בני בנים
And to my children
Rachel, Yaffa, Deena, Tsvi, Aryea and Miriam
May they follow in their grandparents' footsteps.
—Susan Aranoff

*In Memoriam*

It is with love and sadness that we write this dedication on behalf of our mother, Rivka Haut, z"l, co-author of this book. This book is a culmination of a lifetime of work that our mother performed on behalf of *agunot*. While she did not live to see it through to publication, it gives her voice and her spirit a way to live on.

Our mother, though, would undoubtedly say that this book needs to give voice to the *agunot* most of all. It is for them that she worked tirelessly, with an unwavering focus, for as long as we can remember. Many a childhood dinner was interrupted by a woman calling in distress; our mother would speak with the woman immediately. She never asked anybody to wait, she never took a penny in payment for her time. Our mother had other passions and other projects, but she always came back to the need to end, as she would put it, *agunah* agony.

She tackled the issue on both a global and an individual scale. First and foremost, she believed that a *halachic* solution was necessary, feasible and within reach, and she tirelessly advocated for change on a rabbinic level. Simultaneously she worked with individual *agunot*, making calls to rabbis and community leaders, organizing demonstrations, accompanying them to the *beit din*. As a prominent *beit din* Rabbi commented to us after her passing, they weren't necessarily "happy" to see her but they always respected her. Through her tireless efforts towards these goals, we believe she truly changed the culture of the Orthodox Jewish world.

It feels incomplete to talk about our mother without also talking of our father, Rabbi Yitzchak Haut, z"l. Our father devoted himself to the cause of *agunot* with the same fervor that our mother did. He was co-author of one of the original prenuptial agreements, he worked with many women to provide legal advice, and he wrote a book called *Divorce in Jewish Law and Life*. We remember being alarmed when our parents returned from a demonstration against a recalcitrant husband, and told us that our father had been accosted and knocked to the ground!

Our parents were partners in fighting for the *agunah* cause with body, mind and soul. They both had an amazingly deep love and commitment to Torah, and this love is what drove them to seek change for *agunot*. They absolutely could not abide *halachah* being twisted in a way that hurt families. They had a complete faith that a solution could be found within Orthodoxy to right this wrong.

We pray that this book can be one more step towards that solution. The work of raising awareness was started by our parents and Susan Aranoff long ago. Now we need those of vision and courage to take this further into the next generation. Our mother believed in a world where her beloved children and grandchildren would be proud to live and practice as spiritual and *halachic* Jews. It is up to us to make that vision real.

—Sheryl Haut and Tamara Weissman

# Table of Contents

*Acknowledgments*   ix
*Preface*   1
*Prologue*   5
*Introduction*   9

1. The Founding of Agunah Inc.   17
2. Our Initiation   21
3. We Take to the Streets   28
4. Surveying *Batei Din*   39
5. The Phantom *Ketubah*   52
6. Extortion: Every Man Has His Price   70
7. When the Recalcitrant Is a Rabbi   79
8. Two Thanksgivings in Parsippany   93
9. Violence and Sexual Abuse   107
10. Conferences   120
11. Child Brides   131
12. The *Beit Din* That Couldn't   145
13. A Success Story   156

| | |
|---|---|
| 14. Civil Remedies: The New York State Gett Laws, or, Less Than Meets the Eye | 161 |
| 15. Prenuptial Agreements | 172 |
| 16. The Rackman *Beit Din*: A Watershed | 194 |
| *Conclusion* | 218 |
| *Glossary* | 225 |
| *Pseudonyms* | 232 |
| *Bibliography* | 233 |
| *Index* | 235 |

# Acknowledgments

First and foremost I wish to acknowledge the impact that my *agunah* advocacy had on my children during my decades long involvement with this issue. Looking back, I cannot begin to calculate the hours that this work took away from time spent with them. Sadly, it also exposed them to a very dark and disturbing aspect of Orthodox Jewish life. For all the time stolen and the troubling things they heard and saw, I apologize.

I lament the loss of the late Rivka Haut, my co-author, just before we entered the final stages of writing the book. Our shared hope was that this book would help bring about, at long last, justice and freedom for *agunot*. What the future holds is unknown, but as this book testifies, Rivka devoted every fiber of her being to this struggle. Only the countless *agunot* whom Rivka counseled have a true sense of her selfless dedication to their cause. May her family be consoled by this book as a memorial to her life's work. May her memory be a blessing.

Though I completed the book on my own, I continued throughout to write in both our names, using the first person plurals "we," "our," and "us." When Rivka passed away, there were chapters yet to be completed and chapters yet to be written. We never had a chance to write the Conclusion or edit the manuscript together. The responsibility, therefore, for any omissions or errors in this volume, falls squarely on my shoulders.

I wish also to acknowledge the dedication and precious camaraderie of the late Honey Rackman, another tireless worker for the cause of justice for *agunot*. Much of this book transpires before Honey and I began to work together so her representation in this volume conveys only a small sample of her unflagging efforts to free *agunot*. The same is true of my dear friend and Agunah International co-director Estelle Freilich, who has done more than her share of Agunah International's recent work. Thanks also to my co-director and dear friend Rachell Maidenbaum Gober for her support in the battle to free *agunot*. The contribution of Dr. Elona Lazaroff, a friend and colleague, who was part of the Agunah International team for several years, should also be acknowledged.

    I owe thanks to several people who read all or part of the manuscript of this book and offered comments and corrections. Most of all, I am greatly beholden to Nechi Sirota, who meticulously read and critiqued both the original and a revised version of the manuscript of this volume. Her astute questions and insights led to invaluable improvements throughout the book. Dr. Susan Weiss, an outstanding attorney and *agunah* advocate, read several chapters of the manuscript. I was particularly fortunate to be able to draw on Dr. Weiss's expertise pertaining to prenuptial agreements and civil remedies. Thanks also to Dr. Phyllis Chesler and Dr. Sheryl Haut whose comments enhanced the book. None of these people, of course, should be implicated in any of the shortcomings and errors that may remain in this book.

—Susan Aranoff

# Preface

This book chronicles the plight of *agunot* (sing. *agunah*), Jewish women chained to dead marriages because their husbands refuse to give them a *gett* (pl. *gittin*), a Jewish divorce. This volume also records our thirty years as advocates for justice and freedom for these women. We begin with the story of how we first became aware of the neglected suffering of *agunot* and decided to set up Agunah Inc., an organization whose mission was to advocate for the rights of *agunot* and their children. Subsequent chapters comprise case studies through which the reader learns about the emotional and spiritual trauma and unconscionable choices that confront *agunot* when they turn to rabbis and rabbinic courts for help. These case studies also recount our role in assisting these women in their attempt to escape their intolerable marriages. The cases illustrate the *agunah* abuses we encountered repeatedly in the rabbinic court system: financial extortion, pressure to drop charges of domestic violence or to agree to custody and visitation rights for unfit fathers, procedural irregularities such as a rabbinic court issuing an invalid divorce document or a rabbinic judge adjudicating a case despite close ties to one of the litigants. As these stories unfold, we also describe the slurs and threats that were directed at us because we challenged this system. Finally, this book includes chapters that recount efforts to provide remedies for the *agunah* problem through civil legislation, prenuptial agreements and the establishment of a new, bold rabbinic court dedicated to solving the *agunah* problem.

We have counseled approximately two thousand women from all over the world, the United States, Israel, Europe and Latin America, but this book deals only with American *agunot*, who constitute the vast majority of our caseload. In 2013, Dr. Susan Weiss published *Marriage and Divorce in the Jewish State: Israel's Civil War,* an excellent book dealing with the *agunah* scene in

Israel, the country with the world's largest Jewish population. There are numerous newspaper and periodical articles covering the situation in other countries.

While this book contains a good deal of material explaining the *halakhot* (Jewish laws, sing. *halakhah*) dealing with marriage and divorce, it is far from a full analysis of this vast body of law. For a more comprehensive presentation of these laws the reader can turn to the following books: *Divorce in Jewish Law and Life* (1983) by Irwin Haut, *Women and Jewish Divorce* (1989) by Shlomo Riskin, *The Tears of the Oppressed* (2004) by Aviad Hacohen, *Agunah: The Manchester Analysis* (2011) by Bernard Jackson and *Za'akat Dalot* (2006) by Monique Susskind Goldberg and Diana Villa. These five books are just a sampling of the numerous books and articles written on the *halakhot* concerning Jewish marriage and divorce. *Za'akat Dalot* is in Hebrew but has a useful English summary of the contents of the book. The bibliographies of these books will provide the reader with a myriad of additional sources to pursue both in English and Hebrew.

What is unique to this book is our extensive day-to-day experience with and intimate knowledge of the deeply flawed rabbinic court system and its impact on *agunot* and their families. This knowledge has enabled us to present, not an academic, theoretical analysis of Jewish jurisprudence, but rather the real life stories of how this ancient legal tradition impacts the lives of women and children in a 21st century Western democracy. It is the story of how a subculture in the United States, the Orthodox Jewish community, persists in complying with its own legal system though its laws deny women and children rights that are theirs under the civil legal system.

To assist the reader, we have included a glossary of Hebrew and Yiddish words and Jewish communal institutions and media. We did not follow any strict scholarly rules for spelling these words. Our aim was to choose a spelling that made it easiest for those unfamiliar with these languages to correctly sound out the words.

In most of the chapters, we have used pseudonyms, including for rabbis. Some background details about the cases in this book have been modified or omitted so that the identities of individuals are protected. The cases we present are representative of scores of others in our files with similar story lines. We regret having to use pseudonyms for rabbis, for naming them would hold them accountable as individuals for their conduct. We have provided an alphabetical list of the pseudonyms at the end of the book. Any name that does not appear on that list is a real name. Specifically, in some chapters (Rubin, Chapter 6; Zitrenbaum, Chapter 9; Goldstein and Shereshevsky, Chapter 11; Light, Chapter 16) we felt at liberty to use the real names of those involved because the information in those chapters had been reported in the media and was widely known by the public. We also felt free to use the real names of rabbis whenever their names did not provide a clue to the identity of a specific case.

# Prologue

> "I (God) will go down and I will see whether they have acted according to ***her outcry*** that has come to Me"—Genesis 18:21
> Rashi ad loc. "...and our rabbis taught '*according to her outcry*' the cry of *one* woman whom they murdered in a cruel way."

According to the Babylonian Talmud in the Tractate Sanhedrin, page 109b, as well as the Midrashim, the anguished outcry of one persecuted woman in Sodom reached God's ears causing God to descend from the heavens to investigate. The citizens of Sodom, angry that one woman, contrary to the city's cruel public policy, had dared to distribute food to the poor, punished her by smearing her with honey and exposing her to swarms of bees who stung her until she died. In a straight reading of the verse the antecedent of the possessive pronoun "her" is the city of Sodom, but the Talmud and Midrash interpret the use of the singular possessive, "*her outcry*" to teach that the cries of *one* abused woman were sufficient cause for God to become involved. Upon confirming the cruelty of Sodom's inhabitants toward that woman, God destroyed the entire city.

Countless *aqunot*, innocent of any wrongdoing but sentenced to years of loneliness and suffering, have been crying out in pain. They live in a state of limbo, forbidden to remarry and bear children. The Orthodox rabbinate, entrusted with providing moral leadership and interpreting and implementing *halakhah* (Jewish law), has failed to respond to these women's cries, insisting that under Jewish family law a man is empowered to keep his wife in marital chains even if he has abused and abandoned her. God has commanded, the rabbis maintain, that these women can only be freed from their marriages when their husband-tormentors consent to freeing them. The rabbis, saying that they must be faithful to God's commandments, insist they are powerless to help these women.

One of these women is Blima Zitrenbaum. In February 1996 on a *Shabbat* (Sabbath) morning, Blima, a 33-year-old mother of seven children, was found in her bedroom, bludgeoned by a heavy instrument, unconscious in a pool of blood. Her young daughter who found her and ran to a neighbor, who called for help. The police suspected Blima's estranged husband Joseph was the assailant. Local police in Monsey, New York, were not unfamiliar with the family because Blima had previously obtained an order of protection against Joseph, and the police had been at the Zitrenbaum home numerous times to deal with disturbances. Joseph, a known drug addict, was sought by the police in connection with other crimes as well. A manhunt was launched and Joseph was apprehended by a group of religious Jews in an Orthodox neighborhood. Blima remained in critical condition for weeks and it was unclear if she would survive. She emerged from a coma and was able to return to her family.

Jewish media covered the story, as did the secular press, including *The New York Times*. The Orthodox world was shaken by this vicious crime, so rare in religious circles. We were deeply distressed by the news because we were alerted to Blima's situation by a concerned person who had contacted us several months before, in the hope that we could help Blima obtain a *gett*, a religious divorce. Blima had appealed to several rabbis to help her in obtaining a *gett*. Her community was aware of her problems and her effort to secure a *gett*. They provided financial assistance, but the rabbis maintained that, without Joseph's consent, they could not release her from her marriage bonds. Even after Joseph was convicted of attempting to murder her, the rabbis held that Blima must remain married to him until he agreed, of his own free will, to give her a *gett*.

Chana's case is less graphic but heartbreakingly compelling. Chana was briefly married to a violent man who abused her. She obtained a civil divorce, but was unable to obtain a religious divorce. Her ex-husband was demanding a large sum of money in exchange for a *gett*, money she couldn't and didn't want to pay. Chana was 38 years old and childless. Unless she was freed soon from her dead marriage, she might remain childless forever. This was particularly cruel since Chana was the child of Holocaust survivors whose entire families had been murdered. Time was on her husband's side; he had the luxury of delaying indefinitely while her biological clock was ticking. Chana had spoken to many rabbis. After perfunctory efforts to help her, they all said the same thing: "Our hands are tied. That is the *halakhah*. We can do nothing."

We believed, however, that the rabbis could do more within the bounds of the *halakhic* (Jewish legal) system to help *agunot*, and we challenged them for their inaction. We heard the outcry of innocent *agunot*, and we resolved to do something about it.

# Introduction

At Orthodox weddings, prior to the marriage ceremony, the groom surrounded by dancing and singing friends and family, approaches his bride and lowers a veil over her face. Known as the *badecken*, veiling, this ceremony symbolizes the importance of the groom's informed consent to the marriage. The groom must see with his own eyes that the bride is really his intended, a prudent precaution to avoid being fooled like the biblical patriarch Jacob who mistakenly wed Leah, believing her to be his beloved Rachel. As for the bride— the bright lights, beautiful gowns, dancing crowd, joyous music, and lowering of the veil over her eyes obscure the dangerous realities of the imminent wedding ceremony. She is about to enter a marriage that may lock her into lifelong imprisonment. Should the marriage fail, her husband has the power to withhold the key to her freedom. She may become an *agunah* (pl. *agunot*), a woman whose marrigae has become an anchor (*ogen*) that chains her down.

Orthodox Jewish law, *halakhah*, rules that a *gett*, a religious divorce, is valid only when a husband willingly grants it to his wife. Even if the wife has obtained a civil divorce, she remains married under Jewish law. Should the husband withhold the *gett*, and the wife remarry a Jewish man in a civil ceremony or begin an intimate relationship with a Jewish man without the *gett*, she is considered, according to *halakhah*, an adulteress. Any children born of her new union will be stigmatized as *mamzerim*, bastards, *halakhically* barred from marrying Jews except for other *mamzerim*. This stigma clings to the offspring of that woman for ten generations, meaning forever. The husband, on the other hand, though he continues to withhold the *gett*, is not similarly restricted. If he remarries in a civil ceremony to a Jewish woman or fathers children with her out of wedlock, the children bear no stigma; they are legitimate and free to marry any Jew.

*Agunot* are forced into the shadowy world of rabbinic courts in their quest to secure religious divorces from their recalcitrant husbands. In guiding women through the *gett* process, we learned that rabbinic judges are not impartial. They are patriarchal, intrinsically biased toward satisfying husbands' extortionist demands in return for the *gett*. Rabbinic court rulings routinely deprive women of income and assets. These rulings are enforceable in civil court and nearly impossible to reverse. In one of our cases, a woman was repeatedly beaten black and blue by her husband, but her community rabbi declared that there was no way to free her until she agreed to her husband's demand that she waive her right to alimony and her share of marital assets. The welfare of children is also put at risk in rabbinic courts. *Agunot* have been pressured into hushing up cases of pedophilia in return for the *gett*. Fortunately, civil courts can reverse rabbinic court rulings that jeopardize the welfare of children.

Securing the *gett* is paramount for the rabbis even at the price of impoverishing women and children and turning a blind eye to domestic violence and sexual abuse. Rabbinic courts, in effect, act as agents for the husband's *gett* extortion. When no amount of cajoling, money or other concessions can induce a vindictive husband to release his wife, the rabbis rule that she is doomed to remain chained to a non-existent marriage, sometimes for decades.

A civilly divorced woman who is a member of a *halakhic* community is still considered married until a *gett* is issued through a rabbinic court. Consequently, rabbinic courts, despite their inequitable treatment of women and children, continue to have a hold on *halakhically* observant women who divorce in the United States or in other Diaspora communities. (In Israel all Jewish women must go to rabbinic courts. There is no civil divorce.) Civil court judges and legislators working with *agunah* activists have taken steps to ameliorate the injustices perpetrated by rabbinic courts against *agunot*. New York State courts, for example, have reversed rabbinic court orders for the immediate sale of the homes of *agunot* who still had young children to raise. New York State, Canada, England and South Africa have laws on the books specifically designed to help *agunot*.

Though civil authorities are aware of the abuses that take place in rabbinic courts, rabbinic courts have been shielded from closer scrutiny because of civil authorities' reluctance to become entangled with religious institutions and laws. Recently, however, the role of religious tribunals and laws with regard to divorce and matters pertaining to children is increasingly coming into question in Western democracies.

The precipitating factor that has raised questions about the role of religious tribunals and religious law is the growing prominence of Muslim communities in Western democracies. Advocates of *sharia* law are striving for greater recognition and legitimacy, and this has stirred up heated debate about what status or recognition civil courts should extend, if any, to customary, religious or "foreign" law and to the decisions of religious tribunals. The flashpoint in this controversy is religious law with regard to divorce, child custody/visitation/support and marital assets. This is because *halakhah* and *sharia* marital law give greater power and control to husbands.

In the United States, several states, including North Carolina, Arizona, Kansas, Louisiana, South Dakota and Tennessee, have passed legislation that prohibits judges from considering "foreign laws" (read *sharia*) in their decisions. Similar legislation has been introduced several times in the Florida legislature where Jewish groups have joined Muslim groups in opposing the legislation, voicing concern that the legislation will undermine the status of rabbinic courts, which have long functioned, with little scrutiny, as legally binding arbitration boards. The problem for rabbinic courts is that anti-"foreign law" legislation may make rabbinic arbitration rulings unenforceable if the tribunals base their rulings on a legal code or system that does not grant the same rights to litigants as civil law or the American Constitution does. Orthodox *halakhah* and rabbinic courts clearly do not grant women the same rights as civil law when it comes to divorce.

A 2008 speech in which the Archbishop of Canterbury explored the possibility of some official status for *sharia* law in the United Kingdom stirred up a storm and drew quick rebuttals from government officials, one of whom said, "Let's be absolutely clear: all British citizens must be subject to British law developed through Parliament and the courts." Similarly, in 2006, in Ontario, after intense controversy, including demonstrations in Canada and Europe organized by Muslim feminists, Ontario Attorney General Michael Bryant said, "When it comes to family law arbitrations in this province, there is only one law and that is Canadian law."

It is not surprising that many devout Jews and Muslims want to see their religious rules and tribunals treated as an acceptable framework and venue for their co-religionists who are divorcing in whatever country they may reside. At first glance it seems reasonable to allow members of a particular religion to settle marital disputes in the familiar setting of their own religious tribunals, following the dictates of their religions. However, as we will describe, the moral values and legal principles of patriarchal, all male religious systems can be shockingly at odds with the core values of modern family law and societal norms of equality before the law and protecting the well-being of children.

We have concluded, therefore, that rabbinic courts should be restricted solely to overseeing the ritual aspects of divorce—the writing and giving of the *gett*. Rabbinic courts should be barred from dealing with custody and visitation of children and have no binding jurisdiction over financial matters like alimony and the division of marital assets. Their decisions on these financial matters should not be enforceable in civil court even when the woman has allegedly "voluntarily" agreed to allow a rabbinic court to arbitrate these matters because women are by definition under duress due to their husbands' power to grant the *gett* or hold their wives captive. Can it be said that a woman forgoing her right to litigate in civil court and going instead to a rabbinic court is voluntary when the price she may pay for not going to a rabbinic court is social ostracism, alienation of her children, and forever being barred from remarrying and bearing children in her community?

The power of civil court enforcement should not be added to the forces pressuring a woman to comply with religious court rulings. Religious court rulings should have the status of recommendations only. Compliance with these recommendations should be completely voluntary. Furthermore rabbinic court judges should be designated mandatory reporters of child abuse.

We are under no illusions about how harrowing divorce in the civil courts can be, with long, painful delays, prohibitively high legal fees, unfair advantages to the party who can afford a more expensive lawyer, arbitrary and abrasive judges, stress and friction over dividing scarce dollars between two households, bitter custody and visitation disputes, and children traumatized by the breakup. But civil court judges do not openly and routinely pressure a wife to waive child support, agree to unsafe custody or visitation privileges to an admittedly unfit father, drop well-founded charges of assault or pedophilia against her husband, cancel an order of protection, or give in to financial extortion in return for obtaining a divorce. Rabbinic court judges, by contrast, regularly pressure women to make such concessions to their husbands in return for their *gett*. As bad as a litigating a contentious divorce in civil court may be, for women, litigating a contentious divorce in a rabbinic court is more perilous.

When the decision of a civil court judge seems unjust, there are several levels of appellate courts to which a litigant can turn for review of the lower court decision. Misconduct and suspected unethical behavior by a civil court judge can lead to an investigation, removal from the bench and even criminal charges. All of this can be time consuming and expensive. But in the rabbinic court system there is no opportunity whatsoever to appeal and no agency that sets standards for ethical conduct and investigates breaches of those standards.

The case we make in this volume for curbing the authority of rabbinic courts to arbitrate matters of divorce is a flashing red caution light to states to protect the fundamental human rights of their female citizens, not to succumb to "multicultural" demands that deny these rights. Our conclusion is not rooted in any animus toward Judaism or any other religion or culture but in thirty years of witnessing the injustices committed by rabbinic courts that are recorded in this book.

"Heretics," "prostitutes," "deserving of being killed on sight," are some of the epithets hurled at us, printed on flyers and posted on trees and lampposts in our neighborhoods. What did we do to merit these accusations? We were Orthodox women, directors of Agunah Inc. We devoted years of unpaid work to free *agunot*. This is generally considered a *mitzvah*, a good deed, of the highest order; however, our efforts were branded as feminist assaults upon Torah and Judaism, and we were considered dangerous heretics, women who refused to accept the authority of our rabbis.

We began our work with *agunot* around 1985. The dimensions and urgency of the *agunah* problem that we discovered quickly led us to found an advocacy organization in 1987—Agunah Inc. In later years, Rivka joined the GET organization and Susan founded Agunah International, both organizations with goals similar to Agunah Inc.'s. This volume is a history of the three-decades-long struggle we waged to bring justice to *agunot*.

We consider ourselves Jewish feminists. Our brand of Torah feminism evolved as our devotion to Jewish tradition and our desire to improve the intellectual, spiritual and family life of religious Jewish women merged. Our love of our heritage led us to immerse ourselves in the study of Talmud, the classic text which forms the foundational basis for Jewish law and which, until relatively recently, was the exclusive preserve of men. We worked to provide other women with the opportunity to study as well. We enjoyed teaching Talmud to women on *Shabbat* (Sabbath) afternoons, around our dining room tables, making its arcane and difficult, but intellectually rewarding, texts readily accessible.

Our quest for more satisfying spiritual expression led us to become leaders in the Orthodox women's prayer group movement in the United States and later in the struggle for women's religious rights at the Western Wall, the *Kotel*, in Jerusalem. In 1988, Rivka organized the first group of women to pray together at the *Kotel*; we two have continued in the leadership of this struggle for religious rights for Jewish women at the *Kotel*. But our most difficult challenge was, and remains, our work with *agunot*. We couldn't close our ears to the cries of women whose anguish was being ignored by the Orthodox community. We wanted our community to live up to Judaism's ideals of justice and kindness.

With the knowledge we had gained from years of studying Jewish law and with our experience of fighting the Orthodox rabbinate to attain greater female participation in prayer and ritual, we became advocates for women who were being held hostage in dead marriages. Because we were conversant with Jewish law, we raised questions that the rabbis could not easily dismiss.

We accompanied many *agunot* through the *beit din* (rabbinic court) system. Along the way, we got to know the major players, including rabbis, scribes, *to'anim* (rabbinic court pleaders/lawyers, sing. *to'en*), matrimonial attorneys and communal leaders. We saw how rigid interpretations of Jewish law were harming women and children, how *agunot* were pressured to cave in to extortion. We met religious women who inspired us with their deep faith and their ability to distinguish between rabbinic malfeasance and Torah values of justice and compassion.

The injustices we witnessed in the name of Torah motivated us to channel our energies into a multitude of activities: speaking and meeting with rabbis, disrupting large rabbinic conferences and elegant yeshivah (a religious school) dinners, leading public demonstrations on city streets. We organized a number of conferences ourselves, allowing *agunot* to speak out and express their anger and pain. We wrote articles in books and periodicals, publicized individual cases, gathered hundreds of signatures on petitions to rabbinic sages. We devoted hours and hours each week to this cause. We put the term *"agunah"* on the agenda of the Orthodox world.

Despite all our efforts and the efforts of others to improve the rabbinic court system and curtail its misdeeds, its power has grown, as have its abuses. The influence of an increasingly fundamentalist Israeli rabbinate over the religious courts in the United States has resulted in ever greater stringency, which enshrines men's power over women and children. The Orthodox religious world continues to downplay the *agunah* problem or accept it as an inevitable result of Divine decree.

After years of activism, we decided that a book chronicling our experiences would bring the closed world of rabbinic courts into the open and serve as a catalyst for change. By 1997, we had written a major part of this volume, but we got sidetracked, and we left it sitting on our shelves, saved on old computer discs no longer compatible with today's computers.

After a lapse of many years, our shared frustration with the unrelieved suffering of *agunot* motivated us to resume work on this volume. The *agunah* situation was more pressing than ever as the high divorce rate in secular society was paralleled by a rising divorce rate among Orthodox Jews, bringing with it a corresponding increase in *gett* problems.

Accurate figures for the number of *agunot* in the United States and around the world are hard to come by because the rabbinic court system is fragmented, and there is no central data collection system. During our decades of counseling *agunot*, we averaged about 60 to 70 calls annually and dealt cumulatively with approximately two thousand *agunot*, mostly from the United States but also from Latin America, Israel and Europe. The Organization for Resolution of Agunot (ORA), a New York based advocacy organization founded in 2002, reported in 2014 that it receives 150 phone calls per year from *agunot* seeking assistance, has an ongoing caseload of about 50 and has resolved over 200 *agunah* cases. A 2011 survey of Jewish social service organizations in the U.S. and Canada found that these organizations had contact with 462 *agunot* that year. A 2013 survey done in Israel, where only religious divorce is available, found evidence of *gett* extortion in thousands of cases. The number of children traumatized and impoverished by the *agunah* calamity is obviously a multiple of the number of *agunot*.

As set forth in this book, we believe that *halakhic* solutions to this problem exist. Over the ages, wise rabbis have devised ways of easing difficulties caused by *halakhic* strictures. In the area of finance, for example, the clear Torah prohibition against Jews taking interest on loans to other Jews has been creatively circumvented, utilizing techniques permitting the practice. Banks in Israel and even some in the United States that serve Orthodox clientele make use of a "*heter iska*," a rabbinically created document which structures forbidden interest as profit from an investment. This book is a call for a similarly resourceful approach to freeing women chained to dead marriages.

It is a double loss that the rabbinic court system is in such lamentable condition. Given some of the litigation nightmares that occur in civil divorce court, it would be a contribution to civil society as well as a boon to divorcing Jewish couples if rabbinic courts set a standard of justice and equity that could be held up as a model for civil courts to emulate. *Batei din* could be a point of pride for the Orthodox Jewish community instead of a source of disgrace.

Our sense of moral responsibility compelled us to write this book, to relate the stories of *agunot*, to recount our efforts to help them, to honor the work of those who fought side by side with us, and to appeal to the Orthodox world and all who read this book to find ways to put an end to these terrible abuses which cause so much human suffering and undermine the foundation of Jewish family life.

# 1

# The Founding of Agunah Inc.

In 1979, the first year of New York City Councilwoman Susan Alter's term in office, she noticed a peculiar pattern—young Orthodox women, with many children, poor and alone, coming to her office seeking help. They needed jobs, financial aid, assistance in applying for city welfare programs and counseling. They complained that they and their children were being socially ostracized by their Borough Park community, which was part of Alter's electoral district. Puzzled as to what was going on and why these women were not being cared for by the tight-knit religious community of Borough Park, Alter spoke one-on-one with these women and discovered that they had a burden in common—they were *agunot*.

Alter was the first Orthodox woman to be elected to public office in New York City. At that time she was also a single mother, recently widowed, raising her two young daughters. Apparently, *agunot* approached her because they felt she would empathize with their misfortune.

Casting around for a way to deal with the growing number of such cases, Alter held a meeting of *agunot* in her office. She assembled a panel of professionals: a psychologist, rabbi, attorney and social worker. *Agunot* were invited through word of mouth. She told those who had approached her to invite their friends. Anticipating that the women would be hesitant to speak out openly about their personal dilemmas, Alter opened the evening with some remarks about her own struggles as a single mother, intending to draw them out. Unexpectedly, women began clamoring to be heard, standing up and raising their hands, spilling out tales of pain.

There were about fifty women present, *agunot* and their mothers and sisters. The meeting went on for hours, with the women's anger directed not only at their recalcitrant husbands but also at the Borough Park rabbis and community, the rabbis for offering no help and the community for ignoring them and their children.

One woman suggested a march down 13th Avenue, the main commercial street in the Borough Park community. Others applauded that suggestion. Another told of her husband sitting in jail in a mid-western state, imprisoned for a violent crime, refusing to grant a *gett*. "Why should you be happy when I can't be?" he repeatedly wrote her.

The meeting was brought to a close before all the women had a chance to tell their stories. The anger that was expressed left the panel and onlookers shaken and saddened.

Among those present were Rivka and Irwin Haut. Irwin, both a rabbi and an attorney, was on the panel. Rivka came along because her close friend Susan Alter had asked her to come. The Hauts drove one of the *agunot* home, and she talked about her suffering all the way home. They felt powerless to help.

Rivka spent three sleepless nights after the meeting, unable to erase the images of the women from her mind. After anguishing over the problem for days, she resolved not to become involved in the issue at all. She felt that the *agunah* issue was too enormous and the problems insoluble. At that time Rivka was very involved with the newly formed Orthodox women's prayer movement and decided that her efforts were better spent in that arena which was experiencing its own problems but also its joys. Irwin, however, who had legal and *halakhic* expertise, decided to make himself available to give advice to *agunot* pro bono.

Alter considered setting up an organization called Agunah but eventually decided that it would be more appropriate for her office to steer clear of religious matters and limit its involvement to guiding *agunot* toward available social services. Moreover, the GET (*G*etting *E*qual *T*reatment) organization was just beginning, and Alter and Rivka felt GET would now deal with the problem. But, through the years, even when Alter was elected in a redrawn, predominantly non–Jewish district, a steady stream of calls to her office from *agunot* persisted, and the stories were more desperate. Alter's staff was instructed to funnel the calls to Irwin Haut or to the GET organization.

At the Haut household, their two young daughters became adept at identifying telephone calls from *agunot* by the women's depressed, lifeless and pleading voices. Often the girls would answer the phone and without being told why the woman was calling would shout, "Daddy, there's an *agunah* on the phone." Rivka felt uncomfortable that her young daughters were constantly exposed to these tragedies. One *agunah* came to Rivka's house in the middle

## 1. The Founding of Agunah Inc.

of the day looking for Irwin. When Rivka told her that Irwin was in his office in Manhattan, the *agunah* responded that she intentionally came to speak to Rivka. Rivka explained that she was not involved in this issue and then was unnerved when the woman got down on her knees on the kitchen floor, took Rivka's hands in hers and implored, "Please tell the rabbi to help me."

About five years passed. More women than ever were calling Alter's office. The GET organization had such a backlog of cases that there was a waiting period of several months before a GET caseworker was available. Many *agunot*, under pressure to make choices that had far reaching consequences, needed someone to talk to immediately. They were distraught and urgently needed advice to avoid mistakes that could irreparably damage their lives. Over and over *agunot* told of extortion demands, problems with child custody and support, in cases that were being adjudicated in metropolitan area *batei din* (rabbinic courts). Some rabbis' names kept recurring in these tales of woe. Many women told of rabbinic corruption, emotional trauma to children, and community indifference to their plight. A pattern was becoming painfully obvious: women entrapped in a *beit din* (rabbinic court) system that they did not understand but whose decisions affected their lives in the most profound way. They desperately needed help.

Alter shared some of these stories with Rivka. Try as they might to remain emotionally distant Alter and Rivka became preoccupied with some of the women's accounts and began investigating. As they heard more cases and spoke to more rabbis and *dayyanim* (rabbinic court judges, sing. *dayyan*), the knowledge they acquired weighed on their consciences and forced them to assume responsibility. Before they knew it, they were in too deep to walk away and ignore the pain.

An organized effort was clearly necessary. Alter had many discussions with Rivka, finally convincing her that they should form an organization and call it Agunah. They decided that only women would serve as directors because the men they had consulted on this issue didn't seem to have the same perspective. Daunted by the magnitude of the task, Rivka and Alter decided they needed another woman to join them. A mutual friend, Susan Aranoff, was the perfect choice. She was an Orthodox mother of six children, a professor of economics who had knowledge that might help guide *agunot* with their money problems. She agreed to complete the troika.

The three of them were determined to make a difference. They were religiously knowledgeable, capable of learning the complex *halakhot* of Jewish divorce, not intimidated by rabbis (two of them were married to rabbis— Rivka to Rabbi Irwin Haut. Alter had by then remarried to Rabbi Gilbert

Klaperman). The three felt Alter's political office would open rabbinic doors to them, and it did. They believed Alter's and Rivka's husbands' rabbinic reputations would afford them credibility with the *batei din*, and they did.

For more than thirty years, Susan Aranoff and Rivka Haut, were to carry on the struggle to right the terrible wrongs that were being perpetrated against *agunot*. Little did we know then how this issue would affect our lives and our souls.

# 2

## Our Initiation

In 1987, shortly after we and Alter incorporated Agunah Inc., we were contacted by an individual who introduced himself as a rabbi, who was also a businessman, and was active in the field of *gittin* (pl. of *gett*). He said he had heard about our work with *agunot* and wanted to present us with a case that would enlighten "you ladies" about the *beit din* system. Thus began our association with Rabbi Shloimy Eisen.

We asked around about Eisen and learned that he had a reputation for being a man of action, not leaving a stone unturned in his efforts to secure a *gett* from a recalcitrant husband. His *agunah* activism intrigued us. We decided we wanted to meet him, and a meeting was arranged at his home.

On the appointed evening, we and Alter arrived at Eisen's house located in a mostly Orthodox New York suburban community. We rang the bell and Eisen, tall, with a booming voice, dressed in classic rabbinic garb, a long black gabardine frock and black hat opened the door, introduced himself and showed us in. He had a full beard and *payot* (sidelocks) and wore a white shirt and a tie. He introduced us to Sarah, the *agunah*, and her older sister, who were both wearing *sheitels* (wigs worn by pious Jewish women) and long sleeved dresses which met their community's *tsniut* (modesty) standard for women's attire. Sarah's sister, fifteen years her senior, had an elegant and dignified air.

Everyone seated themselves around Eisen's dining room table, and Shloimy, as we learned to call Eisen, explained that he wanted to walk us through the details of Sarah's case to educate us. Sarah began telling her story. She had to leave her marriage because of her husband Tulie's violence toward her. He had repeatedly beaten her. She recounted her experiences with the *beit din* system while we sat absorbing the cruel twists and turns of her story.

Her first contact with the *beit din* system was when she received a summons known as a *hazmanah* (pl. *hazmanot*) from a Chasidic *beit din* in Brooklyn, with which neither she nor Tulie were affiliated. The *hazmanah* meant that Tulie was demanding that she appear before these rabbis to settle their marital problems. Sarah consulted with a lawyer who advised her to disregard the *hazmanah* since neither she nor Tulie had any connection to that Chasidic community. The lawyer received a phone call from the administrator of the *beit din*, who insisted, "Jews have to go to *beit din*." Sarah was uncomfortable about ignoring rabbinic authority but was unsure of how to proceed so she did nothing and remained in her troubled marriage. As time went on, however, Tulie became more abusive. She reached a point where she could no longer tolerate the status quo.

Sarah contacted a prominent rabbi in her neighborhood. He advised her to evade the Chasidic *beit din* by summoning Tulie to a *beit din* known as a *zabla*. *Zabla*, she explained to us, is an acronym for ***Z**eh **B**orer **L**o **E**chad*, which means each litigant chooses one judge, known as a *borer*. The judicial panel is completed with the required third *borer* who is chosen by the first two. This ad-hoc court is formed to deal with one specific case and then disbands.

As she explained this to us, we interjected that we had studied *zabla* in our *Shabbat* afternoon Talmud class. The Tractate Sanhedrin discusses this kind of court, and we were interested to hear about a contemporary example. Shloimy, visibly surprised to hear that women study Talmud, restrained his curiosity and informed us that *zabla* is frequently used. He, however, frowned upon people going to *zabla* rather than an established *beit din* with a track record and a community reputation to uphold. We were to discover how right he was many cases later.

Sarah continued with her saga. Completely unfamiliar with the rabbinic court system, she made inquiries and was referred to a well-known *borer*, Rabbi Nissan, whose fee was $100 an hour, a large sum in the 1980s. Tulie chose Rabbi Volin as his *borer*. It remained for the two sides to agree on a third *borer*. Rabbi Nissan told Sarah that the best *borer* to complete the panel would be Rabbi Leventhal. But, Nissan said, "The only problem is that he's dead." Ultimately the third *borer* chosen was Rabbi Shalosh, whom Nissan characterized as "the best of the worst."

A year and a half had passed from the time Sarah first decided she needed a divorce until the *zabla beit din* was put together. Before the first session, Nissan informed Sarah that she must agree to litigate all aspects of the divorce in the *beit din*, not in civil court. Sarah was uncomfortable with this but had no choice if she wanted to obtain a *gett*.

Sarah, accompanied by her sister, went to the first *beit din* session nervous about what would take place. The first order of business was for both spouses to sign an arbitration agreement known as a *shtar berurin* (*shtar* for short). Signing this *shtar berurin* document means that the parties agree to accept the jurisdiction of this court of arbitration with regard to the issues listed in the document and to be bound by its decisions, which are legally enforceable in civil court. The document was written in Yiddish, a language Sarah said she did not understand. It was not translated for her, but she signed it because without it, there could be no hearing. In Sarah's case the *shtar* authorized the *beit din* to decide custody of the four children, visitation, child support, maintenance and division of marital assets. The *beit din* informed both parties that their fee would be $1,000 (in late 1980s dollars) from each side per session. Sarah was astonished and asked how many sessions would be necessary. The *beit din* said there was no way to tell.

These preliminary arrangements took place in an anteroom. Now the rabbis began to move into an adjoining room for the first hearing of the case. Sarah and her sister also moved toward the door. As Tulie passed her on his way into the inner room, Sarah's *borer* turned to her and told her that she, being a woman, was not permitted to be present during the *beit din*'s deliberations. "These rabbis were going to decide my life," Sarah told us. She insisted, therefore, upon being in the room. The rabbis reluctantly permitted her to enter but barred her sister. The rabbis placed a chair in a corner of the room for Sarah while Tulie was seated around the large table in the center of the room together with the rabbis.

Through her *borer* Sarah told the *beit din*, in Yiddish, that Tulie had been hitting her. The rabbis inquired, "When was the last time he hit you?" "Two months ago," was the reply. "Such a long time ago? That's nothing." one rabbi said. They ended the session by advising her, "Go home with your husband and try to make peace." "I was afraid of Tulie," Sarah told us, "but I had to listen to the rabbis. So I resigned myself to continuing to live with him."

Sarah's life soon became unbearable. Tulie tried to turn the children against her by telling lies about her. He tried to isolate her from her family, particularly from her sister, by opening all of Sarah's mail and monitoring her phone calls. During one argument, when Tulie caught Sarah trying to secretly make a phone call, he ripped the phone out of the wall and threw a metal chair at her, breaking her wrist. Fearful, Sarah turned to a local rabbi for help, expecting him to contact the *beit din* and urge them to quickly rule that a *gett* must be granted because her physical well-being was at risk.

"Forget about the *beit din*," the rabbi told her. "You'd better go to civil court for an order of protection. But don't tell anyone I told you to. I'll deny it." We understood his reticence because we knew that Orthodox *batei din* object to women going to civil court, especially once their case is already being litigated before a *beit din*. In more than one case we have dealt with, *batei din* have either barred an *agunah* from seeking an order of protection or pressured the *agunah to* drop an existing order of protection. Sarah, however, knew how serious the danger was and instructed her lawyer to get an order of protection to get Tulie out of the house.

Meanwhile, the *beit din* held more sessions and completely ignored Tulie's history of domestic violence. Sarah recounted some of the details of these sessions that had been translated for her by her *borer*. At one point during the deliberations the judges began referring to Sarah as a *moredet*, a rebellious wife. This is a *halakhic* term applied to women who refuse to cohabit with their husbands. This is not merely nomenclature but has significant financial implications. Rabbinic law denies a *moredet* the monetary value of her *ketubah*, marriage contract (see Chapter 5) the financial settlement of thousands of dollars, traditionally due a woman in case of divorce. The rabbis' use of the term *moredet* might mean that they were going to penalize Sarah financially. Perhaps the fact that she had gone to civil court for the order of protection was being held against her.

At another session dealing with custody, Tulie demanded custody of their two sons. He was not demanding custody of his daughters but insisted that he was *halakhically* entitled to the boys. When Sarah protested, raising questions about Tulie's violence and pointing out that it was best for the children to stay together, one of the rabbis said to her, "Let him have the boys. You can always have more." Ultimately six *beit din* sessions were held, which cost Sarah six thousand dollars, but no decision was rendered about anything.

After a year and a half of *beit din* sessions that yielded no decisions and left her chained to her marriage, Sarah heard about Shloimy through word of mouth. She approached Shloimy and asked for help. Shloimy's intervention made a big difference. He insisted that the *beit din* stop dawdling and issue a *p'sak*, a verdict. Sarah's delight in anticipating the end of her ordeal soon turned to anger. Late one night Shloimy called her and said, "The *p'sak* is out. They sold you down the river." She handed copies of the *p'sak* around the table for us to read.

The *p'sak*, one and a half pages long, was typed in Hebrew with handwritten interpolations. It gave the parents joint custody of the children. On Jewish holidays the children would be separated, the girls staying with Sarah and the boys going to Tulie. Their house was to be sold immediately. The house was deeded in both names, had a market value of approximately $400,000 (late 1980s dollars) with a balance on the mortgage of only a few thousand dollars. The *beit din* decreed that Sarah was to receive $100,000 from the proceeds of the sale, with the rest going to Tulie. The last clause in the *p'sak* made the *gett* contingent on the sale of the house with the money being held in escrow by the *beit din* for distribution after the *gett* was given.

Sarah felt the *p'sak* was unacceptable. She felt that the joint custody provisions would damage her children psychologically since she and Tulie were unable to agree on anything and because Tulie was violent. She also felt that her children should be together on Jewish holidays. She was furious that the *beit din* awarded Tulie three quarters of the worth of the house and that she and her children would lose their home, which had been paid for solely with money she had inherited from her parents. Worst of all, the *beit din* was holding her hostage by decreeing that the *gett* not be issued until the house was sold. Thus, for as long as Sarah fought to protect her children and for an equitable financial settlement, she would remain an *agunah*.

The decision was so unfair that Sarah was considering going to civil court to sue the *beit din*. She could not simply ignore the *p'sak* since she had signed a *shtar berurin*, which would be treated as a binding arbitration agreement by the civil courts, allowing Tulie to sue in civil court to enforce the *p'sak*. She still did not have a *gett* because the rabbis had ruled that it be delayed until the house was sold.

When Sarah finished talking her sister began to speak. She spoke of the pain of seeing her sister, a young woman, not married but yet not single, unable to continue a normal life. This very Orthodox woman expressed her anger at the rabbis' lack of compassion. She said she felt relief at finally being able to have her sister's story told to people who believed her and sympathized.

We sat silently absorbing what Sarah had told us. We had heard similar tales of abusive husbands before. But the culpability of the *beit din* was a revelation. The *beit din* had dismissed Sarah's accusations of violence by sending her back to live with her husband. They neglected the welfare of the children by demanding that the house be sold and by ordering joint custody under these circumstances. They charged high fees and subjected Sarah to humiliating conditions. And they kept Sarah imprisoned in a dead marriage by withholding her *gett* until their conditions were met.

We fixed our glances on Sarah and her sister. The irony of the scene struck us. On one side of the table sat Sarah, her sister, and Shloimy, all of whose strict level of religious observance was apparent from their traditional, modest garb and covered heads. They lived in the same world as the rabbis they were accusing. On the opposite side of the table we and Alter sat, bareheaded, dressed in short sleeves, one of us even wearing slacks (considered taboo for women in Sarah's circles). After years of unquestioning acceptance of rabbinic authority, disillusionment and despair had impelled Sarah and her sister to seek us out. Unlike Sarah's anonymous rabbi who feared retribution, we and Alter were Modern Orthodox "outsiders" whose jobs, social status and reputation did not depend on the goodwill of rabbis. We could afford to openly take up her cause and demand justice.

We expressed our empathy and anger at Sarah's predicament. We asked many questions and learned a great deal about *beit din* process. We had no strategy to offer for obtaining the *gett* because the *beit din*, which should have ordered Tulie to grant Sarah a *gett*, was holding her hostage and had a legal hold over her because she had signed a *shtar berurin*. It appeared to us that there was no route other than a civil lawsuit to overturn the *p'sak*.

Though women, desperate to obtain a *gett*, may accept *beit din* jurisdiction over custody, child support and the marital residence, the civil court guards its jurisdiction over matters affecting the welfare of children so that reversing *beit din* decisions on issues impacting children, though expensive, is feasible. Reversing other financial aspects of a *p'sak* is far more difficult because, in general, civil courts hesitate to tamper with binding arbitration decisions. In a handful of New York cases, judges have scrutinized and modified financial settlements on the grounds that the husband's coercive power of withholding the *gett* may result in "coerced, unconscionable" settlements and intentionally inflict emotional distress, but such civil court interventions are rare.

Sarah did bring a suit against the *beit din* in civil court. She succeeded in reversing the custody aspects of the *p'sak* and in delaying the sale of the house until her youngest child reached the age of 18. Sarah was unable to get any other part of the *p'sak* reversed. With the exception of the child-related matters, the court would not revisit the rabbis' decision since Sarah had accepted their jurisdiction when she signed the *shtar berurin*. The civil court did not deal with the *gett*. Three years after the civil court verdict, Sarah was still an *agunah*. Tulie proclaimed that he had a right to delay the granting of the *gett* because Sarah had improperly gone to civil court and reversed the *beit din*'s decision with regard to custody and the immediate sale of the marital residence.

Every avenue that Sarah pursued was a dead end as far as the *gett* was concerned. The *beit din* didn't and the civil court couldn't mandate an immediate *gett*. We too had no way to help her and spoke to her less and less frequently.

Over the years Tulie called Susan a few times making the case that he was not like other recalcitrants who demanded money. He claimed he was simply asserting his *halakhic* right to custody of his sons despite the civil court's ruling. He made no mention of his history of domestic violence. He said that while he loved his daughters, he accepted the *halakhic* rule that girls should be with their mothers. The civil court's custody ruling meant nothing to him, and he would not grant the *gett* until he got his sons and the money from the sale of the house.

Ultimately, after six years and tens of thousands of dollars spent on legal fees, Sarah finally decided she could no longer struggle for justice. She wanted a normal life free of litigation and with the opportunity to find a new spouse. Her children were approaching marriageable age, and continued strife might damage their chances for a good match in their community. Sarah paid Tulie a large sum of money and received her *gett*.

As for us, we were to encounter endless retellings of this basic story. The anger and sadness we felt that evening are with us still. We have devoted decades to exposing and fighting the *beit din* system which perpetuates the abuse of women like Sarah.

# 3

# We Take to the Streets

Shloimy Eisen was committed to protecting *agunot* from injustice, but he was a "true believer" in the system. Sarah ended up paying a ransom for her *gett* despite his help, but Shloimy had an explanation for that: She had gone to a *zabla* (ad hoc religious court), not to an established *beit din*. He maintained that if correct *halakhic* (Jewish legal) procedures are followed—the case is submitted to a proper *beit din*, the parties follow the rabbis' advice and the community supports the *beit din's* decision—the *gett* will be granted. To prove his point to us, and perhaps to himself, he challenged us to organize a demonstration for Ruth, an *agunah* who, according to Eisen, had done everything right.

Ruth, an observant, 25-year-old Orthodox woman who was a librarian, had been an *agunah* for four years when Shloimy brought her to meet us in the late 1980s. She had a five-and-a-half-year-old son and a civil divorce but no *gett*. She said she had to end her marriage because she was physically abused, to the point of needing extensive medical care. Ruth had already won custody and child support in civil court but was willing to have all aspects of the divorce relitigated in a *beit din* in order to secure her *gett*.

Ruth's husband, Dovid, was a religious Jew from an Orthodox family in New Jersey. He was constantly in court seeking increased visitation privileges. Unlike many men who use the *gett* as a bargaining chip to extort money, Dovid seemed to be delaying the *gett* in order to enhance his chances of gaining full custody of his son in a *beit din*. He was relying on advice that when a boy reaches the age of six, *batei din* often award custody to the father.

Dovid worked as an actuary and made his child support payments regularly, but he was petitioning in civil court to reduce the amount. He complained that an excessive amount of child support had been levied on him and maintained that he could not afford it. It seemed possible that the judge was attempting to pressure Dovid to grant the *gett* by holding out the possibility that the child support payments would be reduced once the *gett* was given.

Ruth applied to a well known *beit din* to begin *gett* proceedings. The *beit din* contacted Dovid, who responded that he wanted Rabbi Wolff, a rabbi who had known Dovid's family for years, to deal with the matter. Wolff headed a *beit din* of his own. Under Jewish law, a litigant who is summoned to one *beit din* has the right to refuse to appear in that *beit din* and may, instead, choose a different one. Ruth, in turn, had the right to refuse to litigate in the *beit din* chosen by Dovid and to opt for yet a third *beit din*. She obviously had good reason to be wary of litigating in the *beit din* headed by a rabbi with close ties to Dovid's family, but she wanted her *gett* as soon as possible and, therefore, agreed to litigate in Wolff's *beit din*. Otherwise the process of agreeing on a *beit din* could have dragged on for a year or more. She waited for Wolff to begin the process, but six months went by with no progress. She felt that Wolff was dragging his feet, because of his close ties to Dovid. Ruth's suspicions made sense to us because Wolff's procrastination was consistent with Dovid's strategy of holding out until his son reached the age of six to strengthen his demand for custody of the child.

Frustrated by the lack of movement, Ruth went to Shloimy for help. Knowledgeable about *batei din*, Shloimy recommended a *beit din* that he felt would deal with her case expeditiously. Sure enough, this *beit din* quickly sent a *hazmanah* by certified mail to Dovid, who ignored it. At two week intervals two additional *hazmanot* were sent and ignored. Under proper *beit din* procedure, after three *hazmanot* are issued and ignored, a contempt of court citation, known as a *seruv* (pl. *seruvim*), should follow. Unlike cases we later encountered in which *batei din*, to the detriment of the *agunah*, delayed or refused to issue a *seruv*, this *beit din* issued the *seruv* right away. The *seruv* is a concrete, authoritative ruling that an individual has defied a *beit din*. It indicates that this person is to be shunned by the community. No one is to do business with him. No one is to speak to him. He is not to be welcomed in the synagogue. The *seruv* represents a call on the community to do everything possible to help the wronged party, who correctly sought redress through a *beit din*.

It was at this point in Ruth's pursuit of a *gett* that Shloimy decided our help was needed. Shloimy believed that now that a *seruv* had been issued by a reputable *beit din*, the time had come to mobilize community support for Ruth. That's where we fit in; Shloimy wanted us to organize a demonstration to pressure Dovid to give the *gett*. Shloimy was sure that the sheer embarrassment to Dovid and his family would motivate him to grant the *gett*. "This," Shloimy said, "is the way the system was meant to work."

For Ruth, publicity meant exposing the personal details of her marriage and divorce to the wider community. Moreover, Shloimy informed her that now that she was going public, he would be less involved because he preferred to avoid the glare of publicity. Nevertheless, Ruth chose the public route.

After meeting Ruth, we analyzed the details of her case. We were impressed with her intelligence and religious commitment. She was a young woman, anxious to get on with her life. Her parents' health was suffering from watching their young daughter struggle to earn a living and care for her child while having no possibility of a social life. We sympathized with her plight and felt that we could help her, particularly since a respected *beit din* had issued a *seruv* against Dovid. We decided to take her case to the streets in the heart of the heavily Orthodox Jewish community where Dovid lived. Still novices, we believed Shloimy was right, that community pressure would force Dovid to grant a *gett*.

Looking back today, almost 30 years later, we, realize how pivotal that decision was for us. It marked our embarking upon a lifetime of *agunah* activism. Bringing the *agunah* issue out of the closet was a first step towards educating the Orthodox community about the problem. At that time, rabbis were denying that the problem existed. They maintained that there were few *agunot*, and those few would be quickly freed if only they followed rabbinic advice. Our taking to the streets would expose this misconception.

We had no idea if a demonstration would help Ruth. There were few precedents. Prior to our action, GET (*G*etting *E*quitable *T*reatment), the other Brooklyn based *agunah* advocacy organization, had conducted a number of demonstrations on behalf of an *agunah* whose recalcitrant husband's family owned a furniture store in our neighborhood. For a number of weeks, people gathered in front of the store on Sunday mornings, demanding that a *gett* be granted. Eventually, the *agunah* was freed by her husband.

We felt we had to walk down every avenue, explore every possibility, to discover how best to deal with the issue. Would public embarrassment really solve this and other cases? We had to try.

## *Organizing the Demonstration*

Prior to actually going out on the street to demonstrate, we took some preliminary actions. First, we asked the *beit din*, that had issued the *seruv*, for explicit, written approval of public demonstrations to help Ruth. The *beit din* sent the go ahead we requested. We then wrote a letter to Dovid urging him to avoid the public embarrassment of a demonstration by granting a *gett* immediately. We attached a copy of the *beit din*'s *seruv* and authorization to demonstrate to our letter, and Susan slipped the papers under the door of Dovid's parents' home, where he spent a great deal of his time. In the letter, we gave Dovid two weeks to grant a *gett* or else plans for the demonstration would go forward. He did not respond.

Susan spoke to Dovid and his family several times by phone, urging them to settle this matter amicably. In return for her efforts she received a letter from Dovid's attorney complaining about her harassment of his client by calling him at work and at his parents' home. The lawyer threatened to sue.

Ruth's family undertook a great deal of the work involved in putting together the demonstration. Her cousin Arthur, in particular, proved to be a tireless worker. Arthur ordered thousands of flyers which reproduced the *seruv* (in English and Hebrew) plus a photo of Dovid labeling him a *mesarev le'din* (one who is in contempt of the *beit din*'s order). Arthur had some copies enlarged to poster size and mounted on sticks to be carried during the demonstration. Ruth mobilized her friends and the congregants of her *shul* (synagogue). The rabbi of her parents' *shul* came to the demonstration and encouraged every member of his congregation to participate.

In a last ditch effort to secure her *gett* before going public, Ruth distributed the flyers to various locations in Dovid's neighborhood, including *shuls*. There was no response. The demonstration was inevitable.

We decided to start the demonstration outside Dovid's parents' home, for although Dovid rented a small apartment somewhere, no one could track down the address. Ruth knew that Dovid always brought their son to his parents' home during weekend visitations. Moreover, it was clear from Susan's telephone conversations with them that Dovid's parents strongly supported his withholding the *gett*. We decided to end the demonstration in front of a synagogue where Dovid's uncle was a board member and which Dovid frequented. Dovid's uncle had attempted to undermine the demonstration by having our publicity flyers removed from local synagogues. Rendering assistance to Dovid despite the *seruv* made his parents and uncle fair game as targets for our demonstration.

Agunah Inc. took responsibility for securing a police permit. We had not anticipated any problems since public demonstrations, a form of free of speech, are a basic civil right in the United States. However, when Susan went to the New Jersey police department to apply for a permit, she was told that a prominent lay leader of the community had called and urged the police captain not to grant a permit to Agunah Inc. We later learned that it was Dovid's uncle who had attempted to stymie our efforts. Susan called Alter for help. Though Alter was unknown in New Jersey, her status as a New York politician cleared the way, and the permit was granted. The police captain told Susan that the demonstrators were not allowed within 200 feet of a synagogue. She laughed and said, "Then your cops may end up arresting some of us because we're bound to pass by a synagogue as we march through that neighborhood." The captain replied, "You just have to keep moving. You can't stay in any one place for too long."

We turned to our Orthodox feminist network to bring out as many demonstrators as possible. Ruth attended a *Rosh Chodesh* (New Month) prayer service organized by a Women's Davening (Prayer) Group. After services Ruth spoke to the assembled women, telling her story and asking for their support. The listeners were appalled at Ruth's predicament, which could potentially befall any Orthodox woman. They were deeply affected when this pious young woman told of her inability to get on with her life because of her recalcitrant spouse's refusal to grant a *gett*. Many of the women who heard her speak later attended the demonstration to demand that Dovid grant a *gett*.

## *The Demonstration*

Sunday morning arrived, with the temperature already in the 80s and forecasted to go to the high 90s, both temperature and humidity. We decided to travel together in Susan's well air-conditioned van. Some of our children were with us, including Miriam Aranoff, then a toddler. We were tense while driving, concerned whether there would be enough people for an effective demonstration. As we drove down the street where Dovid's parents lived, we were happy to see that a sizeable crowd had gathered, waiting for us to begin.

Women and men were milling about, carrying large posters with Dovid's photo and the *seruv*. There were teenagers and children as well. We began organizing the activity. We formed a circle in front of the house. We instructed everyone to keep moving, as we were forbidden to stand in one place and to be careful not to step on the lawn or into the driveway. We didn't want to create any grounds for a charge of trespassing. Some younger people remained on the street corner, distributing our literature to passing pedestrians and drivers who stopped to look. We also set up a table and asked passersby to sign petitions urging the Orthodox rabbinate to implement solutions to the *agunah* problem. Many signed.

Men garbed in black coats and hats, despite the sweltering heat, and women with *sheitels* read our literature with interest. Many of them expressed sympathy for the *agunah* and support for our efforts to help her obtain a *gett*. The only negative voice came from a woman who described herself as a friend of Dovid's family. She said, "There are two sides to every story."

While circling around, we all shouted, "DOVID MEIR! GIVE YOUR WIFE A *GETT*!" The street reverberated with our voices and the chant became the mantra of the day. (Days later, little Miriam Aranoff ran around her house still chanting the same words.) Periodically we quieted the crowd as various women spoke. Ruth began by imploring Dovid to grant the *gett*. She said, "I am young and want to go on with my life." She broke down in tears and could not continue. Other speakers took over the megaphone and kept up a steady stream of criticism directed at Dovid and others like him.

After about an hour, we formed a long line and began to march along our designated route leading to the main commercial strip in the neighborhood. As we walked along the residential blocks, populated almost exclusively by Orthodox families, we distributed flyers. We entered stores and asked merchants to display the *seruv* posters with Dovid's picture in their windows. Many did so immediately. We realized the power of the *seruv* in an observant community. With no information other than the *seruv*, storekeepers were willing to place what amounted to a "wanted poster" in their windows, unafraid of libel suits or loss of business.

Wherever we walked the police accompanied us. They cleared the way and held up traffic while we crossed streets. We were never harassed. The community's instinctive response was sympathetic. Many people joined in and walked with us.

With a lot of tumult, we made our way to the Orthodox synagogue where Dovid's uncle was a board member and where Dovid often prayed. The building was set back from the curb, leaving a wide plaza for us to occupy. Just as we planned, we arrived at the synagogue in time for *minchah*, the afternoon service. As congregants, all male, approached the synagogue entrance, we handed them our flyers and asked them to help enforce the *seruv* in any way they could. We asked them not to permit Dovid to pray with them and to pressure his uncle to influence Dovid to grant a *gett*.

As the crowd marched, chanted, engaged congregants in discussion and handed out flyers, we stood and surveyed the crowd. Many people from the GET organization, which had also tried to help Ruth, were there together with members of numerous women's prayer groups. Congregants from Ruth's shul and her parents' shul were there. Tamara, Rivka's younger daughter, was there with her husband-to-be Seth. Seth's mother had also come, bringing one of her younger children.

Amidst all the hubbub, a woman pulled up in a car to ask what was going on. She introduced herself as a reporter for *The New York Post* who just happened to be driving by. She was intrigued because she read our posters and had some knowledge of the *agunah* issue. We explained to her that our organization's policy was not to speak to the secular press, and we asked her not to report on the demonstration. We said that we didn't want to embarrass the Orthodox community in the secular media. She understood and assured us that she would comply with our wishes. She got out of her car and joined us for a while.

A few years later this same woman, Lucette Lagnado, by then a reporter for the *Village Voice*, wrote a lengthy article about *agunot*, called "Of Human Bondage." She went on to become editor of the *Jewish Forward* newspaper, and is now author of several acclaimed books.

We had planned to enter the synagogue, pray and then leave our flyers on the seats. Many of our women filed into the building, but we found to our consternation that *minchah* services were held in a room which lacked a *mechitzah* (barrier, required in Orthodox synagogues, to separate men and women during prayer). This meant that women could not be present during the service. We and the other women in our group went outside, leaving some of our men to pray with the congregation. We stood outside chatting when suddenly we heard yelling and sounds of furniture being thrown. Alarmed, we ran back inside and witnessed a melee between our men and a few of the regular congregants. Somehow, peace was restored and the prayers continued, but there was a lingering tension in the air.

Our group returned to Dovid's parents' home, circled for a while and resumed our chanting. Someone was definitely in the house because the shades were moved aside and a figure was peeking through. This was their only response to our presence. Exhausted, but feeling that the demonstration had been worthwhile, we began saying our good byes. At a minimum we were gratified that so many people came and stayed the whole afternoon and that our message seemed so well received by the community. We had brought the suffering of *agunot* out of the closet and made it a community affair, but we could not then know if our actions would influence Dovid to grant the *gett*. As the crowd dispersed, Ruth's cousin gathered the large posters and placed them in the trunk of his car saying, "I better save these. We may need them again."

Following the demonstration, we continued our efforts to help Ruth. We launched a telephone campaign to persuade Dovid to grant the *gett*. Numerous people called Dovid's parents urging them to influence their son to give the *gett*. His parents' phone was targeted because Dovid had no phone, as far as we knew.

A woman who had participated in the demonstration contacted us to tell us that, upon seeing Dovid's photo on the *seruv*, she felt she had seen him before but couldn't remember where. When she got home she recalled that she met him at an Orthodox Jewish singles event. By chance, she found a group photo with Dovid seated amongst the "singles." We called the organization that sponsored the event and informed them that Dovid was not single and asked that they bar him from future events. They agreed that if Dovid showed up again they would insist that he leave.

Our demonstration had attracted a great deal of attention and mobilized community pressure on Dovid and his family, but Ruth remained an *agunah*.

Anxious to do everything we could to maximize the pressure on Dovid, we decided several weeks later to make a trip by ourselves to visit two rabbis of *shtieblach* (small *shuls* owned by the rabbi in whose house the congregation meets) which Dovid frequented. We knocked on the door of the first rabbi's home. The *rebbetzin* (rabbi's wife), an elderly woman wearing a long sleeved housedress, her hair covered by a *tichel* (kerchief), invited the two us into a small apartment. The living room was dominated by a very large, framed, black and white photo of a European bride and groom. We couldn't help noticing and commenting on it. She proudly told us that it was her wedding portrait which she and her husband carried with them on the boat leaving Europe.

We told her Ruth's story and explained that we wanted to ask her husband to pressure Dovid to do the right thing. Specifically, we wanted her husband to comply with the *seruv* and deny Dovid an *aliyah* (being called up to the Torah) and other synagogue honors like being counted in the *minyan* (quorum for prayers, consisting of ten men). The *rebbetzin* was very sympathetic. Her sadness was evident in her face. But she told us her husband had been ill and was still recuperating from surgery. Without being explicit, she was really asking us to spare him the aggravation of talking with us about this matter. She was comforted to hear that we would not try to see him but would rely on her to communicate the story and give her husband a copy of the *seruv*. We wished her husband a *refuah shelemah* (full recovery) and left.

At the second *shtiebel* the rabbi, a middle aged, bearded, heavy-set American born man, displayed indifference to the whole story. He deflected our request to exclude Dovid from the *shul's* services by saying that Dovid was just a "hanger-on" who moped around the back rows of the *shul* and never received any honors. We were later told by Rivka's future son-in-law, Seth, that this was untrue. Seth at that time worked at a senior citizens' residence in the area and he used to bring some of the residents to that *shul* for Sabbath services. When Seth saw Dovid being called up for an *aliyah*, he made a fuss and pointed out to some of the men that there was a *seruv* against Dovid, but to no avail.

Our final stop that evening was to revisit Dovid's uncle's synagogue. We had learned that there was a membership meeting that evening. We stood in the hallway distributing the *seruv* and asking people to help us motivate Dovid to grant Ruth the *gett*. We soon realized that we were on enemy turf. People refused to take our literature, and some were openly hostile, telling us to mind our own business. We tried to sensitize them by asking how they would feel if this happened to their daughters. One very burly man stuck his finger in Rivka's face in an aggressive manner. Susan admonished him to keep his hands to himself. Suddenly, there was a commotion as a man entered from the street and approached us. We immediately recognized him. Though older and somewhat fuller, it was the face on our posters—Dovid. We realized that Dovid's uncle must have had ducked into the *shul's* office to phone him.

Dovid came armed with dozens of copies of a letter from Rabbi Wolff, whose *beit din* had delayed doing anything, forcing Ruth to turn to the other *beit din* for action. Wolff's letter was short on specifics concerning the *gett* but heaped praise on Dovid, describing him as a good father and observant Jew. This was Dovid's attempt to counter the *seruv* that we were distributing. The same people who wouldn't take our literature eagerly reached for his. Trying to defend Dovid, the people in the synagogue finally engaged in a dialogue with us. They shouted, "You see, there are two sides to every story."

We replied that a *seruv* is proof that an individual is in violation of a rabbinic order. We said that a *gett* should never be used as a bargaining chip to gain increased visitation or custody or anything else. Once there is a civil divorce, the *gett* should be given immediately. Most of the people remained quite cold, but one woman expressed her sympathy for any woman caught in this state of limbo.

This encounter took place in the hallway. Somebody announced that the membership meeting was about to begin. People began to file into the large room, appearing relieved to have a reason to walk away. Suddenly the door to the *shul* office swung open and Dovid's uncle stalked toward us, his face red with rage. At the top of his voice, he demanded that we leave. When we stood our ground he threatened to call the police. Susan, defending freedom of speech, dared him to do so. Totally out of control, he screamed, "I hope he never gives her the *gett*!" And, to our horror, he spit at us and walked away.

We were aghast. The few people remaining in the hallway, who witnessed this scene, were stunned into silence. We turned and left.

Outside the building we caught our breath. We analyzed what had just happened. The spitting was awful but came from a family member in the heat of anger. Even worse was the coldness and indifference of the congregants whose help we sought. To us it was clear that it was the community's responsibility to help an *agunah*. But this congregation only wanted to be left alone.

In later years we were to encounter this same attitude again and again in various local communities. Ultimately we were to realize that the Orthodox Jewish community as a whole was not ready to get involved in helping *agunot*.

Another month passed with no progress. A second demonstration was organized by Ruth's rabbi and her cousin. This time, the slightly smaller but still sizeable group stationed itself in front of the uncle's *shul*. As before the group circled on the pavement, chanting and distributing literature to passersby. It was another blisteringly hot Sunday afternoon, and people began to suffer from the blazing sun. This demonstration ended with a feeling of frustration. There seemed little point in continuing to demonstrate. The community had been made aware of the situation, yet the *gett* remained elusive

Our involvement in Ruth's case stemmed from Shloimy's desire to prove to us that "the system works." He chose Ruth because she had done everything right: She was a pious woman, she had good grounds for divorce, she was willing to re-litigate all issues in a *beit din*, she went to a respected *beit din* she had a *seruv*. We did our part, educating the community about her case and generating public pressure on Dovid to comply. Nevertheless, we had arrived at a dead end. Contrary to what Shloimy believed, the system didn't work.

About two years passed from the day we first met Ruth. After the demonstrations we called her periodically, but there was nothing to report, and, swamped by other cases, we lost contact. We were informed by a friend of Ruth's that she was disappointed that we didn't maintain contact. We felt hurt that she expressed disappointment in us, but we had no other strategies to suggest. Our hurt feelings dissipated almost immediately when we reminded ourselves of the pain and stress she was enduring. We resolved to stay in contact with *agunot* we counseled even if all we had to offer was moral support.

Another year passed. Three years after we met Ruth, we heard that she had received her *gett*. We called her to wish her well in the future and to inquire about the details, hoping to gain insight into how we might help other *agunot*. She told us what had happened. Dovid had come to Ruth's house to pick up some personal possessions that remained in Ruth's house. Dovid became argumentative about an item, grabbed it, knocked Ruth to the floor and rushed off. Ruth fell to the ground with a serious injury. Ruth's neighbors, whom she had wisely asked to be present, witnessed the whole scene.

Ruth filed assault charges in criminal court and had the witnesses to back her up. On the eve of the trial, Dovid offered her a deal. In exchange for her dropping charges he would grant the *gett*. Additionally, he demanded the return of thousands of dollars that he claimed was excessive child support forced upon him punitively by the civil court. Ruth paid the money. She was so tired of waiting for her *gett* that she felt she had no choice. Her parents were not well, and she felt that her years of being an *agunah* had contributed to their ill health. She believed that their condition would improve when she was able to resume a normal life.

In the end, all the hours of planning and demonstrating, of getting hundreds of people out on the street, of talking to rabbis and community members, of distributing thousands of flyers, amounted to nothing. If Dovid hadn't injured Ruth, opening the way to assault charges, who knows how many more years she would have remained an *agunah*?

# 4

# Surveying *Batei Din*

We were picking up information about *batei din* piecemeal from our cases, but after about two years of case work, we felt that we needed to collect information more systematically. We decided we should interview several *batei din* around the New York Metropolitan area. Our goal was to gain insights into *beit din* procedure so that we could provide wise counsel to *agunot* and consult with the rabbis about the egregious problems we had encountered thus far. We developed a set of questions that dealt with key aspects of the *beit din* process and the fears women had when required to appear before a *beit din*. The main topics we wanted to explore were *beit din* policy on issuing a *seruv*, *beit din* stance on litigating some divorce matters in civil court, guidelines for custody decisions, fees for *hazmanot* and *beit din* sessions, and record keeping.

Issuing a timely *seruv* was important because it officially indicated to the community that the recalcitrant husband was defying the *beit din* and should be targeted by demonstrations and other forms of community pressure to give the *gett*. The question of litigating financial matters, child custody and visitation in civil court was crucial because *agunot*, fearful that *batei din* would pressure them to make concessions in order to induce the husband to give the *gett*, often preferred to litigate those issues in civil court. *Batei din*, however, were known to rebuke and threaten women who sought child support and custody through civil court proceedings. Record-keeping was important because we knew of cases in which the records for *gittin* were lost and women were unable to confirm that they had received a *gett*. One client of ours, Chava, couldn't track down proof of the *gett* her first husband had given her 30 years ago. As a result, her daughter Batya had to cancel her wedding because the rabbis said that without proof of her mother's *gett*, Batya might be a *mamzer*, forbidden to marry her groom.

We arranged appointments with rabbis from four *batei din*: Rabbis Aryeh Ralbag and Chaim Krauss who worked with Agudas Harabonim *beit din*; Rabbi Solomon Herbst of the Rabbinical Council of America's (RCA) Beth Din of America (BDA). (Herbst later went on to found his own *beit din*); Rabbis L. Landesman and Chaim Malinowitz of the Beit Din Kollel Harabbonim in Monsey; and Rabbi Reuven Alt of the Bais Yosef Beit Din in Borough Park, Brooklyn. (All fees quoted in this chapter are in 1980s dollars.)

## *Rabbis Ralbag and Krauss*

The meeting with Rabbis Ralbag and Krauss took place in a synagogue on Avenue K in Brooklyn. These two rabbis were associated with Agudas Harabonim of Manhattan's Lower East Side and Rabbi Ginsberg. Their answers to some of our questions were fairly routine. An unlitigated *gett*, where both parties readily agreed to cooperate in the *gett* process, cost between $250 and $300. The *beit din* kept its records in a big black ledger and had been doing so for about fifteen years. Rabbi Ralbag also kept his own records. When we asked about computerized record-keeping, Ralbag and Krauss were firmly in favor of computerizing *gett* records but said that they would refuse to have their *gittin* recorded on the same computer as Conservative rabbis' *gittin*. They also noted that no funds were available for computerization of records. The rabbis reported that the number of *gittin* was on the rise and advocated more attempts at *shalom bayit* (counseling to reconcile couples).

One bright spot for *agunot* was that this *beit din* claimed that they usually awarded custody, even of boys over six, to the mother. The rabbis also said that they tried to work with cooperative judges to have husbands who withhold *gittin* cited for contempt of court.

On the negative side, we were told that this *beit din* did not issue *seruvim*. This was a serious deficiency because without a *seruv*, a wife would have great difficulty mobilizing community pressure against her husband. Many people didn't understand that even if a couple had contentious issues to resolve, using the *gett* as a bargaining chip was extortion. Even when people understood the injustice of *gett* abuse, the old "there are two sides to every story" would allow them to sidestep the socially uncomfortable situation of confronting a recalcitrant husband.

Ralbag and Krauss also admitted to encouraging women to give in to extortion since that might be the only way to secure a *gett*. Otherwise, the rabbis explained, the women would remain *agunot*. They told us that women often paid the *beit din*'s fee for the *gett* despite the fact that the husband should pay, again because otherwise the woman might remain without a *gett*. The unfair advantage that men had in *batei din* couldn't have been clearer.

If a woman went to civil court, this *beit din* recommended that a husband summon her to *beit din*, forcing her to abandon litigation in civil court where she might do better financially. If, however, both spouses took part in civil proceedings without summoning the other to *beit din*, the *beit din* would not re-open issues already settled in civil court. We did not get information about the guidelines the *beit din* followed for financial settlements. Rabbi Ralbag said he did not use a religious prenuptial agreement when performing weddings. Religious prenuptials aim to rein in the power of husbands to withhold the *gett*. These prenups are of limited value but better than the woman having no protection at all (see Chapter 15).

We then asked about the number of cases that the *beit din* handled annually and how many women are unable to obtain a *gett*. We were trying to get an estimate of the number of *agunot* so that we could counter rabbis and others who persisted in denying the magnitude of the *agunah* problem. Ralbag and Krauss reported doing about one hundred *gittin* a year and said that about 5 percent remain unresolved. They lamented the limited enforcement powers of *batei din* in the Diaspora.

All in all, the Ralbag/Krauss *beit din* did not seem satisfactory for women. Without the issuance of a *seruv*, months of litigation before this *beit din* could lead nowhere since, in the absence of a *seruv*, it would be almost impossible to mobilize community pressure on the husband to comply. These rabbis also admitted that they might press women to give in to extortion, for their own good, the rabbis explained.

## *Rabbi Herbst of the Rabbinical Council of America's (RCA)/Beth Din of America (BDA)*

The price of a *gett* at the RCA's Beth Din of America (BDA) at that time was $350. Rabbi Herbst said the *gett* would be done for free if money was a problem. (Up to 2015, we have found this to be true in the BDA.) Herbst supported the idea of computerizing *gett* records but echoed Ralbag and Krauss's statement that no money was available for doing this.

Interestingly, the RCA/BDA seemed to rely on civil courts quite a bit wherever possible. When a case came before them, Herbst said they tried to contact any lawyers involved. They tried to engineer things so that the husband would be the plaintiff in the civil divorce, thus bringing the New York State Gett Law I into play. This 1983 law (New York State's Gett Law II was not passed until 1992) requires that the plaintiff remove "barriers to remarriage," read: cooperate regarding the *gett* (see Chapter 14 for a full discussion of New York's Gett Laws). The RCA/BDA also attempted to educate attorneys to have an agreement to give the *gett* included in any civil separation or divorce agreement. The *beit din* left custody matters to the civil court, Rabbi Herbst told us, because *batei din* don't really have jurisdiction over the children, and the *beit din*'s decision, therefore, could be overturned by civil court, diminishing the dignity and image of a *beit din*.

The RCA/BDA's generally positive policy regarding litigating financial and child related matters in civil court was confirmed in interviews we had at the time with other rabbis associated with the RCA/BDA. In fact, one rabbi in a leadership position at the RCA/BDA told us that they encourage the couple to first settle everything in civil court and to come only then to the *beit din* for the *gett*. Later chapters in this book will reveal that the BDA has moved away from this positive attitude toward litigating in civil court.

Regarding *seruvim* and the enforcement of *seruvim*, Herbst said that the RCA/BDA issued *seruvim* in very few cases and then only as a last resort after all other efforts have failed. The RCA/BDA had not issued a *seruv* in more than ten years, Herbst told us, in compliance with the policy of a deceased, longtime head of the *beit din* who felt that issuing a *seruv* when the *beit din* lacked any enforcement power would make the *beit din* a laughingstock. As for *beit din* efforts to pressure husbands, Herbst said that he had on occasion called employers of recalcitrant to inform them that the husband was withholding a *gett*. Herbst, however, opposed issuing a verdict of *chayav* (requiring the husband to give a *gett*) or *kofin* (coercing the husband to give the *gett*), for like a *seruv*, such strong verdicts would only make the *beit din* look foolish in the absence of any ability to enforce them. *Batei din* in the Diaspora are regrettably weak, Herbst observed.

To illustrate the futility of using coercion, Herbst recounted a story of a recalcitrant husband being beaten and the FBI coming to the RCA/BDA to investigate if their *beit din* was involved, which it was not. We had already heard about that case and were told that the husband had been hospitalized, with both arms and legs broken, but still refused to give the *gett*.

It was clear from Herbst's reticence with regard to *seruvim* and decisive rulings ordering the husband to give a *gett* that the RCA/BDA would do little to help secure a *gett* from a recalcitrant husband.

Once again, we tried to get a handle on how many *agunot* there might be. Herbst told us that the RCA *beit din* dealt with about 500 *gett* cases per year and that 20 percent, or 100 cases per year, remained unresolved. He acknowledged the existence of "factories" where for a price unscrupulous rabbis would issue a *heter meah rabbanim*, permission for a man to marry another woman without giving the first wife a *gett*. No such escape hatch exists for women.

Like Ralbag and Krauss, Herbst said that he counseled women to pay extortion money because otherwise they might remain *agunot*. Herbst seemed to describe a way to avoid extortion by having the *beit din* decide financial matters first but not announce its verdict until after the *gett* is given. In this way, the husband could not use the *gett* to modify the financial settlement because the terms of the settlement would be unknown until after the *gett* was given. The reality of such a sequence seemed questionable to us since Herbst admitted that he recommended capitulating to extortion. In all likelihood, in difficult cases, the husband would never agree to give the *gett* until he was certain that the financial settlement met his demands.

In sum, the RCA *beit din* was not a safe haven for women either. Long proceedings could end without a *seruv* or even an explicit decision that the husband must give the *gett*. And, once again, the woman might be pressured by the rabbis to give in to extortion since she needed the *gett* while the rabbis viewed themselves as powerless to help her in any other way.

## *Kollel Harabbonim of Monsey*

Rabbi Landesman, Rabbi Malinowitz and a third rabbi greeted us upon our arrival in Monsey. In response to our query about the step-by-step procedures of the *beit din*, Landesman told of how the *beit din* attempted to effect a reconciliation of the couple, unless there was already a civil divorce. He said that he advised women who came for a *gett* to speak to one or two divorced women in order to understand what divorce really entails. He referred them to other women if they requested it. Landesman felt that this is more important for women than men, though he referred men as well.

If reconciliation proved impossible, the *beit din* sent a *hazmanah*, if necessary, to bring the parties to the *beit din*. The parties were advised to bring all documentation with them. In Monsey, the rabbis said, most men came to the *beit din* because otherwise signs were put up in the shuls citing them for refusing to appear. Landesman conceded, though, that if the husband had a good *to'en* (rabbinic pleader/lawyer; plural *to'anim*), the *to'en* could delay proceedings for many months with various maneuvers. Each *hazmanah* cost $25, a seruv was $50–$100, and the hourly fee for a *din torah*, a *beit din* hearing, was $80 each for the husband and wife, a total of $160 per hour. The hourly charge was only for the actual session. The parties were not charged for the time the rabbis might spend doing research.

As for a computerized registry, they liked the idea. But the computer would have to be at a non-affiliated Orthodox setting. Yeshiva University, for example, was not acceptable.

When we asked about the cost of a *gett*, the conversation took a surprising turn. A *gett* arranged on Monday through Thursday was $350, but a *gett* done during off hours, on Sunday for example, was $400. Regular *gittin* required only one *dayyan*, two witnesses and a *sofer*. But, if the parties wanted a full *beit din* at the proceeding, three top *dayyanim*, super *edim* (witnesses), and a scribe who wouldn't write the *gett* in a hurry, such a deluxe, neatly written *gett* could cost anywhere from $500 to $750.

We had never heard of such gradations of *gittin* for different prices. Was one *gett* more valid than the other? Impossible. Every valid *gett* must be flawlessly written, and, the *gett* never leaves the *beit din*. And what are "super" edim? We were nonplussed.

The Monsey *beit din* demanded that the parties sign a *shtar berurin* (binding arbitration agreement) that legally binds the parties to abide by the *beit din*'s rulings.

The parties could decide not to litigate custody and assets in the *beit din*, but the *beit din* did not look kindly on this. The rabbis believed that everything should be settled in a *beit din*, not in civil court. But if both parties agreed to settle these matters outside the *beit din*, the *beit din* would still deal with the *gett*. The rabbis also stated their opinion that *zablas*, ad hoc *batei din*, should be avoided.

Landesman said that there were many men whose wives will not accept a *gett*. He said that the more right-wing a couple was, the more problems there were with women refusing to accept a *gett*. Often they asked for a more generous financial settlement than the husband was willing to give, Landesman explained. He added that he believed that there were probably as many men as women with *gett* problems. The third rabbi at the meeting added that when wives assault their husbands it is actually worse than when husbands hit their wives because women, physically weaker, will probably pick up something to use, whereas men hit their wives only with their bare hands.

We were surprised to hear Landesman say that there were many women who refuse to accept a *gett*. At the time of this interview with his *beit din*, we had heard of only one such case. Since Landesman had said the problem in such cases often was women asking for better financial terms, we speculated that, perhaps, women in *Haredi* communities like Monsey, with the typical family of 7 to 10 children, might fear not getting adequate child support after divorcing. Over our thirty years of involvement, we heard of only one additional case of a wife refusing to accept a *gett*, and we had no idea of the facts in that case.

Next we had a major procedural policy that we wanted to propose to the rabbis for consideration: making its standard operating procedure that the *gett* must be given before the *din torah* (rabbinic court hearing) litigation over children and assets so that the husband could not use the *gett* as a bargaining chip. The *gett* would be signed, sealed and delivered, no longer available to be used as leverage to extort concessions from the wife. One of the rabbis was supportive of this idea. But then an argument broke out amongst them over this point. They could not reach an agreement. At our next interview with Rabbi Alt's *beit din*, we were to learn more about why our proposal, which seemed like common sense, was controversial.

The Monsey *beit din* was different than the previous two in that they would issue a *seruv* when a husband refused to comply with the ruling of the *beit din*. But that was as far as it went. After the *seruv* was issued the *beit din* would do nothing to enforce it. At most they might make a phone call or two to the husband's family or to another rabbi, but they made clear that the phone call was not an official *beit din* action. The *agunah* was basically left completely on her own to try to use the *seruv* to generate community pressure on the husband to give the *gett*.

As we were learning, planning and sustaining demonstrations and community pressure is extremely difficult. Furthermore, many synagogue rabbis ignored *seruvim* from *batei din* so that the husband was often able to maintain a perfectly normal life within an Orthodox community despite the existence of a *seruv*. Giving credit where credit is due, however, at least the Monsey *beit din* issued a *seruv* and made clear who was the villain and who the victim when a man kept his wife an *agunah* by refusing to obey the *beit din*.

On the question of custody, the rabbis told us that all things being equal, boys over six go to the father and girls go to the mother. However, they added, all things are rarely equal. The children's wishes are also taken into consideration. They declined to give us any statistics on how often custody is awarded to mothers vs. fathers.

By the time we did this Monsey interview, a new question had arisen about the possibility of an "irur," a doubt cast on the validity of a *gett*, by a husband after he has given the *gett*. The Monsey rabbis said that this is very rare, but it could happen. If a husband claimed his wife was not fully complying with the terms of the settlement, he could challenge the validity of her *gett* and her freedom to remarry. This possibility of a husband attempting to revoke the *gett* is a powerful threat against a woman who fears her husband will re-imprison her in their marriage should she challenge any aspect of the divorce settlement. A wife, of course, has no such recourse should a husband fail to pay child support or fail to comply in any way with a divorce settlement (see Chapter 7).

Like the other *beit din* rabbis, the Monsey rabbis lamented the fact that the community was not more responsive to the *agunah* problem. They felt the community should give more support to a *seruv* issued by a legitimate *beit din*.

Relatively speaking, the Monsey *beit din* seemed like the best of the three *batei din* we had interviewed so far. In contrast to the other *batei din*, they did issue *seruvim*. This fact led us to refer several women to them after this interview. But even this *beit din* had serious problems. Custody decisions were questionable, criteria for decisions on financial matters were unclear, *to'anim* could create long delays in the *agunah*'s quest for a *gett*, civil court was frowned upon, and the *beit din* gave virtually no assistance in putting some muscle behind their *seruvim*.

## *Rabbi Alt of the Bais Yosef* Beit Din

The Bais Yosef *beit din* was located in a run-down two-family house on a tree-lined street in Borough Park, Brooklyn. Our meeting was with Rabbi Alt, who was one of the three senior members of the *beit din*. The *beit din* had been in existence for ten years.

Alt told us that the *beit din* handled about fifty *gett* cases a year. About ten of the fifty develop into problem cases, the same 20 percent problem rate as that of the RCA/BDA. The step-by-step process at Bais Yosef was as follows. When a woman approached the *beit din* for help in securing a *gett*, a *hazmanah* was sent to the husband. When it appeared to the rabbis that this would be a contentious divorce, they insisted that the spouses sign a *shtar berurin*. The fees involved were $20 for a *hazmanah* and $200 per hour for *din torah* sessions, with $100 being paid by each party. The cost of a *gett* was $400.

If the husband failed to appear after the first *hazmanah*, a second and third were sent. If, after the third *hazmanah*, the husband still failed to appear, an "*azharah*," a warning, was issued. Next, a *seruv* was issued. The cost of a *seruv* was $25. Alt reported that no husband had ever sued the *beit din* over the issuance of a *seruv*, although there had been some threats of lawsuits. The time that elapsed between the first *hazmanah* and a *seruv* is four weeks.

Alt mentioned one familiar delaying tactic that litigants can use—asking for a *zabla*. The obstructionist party can choose a disreputable rabbi for the *zabla* so that no other rabbi wants participate in the panel thus causing a long delay. This was reminiscent of Rabbi Landesman's remark that a skillful *to'en* can find ways to delay the *beit din* process for months or more. Fear of this kind of delay tactic is what motivated Ruth to accept her husband Dovid's choice of Rabbi Wolff's *beit din* though Wolff had close ties to Dovid (see Chapter 3).

Alt's position on litigating in civil court was similar to the Monsey *beit din*'s, but a bit more tolerant. Like the Monsey *beit din*, Alt held that if one party began divorce proceedings in civil court and the other party objected and demanded that everything be litigated in *beit din*, the *beit din* should force the party who initiated civil action to withdraw from civil court, waive anything they had won in civil court, and re-litigate everything in *beit din*. However, if both parties agreed that some matters should be settled in civil court, they could come to the *beit din* just for the *gett*. Unlike the Monsey *beit din*, Alt did not seem to frown on couples that elected to litigate some issues in civil court rather than in *beit din*.

We were not able to ascertain from Alt what criteria the *beit din* used for deciding custody and financial matters.

Alt was receptive to the idea of a central registry for *gittin*, agreeing that it was necessary.

It was during this Bais Yosef interview that we heard the most troubling concept of a husband challenging the validity of a *gett* that he had already given his wife. In Monsey the rabbis called it an "*irur*." Rabbi Alt termed it "*motzi la'az*" (calling into question). Alt's statement was extreme. The Monsey rabbis said a man could challenge a *gett* if the wife failed to fulfill the terms of the divorce settlement. Alt, on the other hand, was saying that a man could be *motzi la'az* if he was unhappy with a *beit din p'sak*, even if the wife was obediently complying with that *p'sak*.

The issue of *motzi la'az* came up when we suggested to Alt, as we had to the Monsey rabbis, that the *gett* be given before finances were litigated so the *gett* would be removed as a bargaining chip during the litigation of custody and financial matters. Alt responded that the sequence of the *gett* first and then the financial settlement was impossible because if the husband didn't like the way the *beit din* divided the financial assets, he could say, "If I had known that my ex wife and children would continue to live in our spacious apartment while I would have to live in a one room apartment, I would never had given the *gett*." This is an example of motzi la'az, and such a statement by the husband casts a cloud over the *gett*. Therefore, said Alt, the *gett* cannot be given until all issues are settled to the husband's satisfaction. Only then can the *gett* be given without fear of *motzi la'az* developing.

The way Alt described the *gett* process, it seemed that pressuring the wife to yield to her husband's demands was not aberrant behavior but, rather, an essential part of the *gett* process. If the husband's demands were not met, he was within his rights to withhold the *gett* or even challenge a *gett* after it had been given.

Like the Monsey *beit din*, Alt's Bais Yosef distinguished itself by the fact that it issued *seruvim*. But, also similar to Monsey, Alt's *beit din* did nothing to enforce the *seruv*. The *agunah* was on her own. To his credit, Alt did not say that his *beit din* encouraged women to give in to extortion. Because of the willingness to issue a *seruv*, we began to recommend women to Alt's *beit din*. But his approach to *motzi la'az* was disturbing, for it clearly made the *gett* into an extortion tool. And it seemed like a *seruv* would not be issued against a husband who said he was withholding a *gett* only until his wife complied with his demands regarding money and the children, for satisfying his demands was a prerequisite to a valid *gett*.

Alt's *beit din* was perhaps better than Ralbag's or the RCA, but it still exposed women to unpredictable and far-reaching risk.

In short, none of the four *batei din* we interviewed provided justice for *agunot*.

## *The Unfair* Beit Din *System*

When we interviewed the *batei din*, we were in the early stages of our struggle to free *agunot*, and we arranged the interviews naively thinking that disclosure of *beit din* procedures could lead to examination and improvement of the *beit din* system. The information we gathered revealed that the *beit din* system was far more inequitable than we imagined. There were no uniform rules governing the system; each *beit din* had its own rules, which were largely unknown to *agunot* who had to navigate the system. Some *batei din* issued *seruvim* and some did not. Some tended to award custody of children to mothers while others favored fathers' custody of sons. The criteria used to decide custody and visitation were vague and established without the assistance of psychologists or social workers. Some *batei din* encouraged capitulating to extortion as the only way to secure a *gett*. None of the *batei din* did much to mobilize the community against a recalcitrant husband. A phone call or two or a conversation with a synagogue rabbi was about the most any of the *batei din* rabbis undertook to pressure a husband. Women who won custody or financial support in civil court could be forced to sign it all away when they sought their *gett* in a *beit din*.

Yet all these problems we learned about through our interviews were only the tip of the iceberg. What the rabbis told us was a sanitized version of what goes on in a *beit din*. In our case work, we learned what *batei din* would never reveal in an interview—that some demanded extra pay for expeditious service, that they took on cases where one of the litigants had a close family or friendship tie to the rabbinic judges, that *batei din* withdrew *seruvim* after an *agunah* was able to mobilize significant community pressure against a husband, that in return for the *gett* they urged women to be silent about such matters as pedophilia, that rabbinic courts repeatedly sent women back to abusive marriages. Some *batei din* were better than others, but only in the sense of being the lesser of evils. In truth, no *beit din* was safe for women and children.

## *The Road Not Taken by* Batei Din

Is there a different *halakhic* path that the *batei din* could follow to free *agunot* from these nightmarish marriages? Can a rabbinical court do more to sever the marital bond a wife agreed to as she circled her husband seven times under the *chuppah* (marriage canopy)?

The Talmud lists conditions which require a man to divorce his wife, mandating that a rabbinic court force him if he refuses to give the *gett*. The great 12th century *halakhic* authority Maimonides ruled that when a wife declares "my husband is repulsive to me," "*ma'ees alai*," and she refuses to have sexual relations with him, then "we force him to divorce her immediately, for she is not as a slave that she should be forced to have intercourse with one who is hateful to her" (*Mishneh Torah*, Laws of *Ishut*, Paragraph 14, Section 14). Since she refuses to fulfill her wifely duty of providing her husband with sexual relations, she may lose the value of her *ketubah*, divorce settlement (see Chapter 5) but her feelings of revulsion toward her husband are validated and he is forced to grant her a *gett*, even by beating him up or jailing him. However, Maimonides's contemporary, Rabbenu Tam, limited forceful coercion of a *gett*. Today, whether you're in the Maimonides or Rabbenu Tam camp, beating a recalcitrant husband is illegal, to say the least. Only in Israel do *batei din* have the power to jail recalcitrant men. This is rarely done, and some of these men hold out for years rather than grant a *gett*.

Are there *halakhic* methods for rabbinic courts to free women without jailing or beating a recalcitrant husband until he consents to a *gett*? The answer is, "Yes." The most well known method is for a *beit din* to find grounds to declare that a *ta'ut* (a mistake) occurred at the time of the wedding that renders the marriage void *ab initio*. In such a case, there is no need for a *gett* because no binding marriage bonds ever came into existence.

The late, renowned Rabbi Moshe Feinstein voided marriages when a husband had mental defects or physical conditions that predated the marriage, which the wife was unaware of at the time of the wedding, conditions severe enough that most women, had they known of these problems, would not normally have agreed to such a marriage. Feinstein also voided marriages where the husband was discovered to be homosexual, stating that a typical woman would not knowingly wed a homosexual. In such cases, Feinstein held that the bride's consent to wed was a mistake, null and void. Additionally, he used other criteria to cancel marriages, such as invalid witnesses or other technical flaws in the marriage ceremony itself.

Unfortunately, few rabbis have followed his example. The *batei din* that we have dealt with over the last thirty years rarely, if ever, pursue Rabbi Feinstein's strategy for voiding a marriage based on *ta'ut* despite the fact that many recalcitrant husbands appear to have serious personality disorders. We have dealt with quite a few cases in which the grounds Feinstein relied on for voiding the marriage existed, but the *beit din* rabbis never asked the *agunah* the pertinent questions that would elicit information in support of voiding the marriage. The *agunot* are generally not knowledgeable enough to raise this possibility with the rabbis so this route to freedom remains unexplored. For example, two *agunot* who had tried in vain to obtain a *gett* in the BDA turned to us for help. We studied their cases and concluded that there were grounds for a declaration of *ta'ut*, that the marriage was void, and the women could be freed without a *gett*. We helped the women organized and submit the relevant information to the BDA. Only after we exerted prolonged pressure on the BDA, in one case openly and in one case behind the scenes, did the BDA agree to void the marriage and free the women. In one case, the husband was homosexual (and, in addition, a pedophile jailed for molesting his own children); in the other there was abundant evidence that the wedding ceremony did not comply with Orthodox *halakhic* procedure. Both cases clearly met Rabbi Feinstein's well-known criteria for *ta'ut*, voiding a marriage.

Rabbis who free an *agunah* by a decree of *ta'ut* tend to prefer that their work be kept quiet, even secret, for fear of being denounced by other rabbis. After Rabbi Feinstein's death, his grandson, Rabbi Mordechai Tendler voided marriages but kept his activity under wraps. We learned accidentally that he was following in the footsteps of his grandfather and referred some *agunot* to him, whom he freed. Unfortunately, a scandal put an end to his work (see Chapter 16).

Beginning in 1996, the Rackman *beit din* voided marriages based on domestic violence, sexual infidelity and abandonment, and its work was widely publicized so that *agunot* would know where to turn for help. Hundreds of *agunot* brought their cases to Rackman and were freed. Rackman and the *beit din* were pilloried by the Orthodox rabbinate which declared that the *agunot* who remarried on the strength of Rackman's rulings were committing a terrible sin. Rackman was undeterred, but the *beit din* ceased functioning in 2007 when Rabbi Rackman's advanced age prevented him from continuing (see Chapter 16).

More recently, beginning around 2010, Susan and a colleague, Estelle Freilich, have worked for several years with Rabbi Gedalia Dov Schwartz, who has quietly voided marriages, including on the basis of a husband's history of domestic violence. However, Rabbi Schwartz does not publicize this work and has not issued any of the decisions in our cases through the BDA over which he presides. This limits the impact of his work because it is not institutionalized through the BDA and is, consequently, little known to the Orthodox community.

In 2014, Tamar Epstein, an *agunah* whose years-long ordeal received extensive media coverage in the United States and Israel, was freed by an anonymous panel of rabbis without her husband delivering a *gett*. Rumor has it that the grounds for freeing Tamar were *ta'ut*, but the names of the rabbis and the *halakhic* grounds for freeing Tamar have all been kept secret.

A new *beit din* formed in 2014, headed by American/Israeli Rabbi Simcha Krauss, offers some hope for progress in applying more lenient and compassionate *halakhic* approaches to freeing *agunot*. In addition to using *ta'ut* as grounds for freeing *agunot*, Krauss has said that he intends to use another *halakhic* tool, a *gett zikkui*, which means that the *beit din* will itself issue a *gett* when a husband refuses to do so (see Chapters 10 and 16).

It remains to be seen what the impact and lifespan of the new Krauss *beit din* will be and whether the rulings of that court will be accepted by the Orthodox rabbinate or whether this new *beit din* will be attacked and delegitimized like the Rackman *beit din*. In the meantime, Orthodox women who are pleading their cases in more established *batei din* find themselves trapped in a system that produces the cruelty and injustice recorded in the pages of this book.

## 5

# The Phantom *Ketubah*

In the years that we began working with *agunot*, we were spending every *Shabbat* afternoon around our dining room tables studying the Babylonian Talmud (BT) with a group of women from our newly formed women's prayer group, *The Flatbush Women's Tefillah Group*. We were engaged in an intensive study of the BT Tractate Ketubot, which deals with the laws of Jewish marriage. It took us six years to complete the entire tractate. The more we learned, the more it became clear to us that Prof. Judith Hauptman's "rereading" of the rabbis of the Talmud was correct. These rabbis of late antiquity upheld the patriarchal structure of Jewish marriage, but they were also intent on developing provisions for some measure of economic security for women. Sadly, contemporary *batei din* do just the opposite, they undercut the economic security of *agunot* and their children.

## *The* Ketubah: *An Ancient Prenuptial Contract*

The rabbis of the Talmud understood that marriage is an economic arrangement. In column after column of the Talmud, the rabbis laid out numerous laws governing this arrangement. The husband is obligated to provide his wife with material support that maintains or enhances her accustomed standard of living and to pay to redeem her from captivity, but the wife has no claim beyond that on his income or on any assets accumulated during the marriage. The wife is obligated to perform certain domestic chores such as baking, laundering and nursing her child (Mishnah Ketubot 5:5) and must also give her husband any income she earns during the marriage. Any property that the wife brought into or inherited during the marriage remains hers, but any income generated by that property belongs to the husband. For example, if she owned an orchard prior to the marriage, the income from the sale of the annual produce belongs to the husband, but she retains title to the property itself and regains full possession should her husband predecease her or in the event of divorce.

A key document regarding these financial rights and obligations is the *ketubah*, the marriage contract, in which the husband pledges to feed and clothe his wife and provide her with her conjugal rights. The *ketubah* also specifies the sum that the wife will receive should her husband pre-decease or divorce her. In the event of divorce, the rabbis, perhaps, thought the husband might need time to put together the requisite funds for the divorce settlement, which might result in delaying the divorce, providing a cooling off period, giving the husband time to reconsider and sparing the wife from being suddenly left adrift. Note, however, that a husband could divorce his wife at will as long as he paid the requisite *ketubah* financial settlement. A woman had no such power.

Talmudic law is based upon the societal norm that women would generally move directly from their fathers' homes to their husbands' homes. The Talmud envisions most women spending their lives under the care and jurisdiction of a man. They viewed single women, widowed and divorced women as unfortunate and vulnerable. The *ketubah*, a document created by the rabbis, provided for a standard sum to be given to a widow or divorcee to sustain her for at least a year, giving her time to stabilize her financial situation, perhaps by remarriage or employment. Moreover, the Talmud reports numerous *ketubot* (plural of *ketubah*) containing variations, additions and enhancements of women's economic rights that go beyond the standard *ketubah*'s terms.

For example, Mishnah Ketubot 12:1 discusses a situation of a man (let's call him Reuben) who married a woman who had a daughter from a first marriage. Reuben committed to an enhanced *ketubah* in which he pledged, in addition to the standard financial obligations to the wife, to support the woman's daughter for five years. This second marriage ended in divorce, and the woman married a third husband (let's call him Simeon), who also pledged in the *ketubah* to support the daughter for five years. We might assume that Reuben's financial obligation to the daughter ended when Simeon, the third husband, assumed responsibility. Yet, surprisingly, the Mishnah decrees that Reuben is still bound to support the daughter for the full five years. Both men must fulfill their pledges to provide support to the daughter: One provides her material needs in kind—her food and clothing—and the other provides the cash equivalent.

The financial pledges made by husbands in the *ketubah* were backed up by all the assets he owned. The *ketubah* gave the wife a lien on all the husband's property. Even property that had been sold by the husband after the marriage could be repossessed by the wife to satisfy her *ketubah*.

We were struck by the lengths to which the ancient rabbis went to preserve and ensure the *ketubah* clauses negotiated by individual women at the time of marriage.

We learned that Tractate Ketubot contains a discussion that is surprisingly relevant today, when women often have careers and significant, independent sources of income. The Talmud (BT Ketubot 58b) presents the case of such a woman, talented and able to support herself, who says to her husband: "Don't support me and I have no obligation to turn over any of my income to you." By making this declaration, the wife waives the pledge her husband made in the *ketubah* to support her and consequently extinguishes her husband's claim to 100 percent of her income.

After working with *agunot* who had been deprived of marital assets by rabbis adjudicating their *gittin*, we were frustrated that some rabbis continue to follow the rule that all marital assets belong to the husband even when both spouses had worked outside the home and generated the income to acquire those assets. After all, the Talmudic model just described above provides the *halakhic* framework for women who earned income to retain that accumulated income or the assets purchased with that income in the event of divorce. Of course, civil divorce law goes even further and treats a homemaker wife, who has no outside income, as a full economic partner with regard to the division of marital assets upon divorce.

Over the centuries, civil law regarding the financial aspects of marriage overtook and displaced the *ketubah*. Viewing the *ketubah* as a type of limited compensation owed to a wife upon divorce, the civil court's awarding the wife a share of marital assets and alimony may be viewed as substitutes for the *ketubah* money. However in a number of cases that we handled, it became apparent to us that the *ketubah* still remained relevant either because the *agunot* agreed to litigate the divorce in *beit din* only or were forced to give up assets that were theirs under civil law in return for the *gett*. These cases revealed that today's rabbis and *batei din* trample on women's financial rights, in stark contrast to the efforts the rabbis of the Talmud made to protect women financially.

## *The* Ketubah *at Modern Wedding Ceremonies*

At every Orthodox wedding, much care is given to having kosher (*halakhically* qualified) witnesses, two men known to be observant of Jewish law, sign the *ketubah*. It is read aloud, with great gravity, under the *chuppah* the marriage canopy. Then it is presented to the bride who is instructed to keep it with her always.

The solemn reading of the *ketubah* in its original Aramaic is a ritual traditionally offered to a rabbi or other learned person that the couple wishes to honor. Technically, this reading serves to separate the *erusin*, betrothal (similar to engagement, but more binding), from the *nissuin*, the actual marriage. In the Talmudic era, the *erusin* period lasted about a year and afforded the groom time to prepare financially for the responsibilities of marriage, particularly to give him time to amass the money to underwrite the financial pledge he makes in the *ketubah*. Today, the *erusin* is no longer a prolonged preparatory period that precedes the marriage. Rather, the *erusin* and the *nissuin* take place minutes apart under the marriage canopy at the wedding, separated only by the reading of the *ketubah*. The rabbis made this change because after *erusin* a *gett* is necessary to free the woman even though the couple has not cohabited. To avoid exposing betrothed women to the risk of becoming *agunot* should the groom disappear or hard feelings set in during the prolonged betrothal period, the two stages, *erusin* and *nissuin*, were telescoped into one ceremony, one after another under the marriage canopy.

All the solemnity surrounding the reading of the *ketubah* and the importance of the bride safeguarding it after the marriage serve to elevate its status, to emphasize the *ketubah* as a symbol of rabbinic concern for protecting women's financial interests in the context of marriage. Our research uncovered what a charade this has become today.

## *Women Forced to Waive the* Ketubah

We first began to investigate the *ketubah* and related issues because of our experience with Joan. Joan was a young woman who had a brief marriage of only a few months. Her husband disparaged and humiliated her on a daily basis. She tried to convince him to go to marital counseling, but he refused. After months of mental cruelty, she ended the marriage.

The civil divorce proceedings moved along quickly as there was little to litigate—there were no children and few marital assets from this marriage of short duration. However, Joan's husband was withholding the *gett*, and the rabbi of his synagogue, where his parents were generous donors, seemed to be contributing to the delay by agreeing to countless meetings at which nothing was accomplished and empty promises were made.

On the advice of a mutual friend, Joan contacted us. After hearing her story, we contacted her husband and his rabbi to protest the delay. Yet another meeting was scheduled, but again with no progress toward the *gett*. We kept up the pressure. The prospect of public exposure was very distasteful to the husband's family, and, after a few weeks, a date was set for the *gett* proceeding.

The *gett* was to be given at the Rabbinical Council of America's (RCA) Beth Din of America (BDA). Joan and her parents asked that someone from Agunah Inc. accompany them. Susan agreed to go. When Susan arrived at the *beit din*, she was directed through a narrow hallway to a small room where Joan and her parents were already seated in front of a desk. A *beit din* official, Rabbi Kis, was sitting behind the desk. As Susan entered the room, Rabbi Kis asked who she was. Joan and her parents immediately explained that they had invited Susan to be there with them. Rabbi Kis didn't look happy, but he was quiet. Susan was informed that the *gett* was being written by a scribe in the next room. She knew that this ritual would take about an hour.

At every *gett*, a *sofer* (scribe) carefully writes the *gett* document, on parchment paper, with a quill pen dipped in ink. There is a standard form and wording to be followed. The parchment must be ruled with thirteen lines, and the last line should be divided into two for the two witnesses to sign. The *gett* may not be pre-written, nor can it be a preprinted form with the names of the parties to be filled in. The document must be handwritten in its entirety for each couple. There can be no erasures, no mistakes. Again, the rabbis in the Talmud may have thought that perhaps during the time that the scribe painstakingly writes out the *gett*, the husband may have second thoughts and the woman will be spared from being divorced.

There are a limited number of scribes trained to do this painstaking work. We encountered the same scribes over and over again.

While waiting for the scribe to complete the document, Rabbi Kis took out a thin loose leaf binder and pushed it across the desk for Joan to look at. He referred her to the script inside, which she was to recite during the *gett* proceeding. After he read a few innocuous lines in the script about her Hebrew and English names, any nicknames Joan had, her parents' names, etc., Rabbi Kis said "at this point in the proceedings you will be asked if you waive your *ketubah*." He instructed Joan to answer "Yes," as indicated in the script. Susan's ears perked up. She was surprised to hear this. After all, a *ketubah* embodies the financial settlement to which a divorced woman is entitled. As a condition for the *gett*, Joan's husband was demanding that she return her engagement ring which, under civil law, is hers to keep. She was returning it reluctantly, as her parents had footed the entire bill for a lavish wedding. Susan felt, therefore, that it was doubly unfair for her to be forced to give up what was hers under civil law as well as the financial settlement described in the *ketubah*, which was hers under Jewish law.

Susan turned to Rabbi Kis and asked, "How much is the *ketubah* worth?" Rabbi Kis grumpily said that he had no idea. Susan asked how Joan could renounce something without knowing its value. *Halakhah* (Jewish law) requires that a party know the value of anything they are renouncing. Rabbi Kis deflected the question and tried to move along with the script. Susan persisted, asking Rabbi Kis, who was only an administrator, to ask the rabbinic judges, who preside over hundreds of *gittin* every year, what a *ketubah* is worth. Rabbi Kis shot back that they won't know either. "Does that mean that of the hundreds of women who receive their *gett* at the RCA each year, none collect their *ketubah*?" Susan asked. Once again, Rabbi Kis tried to cut the conversation short and return to the script. He ended the dialogue by saying, "These are the words Joan has to say if she wants her *gett*!" He abruptly walked out of the room.

In his absence, Joan and her parents decided that they would go along with renouncing the *ketubah* monies because they just wanted to get everything over with. Rabbi Kis returned and waited to see if the storm had passed. When no further inquiries about the *ketubah* were forthcoming he said that he had just checked and that the scribe was almost finished. In a few minutes Joan could enter the room to receive the *gett*. He added that Susan could not go into the *beit din* room with Joan. Susan, not wanting Joan to go through the experience without a friend next to her, tried to talk her way in, but Rabbi Kis refused. He announced that Joan's husband didn't want Susan in the room, and he strode out. Joan was visibly shaken but walked in alone. When she returned she was pale but relieved that her ordeal was over.

This episode brought home to us the fact that we had never heard of a woman receiving her *ketubah* money. Rabbi Kis's admission that no one at the RCA, in whose offices the Beth Din of America met, would know how much a *ketubah* was worth was surprising, since the BDA had the largest case load of *gittin* in the metropolitan area, about 500 a year, according to their own estimates.

## *Disuse: Rabbis Don't Know the Value of the* Ketubah

We began to do some research. We wanted to know how much a *ketubah* is worth today and, therefore, how much money women are being deprived of. The sum the groom pledges in a standard *ketubah* is 200 *zuz* in silver for a virgin bride, 100 for a non-virgin. Some communities have a tradition of inserting additional, usually quite large, sums as a symbolic expression of the groom's devotion to his bride.

We decided to pursue this issue with the BDA first and called Rabbi Gedalia Dov Schwartz, the head of the BDA, who resided in Chicago. He said he didn't know. "We follow Rav Moshe's approach with regard to the value of the *ketubah*," Rabbi Schwartz explained. He was referring to the late, great Rabbi Moshe Feinstein, an acknowledged authority on Jewish law. When asked what Rav Moshe's formula was, Rabbi Schwartz said that he had to look it up. "Look it up? How can this be? Aren't any women receiving their *ketubah* money?" He replied, "I think I remember one woman, many years ago, who received her *ketubah* money." He promised to get back to us with the amount according to Rav Moshe.

Two weeks passed, and we heard nothing. We called again and faxed our request to Rabbi Schwartz. Finally he answered and informed us of Rav Moshe's formula for determining the value of a *ketubah*. It was linked to the current market value of silver. According to this reckoning a *ketubah* was then worth six thousand dollars. (How interesting that the value of the *ketubah* fluctuates with the price of silver, offering some protection from inflation!)

We decided to continue our investigation. Did other rabbis also not know the value of the *ketubah*? If *dayyanim*, who officiate at hundreds of *gittin* per year, did not know, did congregational rabbis who perform weddings and ceremoniously fill in *ketubot* at each wedding similarly not know? After all, the *ketubah* is not an unusual, esoteric item, seldom seen or referred to. It has a starring role at every Orthodox wedding!

We began calling the major *batei din* in the New York metropolitan area. We found that few rabbis had any idea how much a *ketubah* is worth today and that *batei din* made no effort to collect the *ketubah* from husbands even in cases where the *agunah* is impoverished and has received no civil court financial settlement or has even given in to extortion in return for the *gett*.

We continued our informal inquiry by asking rabbis we met, particularly at weddings, how much a *ketubah* is worth today. The answers we received ranged from two thousand to twenty thousand dollars. A few rabbis, who all claimed to be following Rav Moshe's formula, came up with significantly different sums.

Clearly the *ketubah*, developed by the Talmudic rabbis to provide economic protection for women, had lapsed into disuse, despite the prominent role given to it in the marriage ceremony.

We encountered several other cases that brought the significance of this fact home to us.

## Leah's Ketubah: *Another Broken Promise*

For a number of years, we had been working with Leah, an impoverished *agunah* whose husband, Moti, spent his days lolling around the house, failing to support their large family. Finally, Moti agreed to grant a *gett*. Because Leah was so needy, we resolved to try to collect her *ketubah* money. Our desire was strengthened by an aged rabbi, a champion of Leah, who had stood by her all the years she was struggling with Moti. This well-meaning rabbi was now ill and unable to accompany Leah to the *gett* proceeding, at which Rabbi Hillel Weinstein was to officiate. The night before the scheduled proceeding, the elderly rabbi instructed Leah to tell Rabbi Weinstein, in his name, that Leah is entitled to her *ketubah*.

Rabbi Weinstein knew nothing about the case. He had been drafted at the last minute to be the *mesader*, the officiator, at the formal *gett* ceremony, because the various rabbis who had been involved all along were not acceptable to both parties.

On the morning of the *gett* proceeding, Rivka accompanied Leah to a house in Brooklyn, where the *sofer* lived. The *gett* was to be given in the *sofer*'s house because he was homebound, recovering from eye surgery. Rivka and Leah arrived early and passed the time making small talk in the dining room with the *sofer*'s wife. The two professional witnesses (Rivka had seen both before) chatted with the *sofer*. Two kosher witnesses—adult, religiously observant males—must be present at every *gett* proceeding. Available, usually unemployed or retired men, are often paid a small sum to show up as witnesses. The witnesses are part of the regular cast of characters, along with the *sofer* and the rabbis, whom Rivka and Susan met again and again.

Around 9:00 a.m., the door to the dining room opened and in walked Moti, Rabbi Weinstein, and another tall, heavy set black frocked man with a black hat. Rabbi Weinstein greeted Rivka, whom he recognized from previous *gett* proceedings, and said hello to Leah. He indicated that he was in a hurry and that was the reason for the early appointment. He sat down, eager to begin.

As Leah sat quietly, a little dazed, Rivka asked Rabbi Weinstein for a private word. He motioned Rivka and Leah into the adjoining room, the kitchen. Rivka asked when Leah would receive her *ketubah* money and how much it would be. Rabbi Weinstein seemed startled by the question, clearly taken aback by the possibility that this could turn into a more complicated proceeding than he had anticipated. He responded, rather nervously, that he knew nothing about this case, he was merely the *mesader*, and that the *din torah*—the earlier negotiation or litigation in *beit din*—should have already settled the questions about the *ketubah*. Leah spoke up, insisting that her rabbi instructed her to ask Rabbi Weinstein for her *ketubah* money. She explained her pressing financial needs, that she had to raise eight children on her small salary, had received nothing from Moti for years, and did not expect to receive anything in the future. At the very least, she felt entitled to her *ketubah*. Before she would accept her *gett*, she demanded to know the status of the *ketubah* money, even if this meant a delay. Rabbi Weinstein, clearly sympathetic to Leah, said that he would see what he could do.

The group returned to the dining room, and Rabbi Weinstein asked Moti to come into the kitchen. Moti, his black garbed friend, and the witnesses all went into the kitchen. After some time there, they returned to the table. Moti sat down, opened a *sefer*, a religious text he had brought with him, and focused his eyes on the small print. It was too far away for Rivka to see if it was a book of Talmud. It looked like one, but Rivka wondered if Moti could even pretend to study Talmud in the midst of these proceedings. From this point on until the actual granting of the *gett*, Moti never took his eyes off the book.

Rabbi Weinstein announced that Moti had agreed to pay the amount of the *ketubah*, which was to be determined by Rabbi Spicer. "Why Rabbi Spicer?" Rivka asked. Rabbi Weinstein, the two witnesses, the *sofer* and Moti's friend all responded at the same time that this would save money, as Rabbi Spicer was already familiar with the case, having been previously involved with the negotiations. Rivka asked if Leah had the option to go to another rabbi. "Yes," said Rabbi Weinstein, "but that would be foolish, for the fees of a new *beit din* would dissipate much of the money gained from the *ketubah*." Nevertheless, Leah insisted, she wanted to be sure that she had the option of going to another *beit din*. Rabbi Weinstein assured Leah that she could choose any mutually acceptable rabbi.

The *sofer* began the process of determining the names of the parties and their correct spellings. The proceedings were conducted in Yiddish, which all present except Rivka understood. The *sofer* produced a briefcase containing his writing materials and explained to Moti that he would now "gift" this briefcase to Moti, who, having technically become its legal owner, would "lend" the writing materials back to the *sofer* to utilize to write the *gett*. Moti was instructed to rise, place the briefcase under his arm, and walk around the room with it, demonstrating ownership. Moti did as he was told, never once glancing at Leah. He then handed the writing materials back to the *sofer*, sat down and resumed looking into his book.

The *sofer* took out a piece of parchment, already scored with lines, a bottle of black ink, and two quill pens which he closely examined. He began writing. Everyone in the room began whispering, the men to the men, the women to each other, except for Moti who continued to pore over his text.

After about 45 minutes, the *sofer*, who had been writing diligently, finished. He handed the *gett* to the one of the witnesses, and left the room. This witness, quill in hand, was in the middle of signing the document when he suddenly stopped, clearly upset, and called for the *sofer*. Apparently, he thought he might have smudged the still wet ink text on the parchment. The two witnesses, and the rabbi and *sofer*, studied the *gett* closely, all of them quite upset. The women were curious to see what was happening, but did not get up to look, knowing such curiosity would be considered unseemly.

The men's conversation indicated that the witness's error might mean that the *gett* needed to be rewritten. Rabbi Weinstein announced "I don't have time." The *sofer*, who had remained quite calm in contrast to the witnesses' agitation, took the *gett* into the kitchen, apparently to study it more closely, in a different light. Rivka heard him speaking with his wife but it was unclear what they were doing. After a few minutes the *sofer* returned with the *gett*, and this time sat next to the witness, guiding his writing as he resumed signing. The two men bent over the *gett*. Suddenly, the *sofer*'s wife ran in and started shouting at her husband in Yiddish "Meturnisht!" "You mustn't!" It seems that because of his eye surgery, the *sofer* had been forbidden by his doctor to bend. The two of them returned to the kitchen, where all could hear them quarrelling, the wife's voice loud and upset, the *sofer*'s calm and soothing. Rivka and Leah smiled at each other, at the irony of this scene. In the midst of the dissolution of a marriage, the elderly couple's obvious love and concern for each other had seeped into the room.

Eventually the *sofer* returned to the dining room and sat straighter, careful not to bend. The ceremony resumed.

Rabbi Weinstein instructed Moti to stand and to drop the *gett* in Leah's open palms. Leah was then to put it under her arm and walk around the room with it, signifying acceptance and ownership, just as Moti had previously done with the *sofer*'s briefcase. The ritual of parting was enacted. Never once looking Leah in the eyes, Moti dropped the *gett* into her open palms, thereby ending 20 years of marriage. She, accepting this closure, walked with it a bit, then returned it to the *sofer*. The *sofer* took the document, which he had so carefully labored over, folded it, and, with a small knife, cut it by etching an X shape over the folded surface, as proof that the document was actually delivered. One of the witnesses informed Leah that she would receive a *p'tur* (an official statement indicating a *gett* has been finalized and the woman is free to remarry) in a few weeks. Rabbi Weinstein said to Leah: "*Harei at muteret l'khol adam.*" "You are now permitted to any man."

This ritual phrase, indicating that the woman is now single, is blunt and unlovely. Nothing comparable is said by the rabbi to the man. It is reminiscent of "*Harei at mekudeshet li*," "Behold you are sanctified unto me," recited by the groom, to his bride, under the *chuppah*. A *chuppah* is full of hopes, of prayers, festive and happy. Here now was the bitter end of 20 years, the unraveling of the marriage, the mirror image of the *chuppah*. In contrast to the atmosphere of a wedding, the atmosphere at a *gett* proceeding is designed to be studiously unemotional, very matter of fact.

Whether under the *chuppah* or at a *gett*, the husband is the active party, the wife passive. Under the *chuppah*, the husband speaks and acquires a wife, binding her to him exclusively, and only he can break those marriage bonds with a *gett*. The bride stands silently under the *chuppah*, passively signals her agreement to be acquired when she allows the wedding ring to be slipped on her finger. She acquires no exclusive claim to her husband and has no power to end the marriage. If her husband is willing to release her from the marriage, she passively holds out her hands to receive the *gett* as she held out her finger to accept the wedding band.

Rabbi Weinstein instructed Leah in a sing song manner, indicating that he had recited this instruction many times, not to remarry within 92 days, and never to marry a Kohen (member of the priestly caste). The 92-day interval is in order to prevent uncertainty about paternity that might occur should the woman remarry immediately and bear a child soon after her divorce. As for not marrying a Kohen, divorcees are deemed unacceptable as wives to a member of the priestly caste. Aside from these limitations, she is free to remarry whomever and whenever she chooses.

When all were leaving the house, Rabbi Weinstein asked Rivka about Fay, a former *agunah* whose *gett* proceeding Rivka had attended more than a year ago, at Rabbi Weinstein's *beit din*. The *agunot* are more than mere objects to him, Rivka thought.

Rivka and Leah were subdued on the drive home, discussing the slim possibility of Leah actually receiving her *ketubah* money. A few days later, Rivka called Rabbi Weinstein and asked about the *ketubah*. Rabbi Weinstein wrote a letter to Rabbi Spicer, stating that Moti had agreed to pay Leah the *ketubah* amount that Rabbi Spicer would determine.

Neither Rabbi Weinstein nor Rabbi Spicer followed up to see if Leah received anything. After some attempts, Leah herself gave up trying to collect the *ketubah* money. It seemed a foregone conclusion to all involved that Leah's *ketubah* was a phantom, a promised sum that would never materialize.

It was now clear from Joan's and Leah's stories that, along with doing little or nothing to block husbands' extortionate financial demands in return for the *gett*, *batei din* routinely ignore the provisions of the *ketubah*.

Once we witnessed the routine rabbinic dismissal of the *ketubah* monies, we tried to educate the Orthodox community about it. We wanted to focus attention on this highly visible but widely ignored document that symbolized *halakhah*'s concept of some financial rights for the wife. We published articles encouraging women to inquire how much their *ketubah* is worth. One article was published in *The Jewish Press*, a weekly newspaper widely read in the right-wing Orthodox community. A rabbi responded to our article by ridiculing us since, he said, "Everyone knows that the *ketubah* is a meaningless document today."

Although it is true that a financial settlement in civil court might moot the *ketubah* issue in many cases, we had, and continue to have, many clients who were forced to litigate all divorce issues in a *beit din*. We advise *agunot* against this, but husbands rightly sense that they have more leverage in a *beit din* and consequently force their wives to submit to a *beit din* to arbitrate all outstanding matters. There the women are generally awarded less financial support than they would have been granted in civil court. Some leave the *beit din* with only their *gett*, deprived of assets they would have received under civil law (see Chapter 7). These women are entitled to their *ketubah* money.

## Flash Forward Fifteen Years

The cases described above took place in the late 1980s to early 1990s. Unfortunately, little has changed. How little things had changed was brought home to Rivka when, in 2011, she accompanied Michal to the Beth Din of America (BDA) to receive her *gett*. (The BDA formally separated from the RCA in the early 1990s and reorganized with a separate board of directors. People continue, however, to refer to the BDA as the RCA *beit din*, and the two are still located in adjoining offices.)

Michal was referred to Rivka by the rabbi who officiated at her wedding. He had insisted that the couple sign a religious prenuptial agreement (see Chapter 15); therefore Michal anticipated little problem obtaining her *gett*.

Michal was a young woman whose marriage had lasted only a few years. There were no children and few assets to litigate about. Rivka advised her to obtain a *gett* as soon as possible, before civil proceedings were over, in order to remove the *gett* from the civil divorce negotiations. Interestingly, though all rabbis know how to perform wedding ceremonies, many have no idea about how to advise people regarding a *gett* and, therefore, refer women to Agunah Inc.

The *gett* proceeding was quickly scheduled and Michal asked Rivka to accompany her. The two women met at a Starbucks situated near the *beit din*. Michal told Rivka that her spouse was unemployed and refused for three years to seek work while she worked to support them both. They both wanted the divorce, but he wanted her to continue to support him by paying him alimony. Michal was worried about this. She clearly was not well to do. She dressed poorly and did not even have a cell phone. Her job was not lucrative. Rivka felt that this was a case where the woman should receive her *ketubah*. Her marriage was ending, providing her with no assets or money; in violation of his pledge in the *ketubah*, her husband had never supported her; she had given all her earnings to support the household; and she might even have to pay her husband alimony! Rivka decided to see how the morning would go.

Michal had previously informed the rabbis that she did not want to see her husband face to face, so they arranged to have him come in first, have the *gett* written, and then have a *shaliach* (agent) deliver it into Michal's hands. While Michal and Rivka waited in a small room for the all clear signal, telling them that the husband had done his part and left, Rabbi Weissmann, Director of the BDA, came in and, speaking quickly, prepared Michal for what was to follow. He told her she would be asked questions by the *mesader ha'gett*, the rabbi officiating, and gave her the well-worn BDA script which contained the formulaic answers to each of the questions. He added: "and you will be asked if you waive your *ketubah* and you will say 'Yes.'"

When Rabbi Weissmann left the room, Rivka reviewed the procedure with a nervous Michal. She explained to Michal about the *ketubah*, telling her that, while it is worth some money, women are routinely asked to give it up.

While Rivka and Michal were waiting, the *sofer*, Rabbi Lichter, came in. He addressed them warmly, nodding kindly in recognition to Rivka. Introducing himself to Michal, he gave her a lovely *brachah* (blessing), wishing her a happier life in the future. After he left, Rivka offered Michal a prayer to recite, explaining that, as the *gett* proceeding is dry, matter of fact, legalistic, a total opposite of the wedding ceremony, she felt it appropriate to add a spiritual, emotional moment of meditation by suggesting that each woman recite a prayer, one that Rivka adapted for each woman she accompanied to a *gett* proceeding.

Michal recited the prayer with tears in her eyes and wept a little, an emotional release, mourning the end of her marriage. She was now ready to accept her *gett*.

Rivka and Michal entered the court room which was furnished with a long wooden table. At the opposite end of the room were a few chairs for them to sit on. It was an intimidating atmosphere, appropriate for a dignified court room, but formal and cold. A bearded, black garbed man came in, studiously ignored them, and sat down at the table. Michal whispered to Rivka that his coldness chilled her. Rabbi Weissmann entered and introduced Rabbi Goldman, who was to be the *mesader ha'gett*. The *sofer* came in and informed Michal, in a kindly manner, that as he had been appointed the agent, he would be the one who actually dropped the *get* into her hands.

Everything went as planned. Michal was asked questions and duly followed the script.

When the proceedings were completed, and Rabbi Lichter had dropped the *gett* into Michal's open palms, Rivka and Michal watched while he cut it with an X, then told Michal to fax the final civil divorce papers to the *bet din*, which would then mail her a *p'tur*. At that point, Rivka decided to raise the issue of the *ketubah*.

As the men were getting up to leave, Rivka said: "I have a question. I know that Michal waived her *ketubah*, but I would like to know how much it is worth." The men were quiet. Weissmann looked at Goldman, clearly hoping he would respond. Goldman mumbled that he didn't know the exact amount. Rivka asked, "Do any women ever receive their *ketubah* money in this *beit din*?" Goldman promptly gave a short speech, saying that some women, perhaps many, of course, receive their *ketubah* when appropriate.

"How much do they receive?" asked Rivka. "I don't remember," was the response.

"How much did the last woman who received her *ketubah* from this *beit din* receive?" The men hemmed and hawed and didn't answer. Finally, to break the silence, Goldman said that the amount varies because it is tied to the market value of silver.

Since the *gett* was done and there was no risk to Michal, Rivka barreled on, asking: "Is it *halakhically* acceptable for a person to waive something when they don't know its exact worth?"

At this point, Michal, beginning to understand the significance of the discussion, stood up and said: "I want to know how much money I have just waived." Again, the rabbis were unable to supply a specific sum, stating that the amount varies with the price of silver. "How much is the weight in silver? I want to check in the newspaper when I get home, and I need to know what weight to check," Michal demanded.

Continuing to ignore Michal would have been untenable. Rabbi Goldman said quietly: "The *ketubah* amount is anywhere from a few thousand to $40,000." "Do you mean from $5,000 to $40,000?" Rivka asked. "No," he mumbled, "from $3,000 to $40,000."

Michal repeated: "I just waived a sum from $3,000 to $40,000?" "Yes."

Michal and Rivka left the *beit din* and in the hall Michal mentioned that she was sure that her ex would be demanding money from her in civil court and she felt that the sum she had just waived might be considered part of the divorce settlement. She wanted her attorney to know this. Rivka responded that as Rabbi Weissmann is an attorney, he might be able to help her. The women returned to the *beit din* offices and Michal asked to speak with Rabbi Weissmann. He came out to the waiting room, and she told him her idea. He agreed to speak to Michal's attorney about the *ketubah* money she had waived.

Michal and Rivka parted, with good wishes on both sides. Rivka later asked a matrimonial attorney about Michal's situation. The attorney responded that since Michal waived the money, it is unclear whether she could still use it to her advantage. However, the attorney suggested that the *beit din* should add a phrase to their script. When women are asked to read the statement indicating the waiving of their *ketubah* monies, the statement should include the phrase: "I waive ... except for what I am entitled to in civil court," or some such variant.

## *A Rare Exception*

In one exceptional case in which Susan was involved, a woman actually received her *ketubah* money, because of an unusually compassionate rabbi, who intervened on her behalf.

The case involved an *agunah* who had been married to a wealthy man. The couple had litigated all aspects of their marriage, including custody, visitation, and division of assets, in civil court. The civil divorce had been finalized and the woman, let's call her Tova, had been awarded a generous portion of the assets, yet she still lacked a *gett*. Since Tova was the spouse who initiated the civil divorce, the 1983 NYS Gett Law I, the only one on the books at that time (see Chapter 14), was of no help to her. Her husband, grasping that he could use the *gett* to extort a reduction in the large amount of money Tova was awarded in civil court, insisted on financial concessions in return for the *gett*. Tova, being a very religious woman, was willing to cede a large sum in exchange for a *gett*. Her freedom under civil law was worthless to her if she was unable to have a social life and to remarry under Jewish law.

Eventually, the parties agreed that Tova would accept a much smaller sum than the court had awarded her, in exchange for a *gett*. They chose a very traditional New York area *beit din* to arrange the *gett* proceeding. Tova asked Susan to accompany her to the proceeding.

On a cloudy fall day, the women arrived at the *beit din*, which held its sessions in the building of a large yeshivah. The first thing they noticed were the coat racks, holding many identical black coats, with black broad brimmed hats placed above them atop the racks. "How can they tell them apart?" the women whispered to each other and smiled.

Feeling like outsiders in a male space, the women were ushered into a small side room, where they sat together until the *Rosh Beit Din* (Head of the Court) came to speak with them. He immediately put them at ease, as he was exceedingly pleasant, even warm, looking directly at Tova while asking questions. The building had a separate room for the husband, thereby avoiding the awkwardness of having former spouses sitting together in one space. The rabbi asked Tova the usual questions about the exact spelling of her name, of her parents' names, and everyone's nicknames, at one point necessitating a phone call to Tova's mother to check a detail. Finally, when the rabbi had all the information he needed, he kindly suggested that Susan and Tova take a walk if they liked, as speaking with Tova's husband, as well as the actual writing of the *gett*, would take some time. He instructed them not to drive out of the area, to remain within the confines of the location written in the *gett* itself (where it was written, name of town, etc.). He assured them that there was a restaurant within those boundaries.

Craving a snack and a break, Susan and Tova left the building and tried to follow his directions. They wandered about the quiet streets, asking a number of men, all of whom were garbed in black suits and coats, where they could find a place for a bite to eat. The men walked right past them, barely acknowledging their existence. They soon realized the men would not speak to them and decided to turn back, when they saw a woman walking in their direction. They eagerly asked her to direct them to a coffee shop. She smiled and insisted that they come with her, to her home, which, she assured them, was close by. They demurred, not wanting to impose upon this total stranger.

She insisted, saying that she understood why they were in the neighborhood, and she wanted the *mitzvah* (good deed) of welcoming guests.

Their new acquaintance led them to her large, beautifully appointed home. She asked her household help to bring coffee. Soon they were presented with a lavish repast; coffee, many varieties of pastry, small sandwiches. Susan and Tova engaged in warm discussion with their gracious hostess. It was as though the three had known each other for years.

This chance, fortunate encounter changed the somber mood with which the day began. Upon leaving the house, Tova told their hostess that her kindness was what she would always remember about the day she finalized her parting from her husband.

Indeed, so many years later, this is what Susan still remembers.

Susan and Tova returned to the *beit din*, and were ushered into a large room, where the rabbis, a set of witnesses, the *sofer*, and Tova's ex sat. The proceedings began. The routine questions were asked and answered. At one point, the *Rosh Beit Din* intervened, departing from the regular script. He asked questions that seemed to be highly irregular: How much money had Tova received in civil court, how much in child support, etc. Susan, somewhat alarmed, rose to ask why these questions were necessary. The *Rosh Beit Din* motioned to her to remain silent. He continued questioning Tova, and then turned to Tova's former spouse and asked if he was planning to pay Tova her *ketubah* money.

"How much does it amount to?" "Twenty thousand," was the response. "O.K., I will." "You must pay her the sum within two weeks," the rabbi insisted. "Fine," he agreed.

Needless to say, this unasked for and unexpected award surprised both Tova and Susan.

The proceedings continued, the *gett* was granted and received, and Tova was freed at last. The women called for a car service to take them home. While waiting for the car, the *Rosh beit din* came over and asked for a lift to the train. When all settled in the car, Susan thanked him for awarding Tova her *ketubah* money. He explained that during the preliminary discussions, he came to realize that Tova was giving up a very large sum of money that the civil court had awarded her in exchange for her *gett*. He was morally opposed to this extortion, and so he decided to give some of it back to her. He acknowledged that she was receiving only a small sum compared to what she had given up, but he had done what he could.

He then went on to scold Tova, in a friendly but definitive manner, for having litigated in a civil court at all. "Jews should bring all their disputes to a *beit din*," he stressed. Despite his disapproval of the couple having litigated in civil court, this very religious man, understanding the injustice inherent in the imbalance of power regarding the *gett*, managed to find a way to redress it, even if only a little.

The cases presented here illustrate how far modern rabbis have strayed from the precedents set by rabbis of old to provide some measure of financial security for women in the form of the *ketubah* divorce settlement and the reversion to the wife of assets that she brought into the marriage. Despite Tova's experience of actually receiving her *ketubah* money, the vast majority of deserving women never do. But the injustice goes far beyond rabbis neglecting to assure an *agunah*'s right to her *ketubah*. Remember Sarah, whose violent, recalcitrant husband got more than half the value of the marital residence though the house had been purchased solely with money from Sarah's inheritance. Upcoming chapters will reveal how rabbis actively participate in extorting additional money and other concessions from *agunot* and even cooperate in allowing the husband to extort money from the entire community in return for a *gett*.

# 6

# Extortion: Every Man Has His Price

The evolution of the *ketubah* reveals the efforts of the ancient Talmudic sages to protect women who were widowed or divorced from being plunged into poverty. Modern rabbis have, regrettably, taken the opposite tack. Extortion as the price for a *gett* is routinely accepted by rabbis. In case after case, rabbis cooperate by acting as go-betweens in extorting financial concessions from women as the price of the *gett*. Often, *batei din* leave these women and their children impoverished, on the brink of homelessness.

Rabbis rationalize their cooperation with unscrupulous husbands by citing the *halakhic* requirement that the husband grant the *gett* willingly. Consequently the rabbis are predisposed to satisfy the husband's demands, allowing him to walk away from the *beit din* with major financial gains and other undeserved concessions. Fixated on securing a valid *gett*, even at the expense of justice, the rabbis act as if brokering extortion in return for the *gett* is in a way meritorious. If the woman is no longer chained to her husband, is free to remarry, no longer at risk of committing sinful adulterous acts, the *beit din* has fulfilled its responsibility, the rabbis feel. From the rabbis' single-minded perspective, securing the *gett* is a religious requirement worth almost any concession by the wife.

We knew from our very first cases that unscrupulous husbands try to use the *gett* as a tool for extortion. It took a bit longer for us to realize that rabbis accept the recalcitrant husbands' extortion demands as an integral part of *gett* negotiations. As one *beit din* rabbi said to Susan when she inquired about how he solves contentious *gett* cases, "Every man has his price. The man has to be happy to give the *gett*. If the woman can come up with enough cash, the problem is solved."

## Gett *at a Discount—The Open Institutionalization of Extortion*

The idea that it is acceptable for men to put a price tag on the *gett* was so widely accepted that Rabbi Yehuda Levin, director of Get Free, a short-lived organization, unabashedly described himself as a "negotiator" whose mission was to obtain a *gett* for a woman at the lowest possible price. Get Free was established and funded in the early 1990s by a family whose daughter had a *gett* problem. As a result of their experience, they decided to help others in similar situations by hiring Rabbi Levin to help *agunot* free of charge. Rabbi Levin contacted us and asked us to refer women to him. Unaware of Rabbi Levin's attitude, we were happy to have his help but remained in contact with the *agunot* to monitor their situation. As time passed, we began to feel uneasy with some of the reports the women gave us. One woman complained to us that Rabbi Levin, after talking to her husband, began pressuring her to meet some of her husband's financial demands. Puzzled, we scheduled a meeting in Levin's office.

On the appointed day, we drove together to Get Free's basement office on a residential street in Flatbush. As soon as we entered, Levin, a husky, black-garbed, bearded rabbi, began to tell us about his extensive speaking program throughout the country, sometimes in cooperation with church groups, bringing his anti-gay and anti-abortion message to his audiences. We quickly shifted the discussion to his approach to helping *agunot*.

After over an hour of discussion, it became clear that Levin's concept of helping *agunot* was very different than ours. While we condemned a husband's demand for money in return for the *gett* as illegitimate, Levin was comfortable with negotiating a *gett* for the lowest possible price. In his own words, he said, "I'm not interested in justice for the woman." Once Levin concluded that the husband could not be bargained down any further, he would begin to pressure the wife to give in. Levin freely acknowledged that he did not feel bound by the same code of ethics and confidentiality as a lawyer and had no problem switching from representing the wife to pushing her to capitulate to her husband's extortion.

As the discussion came to an end, Levin couldn't resist returning to the causes closest to his heart. "*Agunah* is your cause, not mine," he said. "My causes are stopping homosexuality and abortion." In 1985, Rabbi Levin ran unsuccessfully for mayor of New York City on the Right-to-Life ticket. He felt the Torah demanded absolute opposition to homosexuality and abortion. With respect to *agunot*, he felt that yielding to extortion was the way to go if it was the best deal the woman could get.

When Levin finished talking, Susan said to him, "Rabbi Levin, you should change the name of your organization to '*Gett* at a Discount' instead of Get Free." There was a chuckle all around, but we returned immediately to the serious implications of our discussion. We told Levin that we were heretofore unaware that he might switch sides and pressure women to agree to "deals" once the husband dug in his heels and that in the future when women ask Agunah Inc. about Get Free we would inform them of this. *Agunot* might still turn to Get Free for help, but they would do so with a clearer idea of Levin's modus operandi.

In 2012, at a demonstration on behalf of the *agunah* Tamar Epstein, Levin was filmed speaking out in favor of the husband's right to withhold the *gett* in order to win concessions from his wife. No longer working as an *agunah* advocate, he openly supported using the *gett* for gain.

## *The Rubin Case—Montreal Pays Off*

*Gett* extortion is so widely accepted by rabbis that they actually solicit "charitable" donations for that purpose. One of Agunah Inc.'s supporters told us that her husband had been approached by a prominent *Rosh Yeshivah* (head of a rabbinic seminary) and asked to make a contribution to help an *agunah* meet the financial demands that her husband had made. Rabbis have openly acknowledged in newspapers that they have collected large sums for payoffs to recalcitrant husbands.

In a case that made headlines in New York newspapers in 1995, the Jewish community of Montreal raised $120,000 to meet the monetary demands of Mr. Avraham Rubin of Brooklyn, whose wife, Chaya, resided in Montreal. It was reported in Jewish newspapers that Rubin asserted that Chaya's brother owed him this sum because of business dealings. Rather than make his case in court, he demanded payment as the price of releasing Chaya. Rabbis launched a campaign to collect this money, and many well-meaning, compassionate Montreal Jews contributed.

The money was conveyed to the Bais Yosef *beit din* in Borough Park, where Rubin resided. The *beit din* set a date for the cash to be handed over and the *gett* to be written. Mr. Rubin demanded to first receive the money and be allowed to leave the *beit din* so that he could put it in a secure place. He said that he feared that after giving the *gett*, he would be attacked and the money would be taken back. He promised to return to the *beit din* after the money was safely stashed away. The *beit din* permitted Rubin to take the money and leave. He returned after a while as he had promised. The scribe then wrote the *gett*, but at the last moment Rubin refused to complete the essential last step of dropping the document into Chaya's hands. Instead, he demanded improved visitation with his children and asserted that the money belonged to him as satisfaction of a debt and had no relevance to the *gett*. He left the *beit din* without granting the *gett*.

The Montreal community was outraged and wrote a letter to the New York *Jewish Press* detailing what had happened and alleging that Rubin was making new and increasing demands for the *gett*. Months passed and there was no *gett*. The Bais Yosef *beit din* that had facilitated the payoff to Rubin did not organize any public pressure on Rubin to return the money. He seemed to have gotten away with his extortion.

In October 1996, the Rubin case made headlines again. It was reported that Rubin claimed he was abducted off the streets of Borough Park, shoved into a van and taken to a cemetery where his ribs were broken and he was subjected to electric shocks and drugged. At some point during this incident, a *gett* was written. Rubin lay on the ground until a passerby heard him moaning and took him to a hospital. In the aftermath of the beating, the Montreal community wrote a letter, published in *The Jewish Press*, announcing that a *gett* had been given and thanking the rabbis for never giving up. No mention was made of the missing $120,000 or the alleged assault. Within days, a group of rabbis condemned Rubin's attackers and declared the *gett* invalid because it was coerced. Rubin blamed Rabbi Mendel Epstein for the attack, but he had no proof. The story faded from the headlines, and it seemed that the Montreal community and its rabbis were satisfied that coercing Rubin to give the *gett* was *halakhically* justified and that Chaya Rubin's *gett* was valid. After $120,000 and some broken ribs and stun gun shocks, the husband realized he "wanted" to give the *gett*. Chaya remarried but had no more children.

In another case of *gett* extortion, also tinged with criminal overtones, Esther, an *agunah* who had been fighting for her *gett* for years, paid rather than continue the struggle. She had broad community support and had mounted several well attended demonstrations in the heart of her ultra-Orthodox neighborhood. At each demonstration, the streets were filled with scores of bearded, black frocked men and *sheitel* wearing women picketing outside the husband's house. Despite the demonstrations, Esther's husband vowed never to give her a *gett*.

Esther seemed to have run into a dead end, but fate gave her another chance if she chose to take it. Rumor had it that her husband was being stalked by loan sharks and needed money fast. She came up with an unknown sum which was conveyed to her husband in return for her *gett*. After receiving her *gett*, Esther published a statement expressing her joy at being free and thanking the rabbis who never gave up on their efforts to help her. Esther paid the price imposed on her by the failure of *batei din* to help her, yet she thanked those rabbis who stood by her.

While Chaya and Esther's cases were highly visible, many other acts of extortion take place quietly, unreported. In one of our cases, the recalcitrant husband was demanding $20,000 from the parents of a young *agunah*, and they decided to pay off after only a few months. At first the parents went from rabbi to rabbi asking for help. All said that there was nothing they could do. One rabbi told them that the best they could hope for was that the husband might become interested in another woman and give the *gett* so he could remarry. With no solution in sight, family and friends began to advise the parents to pay, not to fight. Though the husband deserved nothing, it was a case that was likely to drag on for years. For "only" $20,000 they could avoid years of anguish, unwanted publicity and the risk of escalating demands. Witnessing this payoff was painful for us. But we could not control the *batei din* that refused to condemn such extortion, and we empathized with the parents' fears for their young daughter's emotional state. The parents paid the ransom for their daughter's well-being.

## *Resisting Extortion*

One case in which the husband's extortion attempt failed is instructive and may serve to encourage *agunot* to stand up to greedy husbands even when rabbis advise them to give in.

Roberta, a neighbor of Rivka's, became an *agunah* when her marriage ended and her husband refused to grant her a *gett*. Gradually her husband began making monetary demands in civil court and brazenly through people in the community. One day Rivka received a phone call from a rabbi who had been trying to convince Roberta's husband to grant the *gett* from the time the marriage had ended. The rabbi knew both parties and knew the husband was paying no child support, yet he counseled Roberta to pay up. The rabbi told Rivka that the husband was demanding $200,000 and would grant the *gett* immediately in return. "Tell her to pay," the rabbi said to Rivka. "This is the best deal she will get."

Rivka was dismayed at the outrageous blackmail, but nevertheless conveyed the message. Roberta's reaction was that she would never pay even twenty-five cents for the *gett*. This was reported back to her husband. Furthermore, Roberta told the rabbi to let her husband know that she would not allow him to keep her a prisoner. She would find a way to have a normal life in spite of his withholding the *gett*.

About a month had passed when Roberta received a phone call from a rabbi informing her that her husband had made an appointment to give the *gett* in a few days. Roberta had her doubts about this, but a date was set for the *gett*. Rivka accompanied Roberta to the *beit din* at the appointed hour; her husband arrived, gave the *gett* and left. Roberta had not acceded to any unjust demands, and she had the fortitude to withstand rabbinic advice to give in to extortion. Her husband had tried his best to squeeze some money out of the deal, but finally had to accept the fact that Roberta wouldn't negotiate and wouldn't allow him to control her life even if it meant beginning a new relationship without first obtaining her *gett*. This willingness to transgress the law which declared Roberta a prisoner is what liberated her from the tyranny of the *gett*. Faced with the reality that his wife would not allow *halakhah* to be used as a tool to torture her and that while he insisted that she was still married to him she would be going out with other men, Roberta's husband gave the *gett* with no strings attached.

## Extortion—The Fate of Children

The suffering caused by financial extortion pales in comparison to the angst caused by unsavory husbands who try to use the *gett* to extort unwarranted child visitation or custody. While *batei din* in the United States have no binding jurisdiction over issues concerning children, they will nevertheless support the husband's demand to submit those matters for arbitration by the *beit din*. If the woman refuses, the *beit din* may refuse to take action to pressure the husband to give a *gett* unless she relents. After all, the rabbis say, the husband is complying with the religious obligation of every pious Jew to submit all disputes to a rabbinic court while the *agunah* is wrongly resorting to *arkaot*, secular courts.

Dina filed for divorce in 2008 when she discovered that her husband Judah had sexually molested their young son who was too young to understand what his father had done to him. The civil court appointed a psychologist, physician, investigator and legal guardian to look into the case, and they all recommended that the court issue a "No Contact" restraining order against Judah, prohibiting him from seeing the child. Judah protested his innocence, but the court was convinced that he was a pedophile and left the "No Contact" order standing.

The court proceedings had been a traumatic experience for Dina because the court held a hearing to determine if she was a fit parent in light of the fact that she had not denied Judah any contact with their son earlier. The court was considering removing the child from Dina's custody and putting him in foster care. Dina was beside herself. She explained to the court that her attorney had advised her that until she had a court order denying Judah visitation, she couldn't withhold the child from him. Accepting Dina's explanation and satisfied that she was a responsible parent, the court awarded her custody, but the experience left an indelible mark on Dina. She would never do anything that would raise a shadow of a doubt about her vigilance regarding the welfare of her son.

When Dina turned to a *beit din* to summon Judah for a *gett*, Judah informed Rabbi Roth, the secretary of the *beit din*, that he wanted to litigate all matters, including child support and visitation in the *beit din*. Dina explained to Rabbi Roth that she could never put the civil court's protection of her son in question. She feared that just signing a *beit din* arbitration agreement which reopened the issues of visitation and child support could be grounds for the court taking her son away from her. In that case, Rabbi Roth said, he could not pressure Judah to give a *gett* because Judah was doing the right thing by asking that all matters be put before a *beit din* while Dina was refusing to sign such an arbitration agreement.

Susan spoke several times to Rabbi Roth and kept emphasizing how unthinkable it was for a mother to allow any reconsideration of parental visitation for a father who had molested his son. She reminded the rabbi that the civil court had held an inquiry into Dina's fitness as a parent because she didn't do enough to keep Judah away from their son, but to no avail. Rabbi Roth said there was nothing he could do to help obtain the *gett*.

Several months passed, and Judah retreated to demanding that only the child support be relitigated in the *beit din*, but Dina would not agree. The money was not the main issue for her; it was her intense fear that compromising her son's best interest in any way might cause the court to again question her custody of her son. The rabbi continued to maintain that Judah had a right to refuse to give the *gett* until Dina agreed to relitigate child support, but he held out a slim hope when he said that once the civil divorce was final, the *beit din* would be more forceful in demanding the *gett*.

Judah's attorneys dragged out the civil divorce proceedings with various nuisance motions and adjournments, but finally the divorce was imminent.

Suddenly Susan got a call from a go-between, a Mr. Kablanoff, who said that Judah was willing to give the *gett* but at a *beit din* that Susan had never heard of and whose fee of $1,500 was exorbitant. Susan suspected that Kablanoff was getting a cut from the $1,500, but she continued to try to work out the arrangements for the *gett*. Kablanoff called Susan again and said that Judah wanted Dina to return a fur jacket and some jewelry he had given her as gifts. Susan told Dina and Rabbi Roth about Kablanoff's proposal. Under both civil law and *halakhah* Judah did not have the right to demand the items, Rabbi Roth acknowledged. Dina, however, was desperate for her freedom and agreed to return everything. As suddenly as Kablanoff appeared, however, he disappeared, and the deal was never made.

About two months passed and a civil court session for the divorce was on the calendar. Judah's lawyers declared in their papers that he was in the process of arranging to give a *gett*, and the judge said it would reflect unfavorably on him if he didn't do so. All of a sudden Kablanoff surfaced again, asking Susan to arrange for the return of the jacket and jewelry. At this point, Rabbi Roth came back into the picture and was trying to facilitate the exchange of the jacket and jewelry for the *gett*. But by now Dina, impoverished and struggling to make ends meet, had sold some of the items to pay her lawyer and other expenses. Dina said the items were worth about $1,500–$2,000. But Judah wanted $3,000. And then in the blink of an eye he escalated the demand to $10,000. Agunah Int'l was considering rounding up some money toward the $3,000, but the $10,000 price tag was too much.

When the civil divorce was finalized a month later, Susan called the *beit din* to follow through on Rabbi Roth's pledge to be tougher about pursuing the *gett* once the civil divorce was finalized. Rabbi Roth told Susan that Dina had notified him about the civil divorce and that he had formally summoned Judah to the *beit din* to ask for the *gett*. But Judah informed Rabbi Roth that he was exercising his *halakhic* right to summon Dina to a different *beit din* of his choosing. Rabbi Roth agreed that it would be unwise for Dina to litigate anything in this unknown *beit din* favored by Judah but said that, regrettably, at this point, there was nothing he could do to help. When Susan expressed how morally unacceptable and emotionally painful it was that the *beit din* couldn't find a way to free Dina from her pedophile husband, Rabbi Roth seemed unable to comprehend Susan's exasperation. His face became flushed and tense as he said that the *beit din* had done all it could. He had tried his best to broker the jacket/jewelry trade, but it fell through, he explained. What more could he have done?

Unwilling to jeopardize her son and faced with escalating financial extortion, Dina remained an *agunah*. As another rabbi had said to Susan years ago, Judah had his price like every man, but Dina wouldn't or couldn't pay it.

In the end, Dina gained her freedom by a stroke of luck. Dina signed up for a program that paired her with another woman to study Torah together once a week over the phone. Her telephone partner was Rebbetzin Schlissel, who, sensing Dina was single, began hinting about perhaps finding a suitable match for Dina. Dina explained that she was an *agunah*. Rebbetzin Schlissel was sympathetic and invited Dina to speak with Rabbi Schlissel who wanted to help. When Dina disclosed Judah's full name, Rabbi Schlissel exclaimed that he knew Judah's family and that Judah's father was known as an abrasive, troublesome man in his community. Judah's father was given short term, odd jobs at various shuls and local businesses because he couldn't hold down a steady job anywhere else. Rabbi Schlissel said he would warn Judah's father that if Judah, who was now back living in his father's house, didn't give the *gett*, the community might be less inclined to keep him on their payrolls. The prospect of financial loss did the trick, and Judah gave the *gett*.

Dina was overjoyed to be free and relieved that she was no longer being pressured to re-open any issues that touched upon the safety of her son. But though she was free, Dina couldn't help feeling that the whole system had failed her. The *beit din* became Judah's accomplice, empowering him by legitimizing his demand for re-opening visitation and by brokering his extortion demands. If not for a chance contact with the Schlissels who were total strangers, and by coincidence knew of Judah's troublesome family, Dina might still be an *agunah*. A community that allows the lives and well-being of women and children to be subject to such risk needs to do some deep introspection, Dina thought.

# 7

# When the Recalcitrant Is a Rabbi

When Deborah first called Agunah Inc., she already had a civil divorce and told us that she believed she would soon have a *gett* as well. She was submitting her demand for a *gett* to a *zabla*. She felt that since her husband was a communal rabbi and teacher, a supposed model of probity, he wouldn't risk damaging his public image by defying a rabbinic order to grant her the *gett*. Deborah expressed her *emunat chakhamim*, faith in rabbinic sages, which somewhat eased her fears about accepting the jurisdiction of the *zabla beit din*, which unlike established *batei din* has no track record. Still, she wanted a consultation with Agunah Inc. before the *zabla* sessions were to begin and made a special trip to New York to meet with us.

We met Deborah face-to-face in Rivka's house, seated around Rivka's dining room table. She was a pleasant and refined woman in her late thirties, dressed modestly in an inexpensive yet tasteful outfit. We were impressed with her extensive knowledge of Jewish classical sources. She was particularly learned in Midrash, a genre of rabbinic literature, and her language was the language of Torah, soft spoken but compelling. At this initial meeting and through all the years of our acquaintance, she consistently studded her conversation with gems from Midrashic literature that exactly fit the context.

Our first reaction to Deborah's story was that, in contrast to her belief that the rabbis she respected would do right by her, Deborah was headed for trouble. The rabbis had told her that in order to obtain her *gett*, she would have to waive her civil divorce decree which had awarded her full custody of her five children, a reasonable child support settlement, and exclusive occupancy of the marital residence until her youngest child, then age five, became eighteen. She had to agree to relitigate everything, including custody, before the *zabla beit din* would agree to deal with her request for a *gett*. Deborah planned to go along with these terms. She desperately wanted her *gett*, not so much because she expected to remarry but because she needed a sense of closure. She wanted to sever any remaining connection with the fifteen years of pain she had experienced in her marriage.

Deborah had entered her marriage with high hopes. Raised by parents who were Holocaust survivors, Deborah was given an Orthodox yeshivah education at an all-girls school in Ohio. Her husband-to-be, the pious and learned Rabbi Wax, seemed to be the ideal spouse that Deborah had been raised to seek.

In the early years of the marriage, Deborah was disturbed by certain strictures that Wax imposed on their growing family, but she attributed them to excessive piety. Wax forbade secular books to his children and prohibited them from using the public library. The children would hide their books and read them at night by the light of the moon streaming through their window. He also banned music in the house, claiming that Jews are in mourning for the destruction of the Temple in Jerusalem and may not enjoy music. Art work was also forbidden as unacceptably frivolous. This extreme attitude was particularly harsh on Deborah who was artistic and later gave private art lessons to supplement her meager income. Rabbi Wax went so far as to burn all of Deborah's art books. His temper became increasingly volatile. Plates, cups and glasses flew if Deborah resisted any of his decrees.

Despite the warning signs, Deborah continued to have more children in accordance with traditional Orthodox family life. Her husband's temper was becoming increasingly explosive, but her growing family created pressure on Deborah to preserve the marriage for the sake of the children and for economic reasons. Eventually Wax's behavior became so threatening that Deborah began to realize that divorce was the preferred option. Wax gave Deborah no money for household expenses and had the heat and telephone service cut off. Once when Deborah complained that she had no money for food, he stormed out and returned with two supermarket bags filled only with turnips. He slammed the bags down on the table and shouted, "Don't ever say we don't have food in the house!"

The stress in the house began to affect the children. Their school work suffered, and one of the children seemed to breaking down from the strain. Increasingly, the children were becoming victims of Wax's fits of rage. On more than one occasion he locked them out in frigid winter weather in order to discipline them. He yelled at them and their friends if he overheard them laughing or being light hearted. Deborah became a bundle of nerves and couldn't tolerate Wax's grim presence any longer. She had to put an end to the family's suffering. She asked for a *gett*, but Wax refused.

The situation in the house became unlivable. Deborah consulted with several rabbis who gave her permission to go to civil court. Wax obeyed the civil court's decree to leave the home, but, in defiance of civil court, he failed to pay a penny in child support for four years. Of course, in the eyes of *halakhah*, Deborah was still married to Wax. This enduring link to him had to be severed in order for her to have peace.

We understood Deborah's need for closure but were afraid that she might pay too high a price for the *gett*. She would be risking all she had won in civil court—custody of the children and her right to remain in the house. We suggested that it would be more prudent to hold onto her civil divorce and just wait Wax out without resorting to a *beit din*. As a rabbi teaching at a yeshivah, it would be unseemly for him to continue to hold her hostage and live without a wife. In all likelihood, he would want to give the *gett* and remarry sooner rather than later. But the emotional revulsion of remaining his *halakhic* wife was too much for her. She decided to risk all in the *zabla beit din* as long as two rabbis she respected participated.

Before meeting with us, Deborah had already selected Rabbi Shvach, a well-known rabbi, as her *borer*. Wax's chosen *borer* was Rabbi Bitterman who was widely known as an unprincipled character often chosen by unscrupulous husbands as their *borer*. Since each party's *borer* is expected to lean toward the best interest of his client, the third rabbi, agreed upon by the two *borerim* and supposedly neutral, holds the pivotal position on the *zabla* panel.

Deborah's choice for the third rabbi was Rabbi Beer of Boston. He was well known because of his Torah publications. Bitterman accepted Beer as the third member of the *zabla* panel. Because Deborah trusted Beer's integrity, she was inclined to sign the *shtar berurin* (arbitration agreement) that put her fate in the *zabla* rabbis' hands. We didn't know Rabbi Beer well, but we heard he was a man of means, and this made it less likely that he would be susceptible to bribery. This was important because of Rabbi Bitterman's unsavory reputation. Beer told Deborah he would charge nothing for serving on the panel and he never did.

With trepidation, we wished Deborah well and urged her to call us whenever she felt the need for advice. Over the next few weeks Deborah called often.

Deborah had a relative who was a congregational rabbi in the city where she lived. He accompanied her to the *zabla beit din* to sign the *shtar berurin*.

He was non-committal when she asked his advice about signing the *shtar*. His ambivalence was far from reassuring, but when pressed he said, "If you trust Rabbi Beer, then sign. Beer has the deciding vote, after all." With a stroke of the pen, Deborah gave up her hard won civil court victories, the fruit of three years of litigation, and began anew her struggle to protect her children and win her freedom, this time in a *zabla beit din*.

## *The* Din Torah *and* P'sak

The *din torah* (*halakhic* litigation) consisted of several sessions. Deborah was asked to explain why she wanted the *gett*. She told the rabbis many confidential and intimate details of the marriage. She described how one of her children pleaded with her to ask the *beit din* to "please tell daddy to stop locking us out of the house."

Wax did not deny these actions but feebly excused his behavior as "only a game." He criticized Deborah, accused her of not being a good housewife, not cleaning properly and of looking at pictures of naked women. Deborah insisted that he explain the latter charge. He was forced to explain that he "caught" her reading a book about sculpture. Deborah reported to us that throughout the proceedings, the rabbis treated Wax with kid gloves. They were never harsh with him despite his abusive behavior and admitted failure to support his family over the past four years.

At the sixth and final *beit din* session Deborah and Wax were each asked to state what they wanted. Deborah asked for her *gett*, custody of the children and full ownership of the house. She felt entitled to the house because Wax owed her four years of child support and would probably not pay in the future. Deborah was already more than $60,000 in debt to a Jewish emergency loan fund.

Wax asked for custody of all the children and the house. Deborah, he said, could rent a nearby apartment. He would allow her generous visitation and would even take Deborah back if she so desired.

The *beit din* told the parties that they would be notified when a decision was reached. Deborah's anxiety was relieved somewhat when one of the rabbis told her that the *beit din* would not allow Wax any overnight visitation with the children because they considered him a "borderline" personality.

After about a month, the *beit din* rendered its *p'sak* (ruling). They gave Deborah full custody and limited Rabbi Wax's visitation to daytime privileges. Wax was directed to pay child support of $500 per week, to maintain medical insurance, pay any medical or dental bills not covered by insurance, and to pay yeshivah tuition. Deborah was ordered to return the jewelry Wax had given her before they married. Contrary to civil court, which generally gives the custodial parent exclusive occupancy of the marital residence until the children reach adulthood, the *beit din* decreed that the house be sold immediately, and the proceeds of the sale be split between the parties.

As for the *gett*, the *beit din* made it hostage to the sale of the house. The *p'sak* directed that the *gett* "not be given until the house is sold and the proceeds divided between the parties."

The *beit din*'s ruling put Deborah into a bidding war with Wax. Whoever came up with the most money for the house could buy out the other and take possession. Deborah and the children were now at risk of being evicted and uprooted. Wax, who had shirked his financial obligation to his children for years, could rely on his family's resources to outbid Deborah. Deborah, on the other hand, had already exhausted her borrowing power and her family's meager financial resources to support the children. Ousting her from the house meant six people would be uprooted not only from their home but from their neighborhood, schools and friends. She could not afford to rent an apartment that would accommodate the family in the neighborhood in which they lived. As with many families, the cost of maintaining her mortgage payment was lower than the high rents that often prevail in Orthodox neighborhoods.

Where did this *p'sak* leave Deborah, who had been an *agunah* for five years and had placed her trust in the rabbinic panel? Between a rock and a hard place. If she followed the *p'sak* and allowed the bidding war, she and her children could lose their home. If she defied the *p'sak* and refused to engage in a bidding war or sell the house, she would not receive her *gett*, which was now contingent on the sale of the house. Feeling trapped, Deborah consulted with her lawyer to explore what avenues were still open to her. She asked if legally she had to comply with the *p'sak*. To her dismay, he informed her that she had to obey the *p'sak* since she had signed a *shtar berurin* or else sue the *beit din* in civil court. Deborah knew she could never bring herself to disgrace a rabbinic tribunal by suing it in civil court. That meant that there was no way for her to escape the jurisdiction and rulings of the rabbis.

A few days after the *p'sak*, Deborah poured out her pain to Rabbi Beer, asking how the *beit din* could issue a *p'sak* that delayed the giving of the *gett* until the house was sold. She believed that *halakhah* was geared toward releasing *agunot* as quickly as possible, not letting their husbands keep them in limbo. She became an *agunah* at the age of 37 and was now almost 42. Beer responded that since she had once gone to civil court, which was frowned upon by the rabbis, the *beit din* felt the only way to insure her compliance with the *p'sak* was to be sure that she did not receive her *gett* until it was too late for her to defy their order to sell the family home.

A few days later, Deborah called us and said she had spent a sleepless night. Yesterday, her son's graduation party had been ruined for her because she was in turmoil over what she perceived as Beer's betrayal of her and her children. She had had faith in his decency and integrity but now was forced to realize that he had put her children's well-being at risk by forcing the sale of their home. The civil court had protected her children, but Beer and the other rabbis had stripped away that protection. Deborah was undergoing a crisis of faith, regarding both rabbis and Judaism.

Resigned to having to obey the *p'sak*, Deborah tried to make the best of it. She contacted appraisers to determine the value of the house and how much money she would need to buy Wax out. Wax however defied the *p'sak* by ignoring every responsibility it imposed on him. He sent no child support. He didn't pay tuition. He refused to pay for his children's dental care.

Months went by. The children's yeshivah called Deborah to demand payment. Deborah called the *beit din* to ask that they enforce the p'sak and compel Wax to pay the tuition. After speaking to Wax, Beer told Deborah that the *beit din* would write a letter to the yeshivah explaining that it was the father's obligation to pay, and that they should stop bothering Deborah about the tuition. The yeshivah needed the tuition, not a letter from the rabbis, and they continued to press Deborah. To prevent the yeshivah from refusing admission to her children, Deborah turned to her parents for help. Deborah's parents, Holocaust survivors, dipped into their last savings to assure their grandchildren's precious Jewish education. They began paying the thousands in tuition themselves.

Regarding the dentist bills, Wax told the *beit din* that the children had their teeth cleaned too often, for unnecessary cosmetic reasons. In response to his protest, the rabbis called the children's dentist, who continued to treat the children while waiting for payment, and asked for the children's records to send to another practitioner for an opinion on whether the treatment was necessary. The dentist was shocked by the rabbis' intrusiveness and refused to release these confidential records.

Deborah called us with frequent updates on her situation. At her request, we called and wrote to Beer demanding that a *seruv* be issued against Wax immediately as he was violating every financial clause of the *p'sak*. We believed that Wax, a yeshivah rabbi, would be motivated to fulfill his responsibilities by even the threat of a *seruv*, which stigmatizes a person as being in contempt of a rabbinic court. The *beit din* refused to issue a *seruv*.

Unable to extract a *seruv* from the *beit din*, Deborah tried a new strategy to deal with Wax's total disregard of the *p'sak*, demanding a new *din torah* to which she was surely entitled on *halakhic* grounds. She called Beer constantly to demand this, but to no avail. Though reluctant to go public, Deborah realized that it was hopeless to expect fair treatment from the *beit din* and that only a street demonstration might help her.

Deborah's *borer* Rabbi Shvach did not discourage plans for a demonstration. Rebbetzin Shvach, Rabbi Shvach's wife, who had taken a personal interest in the case, actively encouraged Deborah to demonstrate. We spoke to Rebbetzin Shvach and asked her to join us on the picket lines. She felt it was not appropriate for her but wished us *hatzlocha* (success). Rabbi Shvach wrote a supportive letter for distribution in which he declared that Wax was violating the *p'sak*.

Deborah turned to Agunah Inc. for help with the demonstration. Since Wax was a rabbi, we advised demonstrating at the yeshivah where he taught. We contacted the Rosh Yeshivah (Head of the Yeshivah) for permission to demonstrate in the school's lobby. He gave us permission. We planned a Sunday afternoon demonstration at *minchah* time, when neighborhood people joined the students for afternoon services. We prepared flyers with information about the case to distribute as the men entered the building. We helped Deborah recruit people, and we brought a few carloads of women and a handful of men, including Rivka's husband Irwin. There were about forty women, most of them friends and neighbors of Deborah, who were outraged about her situation.

Deborah's women friends, wearing *sheitels* and long sleeved dresses, were concerned about the propriety of women handing men flyers, raising the possibility of forbidden physical contact. They decided to leave the flyers on a table and ask the men to take them. As the men entered the building's lobby, the women requested, "Please tell Rabbi Wax to grant his wife a *gett*."

The demonstration proceeded uneventfully for quite a while, the women distributing and the men taking flyers and disappearing into the prayer hall without uttering a word. Suddenly the doors burst open and three men rushed into the lobby and overturned the table upon which the flyers had been placed. Next, they began to shove women against the walls, grab the flyers and shout "Get out of here! Mind your own business!" One of the women took out a camera and snapped some pictures. The tallest and burliest of the three men tried to grab the camera, but the women began passing it around one to the other until it was hidden in somebody's pocketbook. During the brawl, Susan, at one point, had the camera in her hands when the burly thug lunged at her, wrenching her shoulder. The thugs escalated their attack. Rivka's husband Irwin tried to defend the women, thrusting himself in the middle of the fray. Two men threw him on the floor and held him down almost choking him. Several women were punched and bruised, but they held their ground. These same women who had worried about violating a religious prohibition by inadvertently touching a man's hand when handing him a flyer now defended themselves by pushing and shoving men back. Not one woman showed any weakness. They all fought back.

The melee ended only when the police arrived, apparently in response to an anonymous call. The police were agitated because other synagogues in the neighborhood had recently been targets of anti–Semitic attacks. They demanded to know what was going on. We were in the midst of explaining that we had the Rosh Yeshivah's permission when he arrived for *minchah* services. At the Rosh Yeshivah's invitation, we all adjourned to his office. He explained to the police that, indeed, we had his permission to demonstrate. Susan, who recognized that the thugs were trying to deter future demonstrations, decided to fight fire with fire. She asked to press charges and showed the police her bruised arm. She described the thugs, told the police we would soon have pictures of them and asked that an investigation be initiated.

The police left, and the two of us remained talking to the rabbi when suddenly Wax's father, Mendy Wax, stormed into the room. We were seated in the front of the rabbi's desk. The first words to cross Mendy Wax's lips were, "Miss, your skirt is too short, please cover your knees." Then we got down to business. We demanded that Mendy, who openly supported his son's recalcitrance, pressure his son to give the *gett* and support his family. Mendy, like Rabbi Wax, said "We're following the *p'sak*. Deborah hasn't sold the house and until she does she won't receive her *gett*." Then he turned and left.

We exited the building and found the street filled with local residents, rabbinic students from the yeshivah and passersby. All were engaged in intense exchanges about the situation, expressing different viewpoints. Most sympathized with Deborah.

A week later when our photos were printed, we proceeded with our plans to press criminal charges against the burly thug. We mailed two copies of the photo to Deborah who passed one copy around the neighborhood surrounding the yeshivah and gave the other copy to the police. Nobody, however, could identify him. Apparently he was an imported goon brought in to terrorize us. But we felt that our tenacity in pursuing the attackers would deter them in the future.

The result of the demonstration was greater community awareness of

Deborah's situation, but in practical terms nothing changed. The *beit din*'s failure to issue a *seruv* despite Wax's egregious violations of the *p'sak*, protected him. In the face of growing community pressure, Wax's refrain was, "I'm just following the *p'sak*." The *p'sak* decreed that the *gett* should not be granted until the house was sold, and Wax hid behind this *p'sak*. He and his father's quoting the *p'sak* confirmed our belief that the *p'sak* was damaging Deborah even though Wax was in defiance of all the financial obligations the *p'sak* imposed on him.

We were frustrated and dismayed because despite the outrage of many in the community, Wax was not removed from his position as a yeshivah teacher, and Deborah remained an *agunah*.

A month passed and we returned to Wax's yeshivah, this time equipped with megaphones, flyers and police protection. Our contingent marched through the neighborhood, past the yeshivah and Wax's block. We ended up outside the yeshivah where Deborah stood, demanding a *gett* through the megaphone. This time, the *beit din* reacted to our activities.

That evening, at midnight, the members of the *beit din* conferred and decided to convene a new session. Beer told Deborah that he had been waiting for the second demonstration to put the necessary pressure on the other *beit din* rabbis for a new session. Although Deborah had been requesting a new hearing because of Wax's flagrant violations of the *p'sak*, it was only the public demonstration that prodded the rabbis into action.

The site of this new *beit din* session became a matter of contention. The two previous sessions had been held at a shabby motel which advertised rooms by the hour. Deborah was uncomfortable even walking into the place and wanted the session held at a more suitable location. She prevailed and Rabbi Beer's Boston synagogue was chosen for the hearing.

On the day of the new hearing, we awoke at 4 a.m. to drive to rendezvous with Deborah before the *beit din* session began. Deborah showed us the synagogue where the session was to be held. We stationed ourselves outside the synagogue so that the rabbis would know that the someone was monitoring their actions. As Rabbi Beer approached the synagogue we accosted him and demanded to know why the *beit din* had not issued a *seruv* against Wax. We also asked him to direct Wax to grant a *gett* immediately. Beer reacted vaguely to us, saying, "We have to be sure that the husband is happy with the settlement so that he'll give the *gett* willingly." "You know," he continued, "I told Rabbi Wax that you two are dangerous women, that I'm afraid of you. I told him that he should watch himself because you ladies have men like him beaten up." We were perturbed by these remarks and indicated our displeasure Beer had unjustly delayed calling a *beit din* session until we went out on the streets. Now he was trying to make us, rather than the *beit din*, the agent for pressuring Wax into complying with the *beit din*'s ruling. (Several days later Beer's foolish lies about Agunah Inc. employing violent tactics resulted in dangerous threats against us.) As we were speaking, the other two rabbis came along and all three entered the synagogue.

The hearing was closed and went on for the entire day. However, Deborah received periodic bulletins about where things stood from an unexpected quarter. Rebbitzen Shvach, whose home was around the corner, periodically entered the *beit din* room ostensibly to deliver important messages to her husband. During these forays, she managed to glean enough information to keep Deborah posted.

At that sitting, the *beit din* amended their previous *p'sak*, eliminating the bidding war and allowing Deborah to buy her husband's share of the house at a price set by an objective appraiser. This small victory was the only tangible fruit of both demonstrations.

Months of haggling over the appraisals of three different appraisers followed. Wax's appraiser, who turned out to be unlicensed, gave the highest appraisal which would have allowed Wax to extort an unfair price for his share of the house. Deborah's appraiser, an established professional in the field, gave a fair appraisal based on comparable houses recently sold in the neighborhood. The *beit din* allowed Deborah to languish during this haggling and suffer from the uncertainty of whether she would be able to afford to protect her home. We wrote and called the *beit din* continuously, asking them to decide on a fair price and resolve the sale of the house so that the *gett* would finally be given.

More than two years had passed since Deborah first went to the *beit din*. She had gained nothing and lost a great deal. Her civil divorce decree ordered Wax not only to pay child support but to pay tuition and health insurance. The *beit din* ignored Wax's failure to pay tuition and medical expenses and eventually freed him from these obligations altogether. Under the civil decree, Deborah and the children would have remained in their home until the youngest child was eighteen. The *beit din*'s *p'sak* forced Deborah to raise a large sum of money or lose her home. And she still did not have a *gett*.

In the midst of the appraisal "war," Wax told the *beit din* that he was going to Australia for a family celebration. Deborah was agitated because she feared that he might not return, leaving her an eternal *agunah*. She begged the *beit din* to insist that he grant her the *gett* immediately or else not be permitted to leave the country. Deborah's already crumbling faith in Beer and the whole *beit din* system suffered another blow when the *beit din* ignored her request and permitted Wax to travel abroad.

In the meantime, we had our own problems with Rabbi Beer. Shortly after Beer told us about his portrayal of us as violent "enforcers," posters began appearing on trees and lampposts in our neighborhood, saying that "The women of Agunah Inc. utilize terrorist tactics and malicious threats" and calling on religious people to kill us on sight. The flyers, signed by an unknown group calling itself "The Rabbinical Organization for the Prevention of Distortion of the Torah" proclaimed that we were informers about whom "Jewish law explicitly states that it is a *mitzvah* to kill the informer after a warning [where possible and if not possible even without warning them]." People who saw the flyer or received it in the mail began calling us to alert us to the danger. Alarmed at the threatening nature of the flyer which left us open to physical attack, we brought a copy to our local police precinct and left Wax a telephone message that the New York police had been alerted to this flyer which we believed originated with him.

The link between Beer's irresponsible remarks and the menacing flyer was apparent. We tried to counteract it by requesting a letter from Beer expressing his approval of Agunah Inc. He agreed to write such a letter, and a few days later he faxed a highly supportive letter to us. The letter, however, was not on stationery nor was it signed. We called to thank him and ask for a signed copy. He said it would be forthcoming, but the signed copy never arrived. Our phone call about the police to Wax, however, seemed to do the trick. No further flyers were distributed.

Incredibly, though Beer refused to give us a signed letter of support, he did furnish one to Wax. Wax felt the need for a letter validating his withholding of the *gett* as community pressure against him was building and growing more vocal. Despite Wax's flouting the *p'sak*'s child support obligations Beer obliged him by writing a letter stating that Wax was following the directives of the *beit din*. Wax made frequent use of this letter which portrayed him as a solid "*beit din* man."

A full half year had elapsed since the *beit din* ordered an appraisal of the house. Finally, the *beit din* sent an appraiser of their choice. The house was appraised below Wax's appraisal, and a sympathetic person who had heard about Deborah's predicament and was concerned that the family remain in the house lent Deborah the money she needed.

It was now the *beit din*'s job to settle the remaining financial details between the couple. Wax owed Deborah thousands of dollars in child support arrears and in compensation for property he had destroyed. In light of the high likelihood that Wax would continue his well-established pattern of refusing to pay child support, Deborah planned to request that the *beit din* hold in escrow a sizeable portion of the money she was to pay Wax for his share of the house. We wrote and called Beer urging him to protect Deborah and the children by holding back money in an escrow account. The *beit din* deducted the arrears Rabbi Wax owed from the money he received, but they withheld only a paltry six thousand dollars in escrow. And most egregiously, the rabbis informed Deborah that her financial claims against Wax would be reduced in the amount of the dollar value of the jewelry which she could no longer return because she had been forced to sell it to buy food for her children. When we challenged the *beit din*'s failure to place at least one year's child support in escrow, Beer assured us that if Wax defaulted again on child support, the *beit din* would issue a *seruv* against him.

The issue of the house was finally settled, and the *beit din* had satisfied Wax's demand to receive his money immediately. He had demanded and the *beit din* had agreed that he would receive either cash or a bank check in his hand at the *gett* proceeding.

At this point, with the *gett* imminent, the rabbis asked Deborah to bring her *ketubah*, religious prenuptial contract, to the *beit din*. Deborah was unable to produce the *ketubah* because Wax had stolen it when he left the house. Wax was asked to bring the *ketubah* into the *beit din*. He refused to do so until he was given a guarantee that the rabbis would not require him to honor the financial obligations stipulated in the *ketubah*. The rabbis, without consulting Deborah, promised him that they were freeing him from any and all such obligations. Only then did he produce the *ketubah*. It was immediately apparent why Wax had stolen it. This *ketubah*, in addition to the standard financial clauses, had an additional provision in which Wax had promised, in the event of divorce, an additional sum (known as *tosefet ketubah*) of $100,000 to Deborah. The *ketubah* contained a statement that the additional sum could not be waived under any circumstances, even if the rabbis told the husband that he need not pay it.

Deborah was deeply shaken. She demanded to know how the rabbis could waive her rights to her *ketubah* without consulting her. The rabbis told her they were sorry, but what was done was done.

After seven years Deborah was finally to receive her *gett*. On that day she stood before the *beit din* and said, "You have condemned me and my children to a lifetime of poverty and debt. When other *agunot* come to me for advice, I will tell them what you have done to me and my children." Three months after finally granting the *gett*, Wax remarried.

## The Aftermath of the Gett

It was no surprise that Wax, with his history as a deadbeat dad, never paid any of the child support ordered by the *beit din*. Even worse, when one of her children required major medical care, Deborah discovered that Wax had lied to the *beit din* and had not maintained medical insurance for the children. This exposed Deborah to financial ruin. She demanded a new hearing before the *beit din* and asked Rebbetzin Shvach to accompany her to the hearing. When Deborah entered the room, Wax went into a tirade shouting that it was *halakhically* prohibited for him to be in the same room as his ex-wife. The rabbis asked Deborah to stand out in the hallway. Rebbetzin Shvach swung into action. She deflated Wax's assertion by suggesting that he stand out in the hallway instead. Deborah was finally admitted to the room. The session ended with no specific action against Rabbi Wax.

Deborah then called Beer requesting access to the six thousand dollars in escrow funds since Wax had defaulted on his financial obligations. To her shock she was told that most of the money had already been released to Wax upon his request. Once again the *beit din* had stripped Deborah of what was rightfully hers, but they had done their utmost to assure that Wax was "happy" about giving the *gett*. She demanded a *seruv* as Beer had promised in the event that Wax was delinquent in his financial obligations. This time the *seruv* was forthcoming but was signed by only two of the three *borerim*. Wax's *borer* refused to sign, thereby weakening its clout.

A *beit din*'s divorce decision has the legal status of an arbitration agreement. As such it can be filed in civil court and enforced through the civil legal system. Deborah sought and received permission from Beer to seek enforcement of the child support and medical insurance the *beit din* had ordered Wax to pay. The civil court ordered Wax jailed on Fridays and Saturdays, releasing him for the rest of the week so that he could earn his salary as a teacher and meet his financial obligations to Deborah and the children. His incarceration resulted in an outcry from his supporters who plastered their neighborhood with posters and flyers decrying and bemoaning the fact that that "Our Rebbe (teacher) Is In Jail." Some of Wax's supporters raised the substantial sum that he owed Deborah so he wouldn't have to serve time in jail, but Wax, vindictive till the end, refused the money, preferring to remain in jail rather than see Deborah get any relief. He continued to serve his weekend time in jail for six months after which the judge gave up. During these proceedings, Deborah represented herself in court while Wax had a pricey Orthodox attorney representing him. Beer testified on Deborah's behalf, but the *beit din*'s earlier rulings had allowed Wax to withdraw and hide all his assets, and Deborah had no recourse.

Deborah was victimized by both her husband and the rabbis but, incredible as it may sound, she was more fortunate than *agunot* who remain chained forever. Wax was a scoundrel. He exploited the *beit din*'s willingness to cater to his escalating financial demands, but when he had squeezed out every possible concession, he cashed in, gave the *gett* and found a new wife as behooves a rabbi. Deborah was lucky to have a circle of courageous friends who were not intimidated by pressure and physical force.

Our contact with Deborah continued after the *gett* was given. We often spoke to her before Jewish holidays to wish each other well. She invited us to a family celebration at which she introduced us to an elderly couple and said, "This couple made it possible for me to get my *gett*. They are the people who lent me the money so I wouldn't lose my home." We thanked the couple, but they humbly interrupted by praising us for our work.

Deborah resumed her life as best she could. She returned to college to complete her degree and improve her earning power to better support her children. She remained a piously observant woman and often reached out to advise *agunot*. She warned them to avoid any dealings with *batei din*.

# 8

# Two Thanksgivings in Parsippany

By 1990, as Agunah Inc.'s activities gained more publicity, the number of *agunot* seeking our help skyrocketed. Overwhelmed, we realized that attempting to deal with the *agunah* problem on a case by case basis was futile. The individual husbands were the ostensible culprits, but the underlying cause of the problem was systemic—the failure of the Orthodox rabbinate and *batei din* to denounce and prevent *gett* extortion and abuse. While continuing to help the increasing number of individual *agunot* who turned to us, we decided to channel some of our effort toward motivating the rabbinate to develop a systemic solution to the problem and to mobilizing the grass roots Orthodox community to press the rabbis in that direction as well.

For several months we considered how best to approach the Orthodox rabbinate in an effort to convince them to acknowledge the existence of the *agunah* problem and to accept their responsibility to help. We had a brainstorming session with a number of interested Orthodox Jews to decide which among the many Orthodox groups to turn to first. One idea was to identify ten prominent rabbis from across the Orthodox spectrum who were considered scholarly authorities and who, if they took a stand, had enough influence over their followers to make a difference. We sat around a table generating lists of such names. We drafted a sample letter to send to them.

In the course of our discussion, we came to realize that our ambitions were too grand. We didn't have the wherewithal, neither the resources nor the access, to reach authorities like the Chief Rabbis of Israel and Diaspora communities around the world. In light of this, we decided that "charity begins at home" and that we would do best to direct our efforts at local rabbis and rabbinic organizations who served the communities in which the majority of our *agunot* lived.

Even this narrower task proved difficult. The Orthodox Jewish community in New York is so fragmented that there is no one obvious central institution to which to turn. We considered approaching the Hassidic Lubavitch and Satmar leadership because we were working with *agunot* from those communities, we were familiar with their *batei din*, and they had centralized authorities that we could identify and contact. But we soon decided these two communities were too insular, and that any measures they might adopt might not spread throughout the broader *halakhic* community.

We seriously considered approaching the Rabbinical Council of America (RCA). This would have been a natural choice for us as the RCA is considered to provide leadership to Modern Orthodox Jews, the movement with which we most closely identified and which on the surface seemed most likely to be responsive to the need for changing the way the *agunah* problem was being handled. Moreover, we had detailed knowledge of their *beit din*, the Beth Din of America (BDA) and all its flaws. After serious consideration, we rejected this choice as well because we felt the RCA's insecurity in the face of constant challenges to its authority from the right-wing of Orthodoxy would make it impossible for them to take a courageous stand.

Ultimately, we decided to focus our efforts on Agudath Israel of America (Aguda for short). Many of our *agunot* came from communities whose rabbis are associated with Aguda and look to their Council of Torah Sages as their *halakhic* authorities. Aguda rabbis are considered to be to the right of the RCA, and we felt that if Aguda dealt effectively with the *agunah* problem, RCA rabbis would follow suit. Aguda was also widely known for its network of social services to the Jewish community, and we hoped they would respond to the needs of *agunot*, as so many become impoverished in their efforts to obtain a *gett*.

In the course of our deliberations, we noticed newspaper advertisements for the annual Aguda Thanksgiving weekend convention. As usual, it was to be held in the Hilton Hotel in Parsipanny, New Jersey, which was able to accommodate the thousands who attended each year. The ads listed the many topics that would be discussed. We felt that the *agunah* issue should be on the agenda. On September 5, 1990, we wrote to Aguda asking that they make room on the program for a session dealing with the problems of *agunot*. We said that many of the *agunot* we dealt with felt abandoned by their rabbis. If a public session was ruled out, we asked that at least a private meeting with *agunot* be held, to be addressed by one of their Torah Sages so that the *agunot* would feel that they were not forgotten. We added that we planned to attend the convention with a busload of *agunot* and their supporters.

We received a quick reply, dated September 12, 1990, inviting us to attend a meeting on October 22 at Aguda headquarters in the heart of Manhattan's busy financial district. We invited Shulie and Frayda, two *agunot*, to join us so the rabbis could see and hear what it meant to be an *agunah* from the *agunot* themselves.

When we arrived we were treated politely, ushered into a room furnished with a large, handsome conference table. A secretary came in with a plate of cookies and asked if we wanted coffee or tea. We declined refreshments and waited a few moments until three men entered, David Zwiebel Esq., the attorney for Aguda, who introduced himself and the two other rabbis.

Zwiebel spoke first. He told us that our request for a session dealing with *agunot* was impossible because the program was full. We pressed him for a private meeting with any member of Aguda's rabbinic leadership. He said that too was impossible and parried by questioning why we were approaching Aguda. After all, he pointed out, Aguda has no *beit din*. We responded that while we recognized that they did not have an official *beit din*, there were a number of *batei din* on which Aguda affiliated rabbis served as *dayyanim* (judges). We began naming them. We also pointed out that many of their rabbis were involved in mediating and settling *agunah* cases. We touched on some incidents in *batei din* that we considered corrupt. Then we asked Shulie to tell her story.

We were eager for these rabbis to hear Shulie's story directly from her because we felt they would be more receptive to her pleas than to our requests. We had reason to think that the leadership of Aguda might be resistant to cooperating with us despite the urgency of the *agunah* issue. We were not part of the Aguda community—our mode of dress alone, our uncovered hair, made that clear. We were identified and deeply involved with the Orthodox women's prayer movement which Aguda passionately opposed. Moreover, as we were not personally affected by the *agunah* problem, we were often accused of using the issue to advance a broader feminist agenda. Shulie, on the other hand, was part of the right-wing Orthodox community, a pious woman who looked and comported herself in the same way that their wives and daughters did. Her husband was a rabbi who attended Aguda functions. While she was speaking for herself, she represented many other *agunot*.

Shulie spoke softly for about fifteen minutes. She recounted her ordeal and her problems with the *beit din* and asked for Aguda's help. She expressed her disappointment with the lack of rabbinic attention to this *halakhic* problem and stressed how important it would be to her and to other *agunot* to have the opportunity to meet with Aguda rabbis to discuss their problems.

When Shulie finished recounting her poignant story there was a brief silence. One of the rabbis broke the silence to express his indignation over our earlier reference to corrupt *batei din*. We were taken aback. The rabbi seemed to have totally ignored Shulie's appeal for help. He addressed not a word to her. We responded by saying how dismayed we were at this apparent lack of concern for Shulie's suffering. Zwiebel then spoke up and expressed his sympathy to her. (In a follow-up letter to us, dated November 6, Zwiebel took pains to stress that those present were "moved by the personal plight" of the *agunot* and admired "the courage and strength they displayed by coming to share their personal stories.")

At that point the third rabbi, who had until then been sitting quietly at the far end of the long table, made a remark whose candor about *beit din* corruption surprised us. He asked why we were so riled up about corrupt *batei din*. This wasn't news. He continued that everybody knows that *batei din* are a *shanda*, a disgrace. Even in *dinei mamonos* (monetary disputes) many observant Jews choose to litigate in civil court rather than in a *beit din*, he said. "Exactly," Susan replied. Nobody could force a party in a business dispute to litigate in a *beit din* rather than a civil court. Pious Jews regularly sued each other in civil court over business matters, and the defendant must litigate in civil court or lose by default. An *agunah*'s husband, however, can force her to litigate the most critical issues of her life in a system that is "a *shanda*," to use the rabbi's words, because that's the only place she can obtain her *gett*.

The conversation reverted to the main point of the meeting—getting some time for the *agunah* issue at the convention. We were informed that there was no possibility of dealing with this issue in any way, not at an open session nor at a small closed session. However, David Zwiebel said if Agunah Inc. agreed to stay away from the convention, perhaps a meeting could be arranged for us with the Council of Torah Sages. We eagerly explored this possibility, trying to pin him down on an approximate date for such a meeting. Zwiebel avoided making any commitment by saying that he could not predict whether the Torah Sages would agree to meet with us at all. We interpreted his failure to make any definite commitment as an effort to deter us from attending the convention while offering *agunot* nothing in return.

We told the rabbis that dangling a vague possibility of a meeting with some rabbis at some indeterminate time in the future was not an adequate response to the needs of *agunot*. *Agunot* had heard vague and unfulfilled promises from rabbis for too many years as their lives slipped by. Aguda's refusal to make any gesture toward helping *agunot* showed us that we had no choice but to bring the *agunot* to the convention. That was the only way that the *agunah* issue would appear on the agenda.

We began to plan our visit to the Aguda convention. This was a much more complex task than planning previous street demonstrations. We needed to know the layout of the hotel and to be prepared to be jostled and harassed. Coordinating group transportation was a time-consuming task. Choosing the best time to show up at the convention was also a challenge. We got lucky when one of our *agunot* told us that she had a friend who worked in Aguda's office and was familiar with the hotel meeting rooms and the program schedule. That inside contact informed us that the Thursday night program during which the Council of Torah Sages sat on the dais was open to the public without any fee or registration and would be the best session for us to attend. There would be a large audience of men and women and we would be able to enter and blend with the crowd.

Our goal in attending was to put the *agunah* issue on the agenda of this major Orthodox Jewish organization. We hoped to stimulate grass roots support among the rank and file attendees by educating them with our literature and exposing them to a face-to-face encounter with *agunot*. We also believed that the rabbis could not persist in denying the *agunah* problem after being confronted with a group of *agunot* in public.

The first practical matter to be attended to was transportation to Parsippany, a good hour's drive from Brooklyn and not readily accessible by public transportation. We anticipated trouble entering and, in those pre–cell phone days, difficulty finding each other amongst the large crowds attending. In addition we needed to instruct our group about how to proceed upon arrival and the best time for that was en route. We opted to rent a bus so that we could brief our group during the trip and we would all arrive together.

Hiring a bus was more expensive than we anticipated, and we turned to a former *agunah* whom we had recently helped. She was a woman of means, we had spent much time on her case, and she received her *gett* directly as a result of our efforts. Upon receiving her *gett* she offered to help our organization when called upon. Rivka called her to ask for $500 to cover the bus rental. Rivka was disappointed when the woman turned her down, saying, "Why don't you car pool?"

The following year, before Yom Kippur, the same woman called us to apologize and pledged to help in the future. We have learned through experience that while most *agunot* are deeply appreciative of our work and maintain contact with us, inviting us to children's bar mitzvahs, holiday celebrations etc., this does not hold true for all. Despite our best efforts, some women feel we let them down if we fail to secure their *gett*, or if we are not as quick as they would like in returning their phone calls. Others go on with their lives and, perhaps needing to forget and heal, don't turn back to offer help to others in similar situations. There are those, however, who never forget their former troubles and become staunch and vocal advocates on behalf of *agunot*.

Faced with the former *agunah*'s failure to help financially, we handled the bus expense by asking all those who rode with us to contribute what they could. We covered the remainder out of our pockets.

We had to be discreet about our plans because we wanted to be able to enter the convention hall without being noticed and stopped. We used only word of mouth to recruit people. Nevertheless, some news about our demonstration leaked out. A few weeks before Thanksgiving, one of the *agunot* who had planned to demonstrate with us was warned by the *beit din* that was handling her case that if she appeared at the convention, the *beit din* would be angry and hold it against her. Even though this was certainly an unfair intrusion, affecting her freedom of speech, we all felt that it would be prudent for her not to attend. This incident showed us the extent of Aguda's concern about our plans.

The night of the demonstration, this particular *agunah* met the bus at its stop in Borough Park, boarded briefly, and wished us success. She felt badly about not coming along, but everyone understood her situation.

To prepare for our demonstration, we formed ourselves into two committees. One committee worked on large posters that we would roll up and hide inside our coats, and then hold up at the convention. The other committee worked on flyers. We produced one flyer that has since had many incarnations, but always with its core intact. It contained a list of our proposals for systemic change. We also wrote an open letter to distribute to the thousands attendees, asking them to insist that their rabbis work to free *agunot*. Lastly, we prepared a petition, calling upon the rabbis of Aguda to immediately form a rabbinic group that would seriously study the *agunah* problem and implement *halakhic* remedies.

Thanksgiving arrived. We kept our family Thanksgiving dinners moving at a brisk pace so that we would be done in time to board the bus. One by one we showed up at the corner of the Young Israel of Flatbush where the bus was parked—Rivka with her younger daughter and son-in-law, Susan with some of her kids in tow. *Agunot* arrived with family and friends. People whom we expected as well as some surprise supporters gradually filled the bus. As the bus was about to depart for our Borough Park pick-up point, a woman none of us recognized climbed the stairs of the bus, looked around and quietly disembarked. As we pulled away, we noticed her using the pay phone at the gas station across the street.

En route we strategized and instructed everyone as to how to behave. We decided to have the bus park in a remote section of the parking lot and to disperse and enter the hotel singly or in small unobtrusive groups. The women were to rendezvous in the ladies' room in the lobby. The few men were to quietly enter the men's section and await our activity. We filled large hand bags and manila envelopes with several hundred flyers each. We rolled up the posters and concealed them under our coats. We decided that if we were stopped by security guards we would obey and not resist. This decision was difficult as some people felt that our cause justified civil disobedience. In the end, all agreed not to engage in physical resistance which might alienate rather than educate and motivate the crowd.

We planned to enter the women's section of the auditorium and position ourselves along the back and side walls. We chose one person to unfurl her poster first as a signal for the rest of us to do likewise. We planned merely to stand silently, holding up our posters facing the speaker's dais where the Council of Torah Sages was seated.

The massive parking lot of the Parsippany Hilton was full of cars and buses. As our bus swung through the entrance of the lot, we noticed a bearded, black frocked man, eyeing our bus and holding a walkie-talkie and speaking into it. At that moment we surmised that the mystery woman who had boarded our bus in Brooklyn had phoned ahead with a description of our bus and our approximate arrival time. We instructed the driver to keep moving and drop us off a few at a time. We noticed more security guards and walkie-talkies at the various entrances to the hotel.

Once inside the lobby, we followed our plan and met in the ladies' room. The men in our group went off by themselves as planned. We distributed the packs of flyers and the posters. We exchanged greetings with some acquaintances we met in the ladies' room. They noted our presence and paraphernalia with surprise and curiosity but didn't seem to comprehend what was afoot. We tried to hurry before they might alert somebody from Aguda, but nothing happened. Once ready, we slowly and individually made our way toward the auditorium and took up our positions along the walls in the women's section at the rear of the auditorium.

As we walked toward the auditorium and filed in, several details leaped out at us. We had been careful to dress in compliance with the *tsniut* (modesty) standards followed by Aguda women. We were dressed simply and modestly, no pants, long skirts. As it turned out we didn't quite fit in as many of the women in attendance were dressed in high fashion.

The auditorium was huge, filled to capacity, men in the front closer to the dais and podium where the Torah Sages in their black suits and hats sat facing the audience. Behind a barrier, the women's section began. It was far away from the podium. There were two large screen TV monitors focused on the faces of speakers so that the women could see them.

The room was dimly lit and the audience hushed as a rabbi spoke. As our eye grew accustomed to the dimness, we located each other across the room and focused on the designated person. When she unfolded her poster we all followed suit. There we stood against the walls, with posters uplifted, silently proclaiming our message. Our posters read: RABBIS PLEASE HELP AGUNOT. AGUDATH ISRAEL HEAR THE CRIES OF AGUNOT OF ISRAEL. The *agunot* in our group carried signs saying: I HAVE BEEN AN AGUNAH FOR FIVE (or THREE or SEVEN) YEARS—RABBIS PLEASE HELP ME.

A rumble of murmuring rolled through the women's section. The men, hearing a tumult but unaware of what we had done, turned around to see what was going on behind them in the women's section. The rabbi continued to speak but the crowd's attention was focused on us. We continued to stand silently holding up our signs. In minutes, uniformed security guards pushed their way into the women's section and told us we had to leave. We tried speaking to some of them, explaining to them what we were doing. They insisted that we leave the hall but said we could stay on the premises outside the auditorium. Susan resisted leaving the auditorium. A female guard was sympathetic when she heard why we were demonstrating but repeated that she was instructed to eject us. When the guard insisted, Susan held her ground arguing that freedom of speech protected our right to demonstrate in the auditorium. The freedom of speech argument was questionable, but the guard relented and Susan remained inside with her poster, distributing flyers and talking quietly with women who began questioning her and expressing sympathy. Women reached out asking for flyers and strained to read them by the dim light of the TV monitors. The murmur was low but continuous, deflecting people's attention from the evening's program.

Our few men who were interspersed in the men's section reported that the men were very aware of the goings on and were able to read our posters. Like Susan, they too felt that our action had captured the attention of the audience.

Meanwhile in the hallways, there was a great tumult around us. The long corridor was divided by low ropes which created separate passageways for men and women to enter and exit the auditorium. There was a continuous flow of people in and out. We were permitted to distribute our materials, collect signatures on our petitions and engage the people in conversation. Our flyers were on bright yellow and green colored paper. In a short time it was apparent that they were being carried and read throughout the hotel. People came over and requested copies. Each *agunah* had a crowd around her asking questions and listening to her story.

We collected literally hundreds of signatures on our petitions. We have them still, signature after signature, on lined legal size white paper. Many of the signers told stories of friends and relatives who were *agunot*. Social workers, attorneys and lay people volunteered to help. It was clear that the crowd sympathized with our cause. One attorney gave us his card and asked that we contact him as he was willing to take an *agunah* case pro bono.

The evening's program ended and the corridor and lobby filled with people leaving the lecture hall. Our colorful flyers were seen in every hand. Conversations overheard were almost always about *agunot* and our protest. Some of the Aguda officials passed us with grim and angry stares but said nothing. As the dais rabbis began to file out, they seemed ill at ease and in a hurry to pass. Rivka noticed Rabbi Pam, now deceased, then a revered member of Aguda's Council of Torah Sages. Rivka knew him personally as he had officiated at her wedding. She approached him and asked if he would meet with *agunot* to discuss their problems. He nodded and said, "Call me."

Conversations between us and the attendees went on for hours. We had clearly succeeded in bringing the *agunah* issue to their attention despite the resistance of Aguda leaders. Many people asked if we were staying for the whole weekend and were disappointed when we explained that we were leaving that night. We ended the evening by gathering our group for a short prayer service in the center of the lobby. We were joined by many others who stood respectfully with us.

On the bus home, the feeling was one of exhilaration and satisfaction. The *agunot* and their families felt, for the first time, that the Orthodox community truly understood their pain. They also hoped that the concern exhibited by the people at the convention would translate into pressure on Aguda to come to grips with the agony of *agunot*. We went home exhausted but proud of ourselves for pulling it off.

## The Aftermath of the Convention

A few days after the convention, we mailed Aguda photocopies of the petition with its hundreds of signatures, men and women, members of Aguda, calling on their organization to help *agunot*. Along with the petitions we wrote a letter asking that the Torah Sages meet with the *agunot*. We had already made a follow up call to Rabbi Pam asking him for a meeting. His response was, "Who am I? I'm a just a small rabbi. I have no power." To us this sounded like an evasion of responsibility. He said that we needed to meet with the whole Council of Sages. He agreed that we could use his name as supporting such a meeting. We included this information in our letter.

David Zwiebel responded for Aguda. In his letter to us he said that Agunah Inc. was the wrong type of organization, not worthy of meeting with their rabbis. We were not disheartened because we knew we had accomplished at least one of our goals—we gave the *agunot* a voice and a platform.

The attorney who had volunteered his services, true to his word, invited us to a meeting in his Manhattan office. We had a long talk with him, and he gave us the profile of the type of case he wanted: an *agunah* with children who could not afford to pay legal fees. We referred one *agunah* to him, and he assigned one of his office's attorneys to her case. The case dragged on and the legal work required was enormous. While his office finished the case, it cost his office much more in pro bono time than he had anticipated.

For a while there was a small ripple of support from people who had seen us at the Aguda convention. We received some small donations and several enthusiastic phone calls offering advice and support. We decided to follow through on this strategy by demonstrating at large gatherings of other Orthodox institutions. We organized squads to appear at the Ezras Torah Dinner, at a fund raiser for a Lakewood Yeshiva and a fund raiser for the new Flatbush Mikvah. (A *mikvah* is a ritual bath in which a woman must immerse herself at the end of her menstrual ritual impurity so that she is permitted to have sexual relations with her husband.)

The annual Ezras Torah Dinner, attended by hundreds of Orthodox Jews who support Torah scholarship, was held at a large Manhattan hotel. Scores of rabbis attended as well as lay people. We stood in a large foyer at the entrance to the banquet room. The *agunot* held their signs, attracting much attention and sympathy. Ezras Torah officials asked us to leave, but passersby entering the hall shouted, "Let them stay." We were allowed to remain. A pattern was emerging of the rank and file supporting our demonstrations in the midst of conventions and dinners while the leadership of the various organizations was infuriated at the disruption of their "business as usual" events.

The potential power of community pressure was apparent to us at the Ezras Torah dinner. One of the *agunot*, Shulie, spotted her husband Meir in the crowd. We decided to find his table and expose him in front of his friends in the hope that they would pressure him to grant a *gett*. The banquet hall was huge and we needed to see the seating plan in order to locate his table. Someone from Ezras Torah let us have a peek at the seating chart, and we made our way through the crowded and dimly lit hall. The audience's attention was focused on a large screen showing a video. We approached the table unnoticed by everyone except Meir. He got up and hurriedly exited the hall. When we reached the table, we asked for him and were told by the men seated there that he had just left.

Shulie spoke to the men around the table and introduced herself as Meir's *agunah*. She asked them to help her by persuading him to grant her the *gett*. They were polite and clearly embarrassed.

At the Lakewood Yeshiva dinner, also held at a large hotel, we were met with anger and barred from entering the building. When we started taking pictures of *agunot* being ejected from the lobby, someone grabbed our camera and ripped the film out. Nevertheless, we stood outside and as limousines and cars drove up to discharge the dinner guests, we distributed our flyers. We later wrote a letter to Rebbetzin Kotler of the Lakewood Yeshiva, expressing dismay at the treatment the *agunot* received and explaining why they felt they had to take such drastic action.

At the Flatbush Mikvah fund raiser the juxtaposition of raising money for a facility that is central to the family life of Orthodox Jewish women with the pain of *agunot* who cannot lead a normal family life was powerful. Many women took our flyers and said *"yasher koach"* (more power to you) for our efforts. But some of the organizers of the fund raiser and other attendees were clearly conflicted due to their desire not to disrupt the festive evening versus their empathy for *agunot*.

During this time we held local meetings attempting to develop a group of people to join us in our work. Women came from the heart of the right-wing Orthodox communities in Flatbush and Borough Park. *Agunot* spoke to them, and we brain stormed about how to become a catalyst for change. A few men attended regularly, especially one young man who became a devoted worker. The people attending the meetings were well meaning and capable, but we had neither the time nor the money to set up the organizational structure and training program necessary to fully integrate them into our efforts. Some of these people did show up at the various demonstrations we held and later at the two conferences we organized.

We skipped next year's Thanksgiving at Parsippany. After our 'non-appearance" we received feedback from people who said that we were missed at the convention. Our absence was noted. When the next Aguda convention rolled around the following Thanksgiving, we decided to attend. This time they were not expecting us, and as our bus pulled into the parking lot it was apparent their security personnel were not on alert.

We had rented a school bus this time in order to save money. The seats were uncomfortable, it was crowded, and our bodies registered every bump in the road. An older couple, the parents of an *agunah*, came with us on this trip. They were members of Aguda and well known in those circles. Their daughter Nechama had been without a *gett* for five years, and they felt that the Orthodox community had let them down. The mother was a spunky lady whose outspokenness enlivened the trip. On the bus we again organized our posters and flyers and planned to meet in the ladies' room. The men with us would station themselves in the men's section and hand out flyers at the appropriate time. Now more experienced in these operations, we had a better plan to synchronize our action. We chose Rachel Aranoff, Susan's oldest daughter, to click on a small flashlight when she felt everyone had time to position themselves inside the lecture hall.

The setting was exactly the same as the last time—the dark room, men up front, women in the rear behind a barrier, large video screens for women to view the Torah Sages who were seated up front on the dais. Some of us, including Rachel, were unaware that the rabbi addressing the gathering as we entered was none other than Rabbi Pam, the rabbi who backed out of his agreement to meet with us after the first demonstration. Rabbi Pam, then a Rosh Yeshiva of Torah V'daath, a large Brooklyn yeshivah, was a venerated figure. When Rachel gave the signal, posters lit up by flashlights appeared all over the women's section. There was an audible gasp, again loud enough to make the men turn around. People were stunned that we dared to demonstrate during Rabbi Pam's speech. Some people in the audience recognized Nechama's mother and yelled at her for having the chutzpa to do such a thing. She held her ground, answering indignantly, "What is Rabbi Pam or any of the other rabbis doing to help my daughter? What is Aguda doing? If your daughter was an *agunah* you would be in my place right now."

Unlike the previous time, many women in the audience responded to us with antagonism. A few tried to rip our posters out of our hands. Once again we were ejected from the hall by security guards and we took up positions in the lobby, distributing our flyers and engaging people in conversation. The flyers we distributed were the same as those we had distributed two years previously, with a box indicating that unfortunately they were still relevant since nothing had improved in the interim. We sensed this time that the crowd's attitude toward us had changed perceptibly. While most people were sympathetic to the *agunot*, people seemed cool to Agunah Inc. The good will that had prevailed at our first appearance had evaporated.

We felt that the Aguda, which rejected our message that rabbis are to blame for the continued suffering of *agunot*, had managed to deflect the blame by focusing criticism on us. People in the crowd called us feminists, an appellation that is anathema to them. Over and over again we were told that the rabbis don't want to deal with us because we are the "wrong people" to handle this problem and that Aguda was now taking care of it.

Milling around at the convention, we heard talk about the organization called Get Free led by Rabbi Yehuda Levin and funded by a wealthy member of Aguda to deal with the *agunah* problem. We knew of Rabbi Levin, since he had called us several times to ask for help when he began working in the *gett* arena. We had been involved in several cases with him and knew that the ultimate solution would not emerge from his work (see Chapter 6). Levin saw himself as a deal maker who tried to reduce the dollar amount of extortion the *agunah* would have to pay, not as an advocate for real justice for *agunot*. He himself told us that his work for *agunot* was a job for him and not his cause. The causes to which he was most dedicated were opposing abortion and homosexuality. He ran several times for political office on that platform. In the 1996 presidential campaign, Levin backed Pat Buchanan, who agreed with his stands against abortion and homosexuality, but whom many Jews viewed as an anti–Semite. Shortly after his endorsement of Buchanan, the Get Free organization disappeared. Levin remains politically active. In 2010 he backed Carl Paladino for governor of New York. Paladino delivered a harsh anti-gay speech, written by Levin. In the face of withering criticism, Paladino retracted the speech, and Levin withdrew his endorsement.

Rabbi Levin and Get Free served as a fig leaf to conceal Aguda's inaction on the *agunah* issue, but we knew long before Levin's extraneous political entanglements that he would not be a major factor in solving the *agunah* problem.

From the time of our first appearance in Parsippany, Aguda made us a target of biting criticism. Long after we stopped showing up at their conventions, they continued to express their disapproval of us in both their magazine and newsprint bulletin. Since our first appearance, some of the Torah sages mentioned *agunot* in various speeches, always stressing how badly they feel but with no effective proposals on eliminating the problem. Our Aguda demonstrations received little coverage in Jewish newspapers. A reporter for one major Jewish newspaper told us she could not write us up for fear that Aguda might cut some of the extensive advertising they ran in the paper she worked for.

On our bus trip home after our second appearance, the *agunot* and their families felt a sense of achievement and release. They brought their issue to the attention of a large group of Orthodox Jews. They felt the sympathy of most of the people they encountered. We, however, were downhearted. We felt the change in the reception we received. Aguda had succeeded in branding us as "feminist troublemakers." We knew that despite all the time and sacrifice involved in mounting the public campaign, we had not succeeded in launching a grass roots movement to free *agunot*.

# 9

# Violence and Sexual Abuse

> "If a man can be forced to grant a *gett* because of bad breath, how much more so because he endangers her life..."—Jerusalem Talmud 9:10

Divorce is a sad ending to what began as hope for a bright future. If and how a marriage ends has serious repercussions for the couple and their children. While divorce is not to be taken lightly, we believe that neither spouse should be forced to remain in a marriage against their will and certainly not when their spouse is violent and dangerous. For pious women, divorce is a last resort, sought only when conditions within the marriage have become intolerable. In all our years of *agunah* activism, we do not recall a single case where the wife sought a *gett* simply because she "fell out of love." Most of our *agunah* cases involve women who need to escape serious mental, physical or sexual abuse. Some involve sexual abuse of children. One notorious case involved a drug-addicted husband convicted of attempted murder. Yet, even in these severe and dangerous situations, the women remained trapped. Rabbis ruled that the abusers retain their rights to hold their wives hostage even when the wives fled the marital residences and civil divorces had been finalized.

## *A Child Molester Goes Free*

Naomi, a computer programmer, contacted us after reading a newspaper account of a demonstration we led for an *agunah*. She was a well-spoken, intelligent young woman, mother of six children, two of whom were girls. She was separated from her husband and was desperately seeking a *gett*. The *beit din* she was working with had offered her a way out of her marriage, but she was unwilling to follow their proposed route.

Naomi told us a hair-raising story. One day she unexpectedly came home early and found her husband on the living room couch, sexually molesting their youngest daughter. She immediately threw him out of the house, screaming at him never to return. Being a pious woman, Naomi then turned to a rabbi in her tight-knit community for advice. The rabbi counseled her to take her husband back. After all, the rabbi insisted, he's a good father to the boys.

Understanding that keeping daughters under the same roof as this father was unacceptable, the rabbi advised Naomi to send her young daughters to live with family or neighbors. Traumatized and accustomed to heeding rabbinic advice, Naomi did as the rabbi suggested. She sent her daughters to live with their aunt and uncle, and she took her husband back into the family home.

Naomi visited her daughters frequently. Despite having lived in a very traditional religious community all her life, she soon began questioning the wisdom of her rabbi's advice. She saw that her daughters were suffering, unable to comprehend why they had been sent away from home. She decided to take the youngest daughter, the one who had been molested, to a therapist. She chose one outside of her insular community, a non-religious Jewish woman who was an expert at treating abused children.

During the course of treatment, the therapist held a session with Naomi alone. She asked Naomi to consider the effect her actions were having on her daughters. "From your daughters' perspective, you have punished them by banishing them from their home, and you have rewarded the abuser by allowing him to return," she said.

In describing the session to us, Naomi said: "A light bulb went on in my head. I suddenly came to my senses, and realized how badly I had been treating my daughters." She sprang into action. She brought her daughters back home, insisted that her husband leave the house, and contacted the police. She filed criminal charges against her husband, firm in her conviction that she would never agree to revive her marriage and jeopardize her daughters again. Then she went to her local *beit din* and started *gett* proceedings.

When Naomi approached us for help, she had been involved with the *beit din* for six months. Her husband had moved out of the community, and the rabbis feared that, in an effort to escape criminal prosecution for sexually abusing his children and others, he might flee the country. They wanted Naomi to obtain a *gett* as soon as possible, before he disappeared, leaving her an eternal *agunah*. They asked her to sign a pledge that she would drop all criminal charges concerning the abuse of her daughter forever in exchange for her *gett*. Only when the threat of going to jail was completely eliminated, they insisted, would the *halakhic* condition that a *gett* be granted without coercion be fulfilled. Only then would the husband be granting the *gett* "of his own free will," freeing her.

Naomi was caught in a terrible quandary. She desperately wanted her *halakhic* freedom. She too was afraid that her husband would disappear. However, her sense of morality was holding her back from dropping the charges and leaving him at large to prey upon other children.

Naomi's dilemma was intensified by the sad fact that after she brought criminal charges, alerting her community to the situation in her household, two other women had confided to her that her husband had molested their daughters as well. These women told no one, but kept their children away from him. They feared that nobody would believe that this outwardly religious man had committed such crimes. They also wished to protect their daughters' reputations as innocent children and not expose them to public attention.

With their permission, Naomi told the rabbis about the women's allegations without revealing their identities. The rabbis did not doubt Naomi's report. Yet, they still insisted that she drop her charges in exchange for the *gett*.

We sat listening to Naomi's story with chagrin, and we had difficulty believing her account of the *beit din*'s behavior. We told Naomi we wanted to speak to the rabbis about her case, and she readily gave us permission.

We set up a telephone appointment with the *beit din* and placed the call. The *Rosh* (head of the) *Beit Din* answered the phone and greeted us politely. He said he had heard of Agunah Inc.'s work so no introductions were necessary—we could get right down to business. As soon as we mentioned Naomi's name, the rabbi told us: "She really doesn't want a *gett*. We told her what to do. We gave her an agreement to sign and she insisted on showing it to a lawyer. If she really wants her *gett*, she'll sign the agreement. She has to drop all criminal charges and promise never to make such charges again."

The rabbi continued, confiding to us that he thought Naomi had made a mistake when she complied with her rabbi's advice to move her daughters out of the house. "Of course it was the wrong idea. She should have come to our *beit din* and not to that rabbi. However," he continued, "there is a great risk that Naomi's husband will soon leave the country. We want her to obtain her *gett*, and signing the agreement is the only way."

We were stunned. Was this the Twilight Zone where the basic rules we live our lives by were suspended, where right is wrong and wrong is right and such perversions are ignored by those charged with safeguarding *halakhic* values? We had just heard a respected rabbi in a position of authority advocate freeing a child molester, who would likely continue to abuse other children. "Aren't you afraid that he will molest other children, as we all know he has already done?" we asked. "No," was the reply. "He will never molest another child in our community because all the mothers know not to permit their children to be near him." We protested, maintaining that such offenders move around and continue their perversions. His answer rings in our ears even now, so many years later: "Let the next mother bring charges against him, not Naomi. Let Naomi get her *gett*."

We reported back to Naomi. We felt we had succeeded in putting an end to the rabbi's unfounded charge that she really didn't want her *gett*, but the *gett* remained out of her reach unless she signed the release. There seemed to be no other option. We couldn't suggest demonstrations against the husband, as he was already persona non grata in the community and not susceptible to further embarrassment. Remarrying without a *gett* was an unthinkable religious violation for Naomi. Unless she agreed to her husband's and the *beit din's* terms, Naomi would remain *halakhically* tied to this reprehensible man, possibly for the rest of her years. Naomi had to make a painful decision. Ultimately, out of the realistic fear that he would disappear unless she dropped all charges, she acceded to the *beit din's* conditions, signed the agreement, and received her *gett*.

Was this the right decision? It is immoral for rabbis to permit misfits like Naomi's husband to retain the *halakhic* right to chain their wives to a dead "marriage" such as this and to press for dropping criminal charges against such an offender. The rabbis put Naomi in a terrible situation, forcing her to decide whether to insure the safety of other children by trying to put the molester behind bars, thereby sentencing herself to remaining single and celibate, or to gain her freedom by freeing him. Who bears responsibility for Naomi's choice?

Although we often lose contact with *agunot* once they receive their *gett*, we did hear from Naomi again. Two years later, she called us. She had remarried and wanted to tell us about the birth of her new baby. She told us that she and all her children were very happy with their new husband and father.

We were elated at her happiness. Her children now had a loving father, which would have been impossible without the *gett*. But we wondered where Naomi's first husband had gone. Since the rabbis' machinations released this criminal into society without penalty or rehabilitation, we were haunted by the fear that other children might suffer at his hands. Shouldn't the rabbis have been able to free Naomi and her children another way? For us, *halakhah* was abused in this case. The rabbis purchased Naomi's *gett* at the price of violating the most basic moral values of society. That is too high a price to pay.

## Had He Killed Her, She Wouldn't Need a Gett

No *agunah* we worked with experienced violence as harrowing as Blima Zitrenbaum, mentioned in our Prologue, whose husband was convicted of attempting to murder her by repeated blows to the head with a hammer. And no case illustrates more powerfully the rabbis' insistence that a husband's unconditional legal control over his wife's life endures no matter how abusive he is.

We first heard of Blima Zitrenbaum after she confided her troubles to her friend Faigie, who recommended that she call us. Blima had told Faigie that she was trying desperately to secure a *gett* from her dangerously violent, drug dependent husband. She had turned to the rabbis in her Rockland County community of Monsey, New York, for help in securing a *gett*, but they told her there was nothing they could do as long as her husband refused to release her from the bonds of marriage.

Blima called us once and told us that she didn't know where her husband was. He was on the run, wanted by the police on some charge. There was nothing we could do for her except refer her to a local rabbi we thought might help her track him down. That was the only time we spoke to Blima, and her case faded from our memories until her frightful story made news.

People in Monsey knew that Joseph Zitrenbaum was a drug addict. They had seen the needle marks on his arm and they knew that Joseph had threatened Blima and stalked her even as she moved to different apartments to hide from him, and that she had secured an Order of Protection from the civil court. (The narrative of this case is based on courtroom testimony given in prosecution of Joseph Zitrenbaum for assault and attempted murder and newspaper coverage of the crime and trial.)

One fateful Friday afternoon in February 1996, shortly before sundown and the onset of the Sabbath, Joseph Zitrenbaum made a threatening phone call which Blima's answering machine recorded. Petrified, Blima called her close friend Sheva Wagschul and asked her to hurry over before Sabbath candle lighting time to stay with her overnight. Sheva arrived within minutes with her young son. She listened to the tape of Joseph's threats and decided to stay.

Early Saturday morning Sheva woke up to the sound of children's voices having breakfast in the kitchen. She got out of bed and tried Blima's door but found it locked. When all the children awoke and Blima still hadn't emerged from her room, Sheva returned to knock on Blima's door, but there was no answer. Concerned, Sheva, together with her son and Blima's daughter, knocked harder and louder, and the door swung open.

The scene in the bedroom was terrifying. Blood all over, Blima lying motionless. Sheva quickly closed the door to shield the children from this gory sight. She ran to the kitchen to call the police. But the kitchen phone, unnoticed earlier because telephone use is forbidden on the Sabbath, was off the hook. She followed the phone cord and found the receiver wrapped in a blanket and stuffed in the oven. She replaced the receiver and waited a moment to pick it up and try again to call the police, but there was still no dial tone. She realized to her horror that the phone in Blima's bedroom must also be off the hook and that she would have to enter the bedroom where her friend lay covered in blood in order to get a phone connection and call the police. She steeled herself, entered, and made the call.

Blima's 11-year-old daughter ran to a neighbor's house for help. "Mommy's dead," she told the neighbor. "She got killed by someone in the middle of the night." The neighbor called the Jewish volunteer ambulance corps, Hatzalah. Police arrived and Blima was rushed by helicopter to the brain trauma center of an undisclosed hospital. When she arrived the doctor noted that her skull had been fractured in numerous places, pieces of bone were embedded in her brain and brain tissue was pouring out of the wounds. But she was alive and able to respond and communicate intermittently. She underwent hours of delicate, lifesaving brain surgery. After a three-week stay in the hospital and therapy, Blima regained the use of her hands and re-learned how to speak, though haltingly, as evident when she later testified on the witness stand.

In the meantime the police began a manhunt for Joseph Zitrenbaum. Rockland County detectives, the New York City police and the Shomrim, an Orthodox volunteer police force, all searched the Chasidic Borough Park and Williamsburg neighborhoods in Brooklyn where Zitrenbaum was likely to have fled. Zitrenbaum had shaved his beard, removed his glasses and donned a hunting hat to disguise himself. But the Shomrim had anticipated his attempt to change his appearance and had circulated flyers with an image of Joseph without a beard. It was not in Brooklyn but in a store in the also heavily Jewish Lower East Side of Manhattan that Zitrenbaum was recognized as he attempted to buy a cup of coffee. Collared by the police, Zitrenbaum was brought to trial on charges of attempted murder, burglary and assault.

Susan and the late Honey Rackman, who had by then joined as a director of Agunah Inc., spent a day in court monitoring the Zitrenbaum trial. The grisly facts of the case emerged in the testimony of the witnesses they heard that day, but random conversations Susan and Honey had with people they met provided further insights into this insular Orthodox community's attitude toward the *agunah* problem.

Upon entering the courtroom Susan and Honey observed a middle-aged man dressed in the black hat and long black gabardine coat typical of ultra-Orthodox Jewish men as well as a younger man with a jet black beard and *payot* (sidelocks), also dressed in the plain black suit and white shirt of the yeshivah world. They were seated apart from each other. Besides these two obviously Jewish spectators, there was a TV reporter who had a large video camera running, a female reporter from the local Rockland County News, a bailiff, and a young black woman seated next to Jospeh Zitrenbaum and with whom Zitrenbaum frequently consulted during the trial. The jury panel consisted of a mix of men and women, some white, some Asian and some black.

Honey and Susan quietly slipped into the rear bench in the gallery. The prosecuting attorney was in the middle of interrogating a police detective. Details about the address of the crime scene, the timing of certain events and the use of a device made up of a wheel and meter to measure the distance and walking/running time between various locations involved in the case were put on record.

The judge called for a short break and Susan and Honey went into the hallway. Susan approached the middle-aged, black gabardined man to query him about the Zitrenbaum case. She was most interested in eliciting his feelings about the irony that, according to the rabbis, Blima was forced to remain married to her accused assailant. Susan asked him if he knew that Blima could not get a *gett* from Joseph, who had almost bludgeoned her to death. He answered, "Yes." "Doesn't it disturb you that despite Joseph's violent attack, she is still forced to remain his wife?" "No," the man answered, without a moment's hesitation. "You are obviously a pious Jew," Susan continued. "Don't you think after such an act of violence, a *gett* should be given?" "A *gett* has nothing to do with what the husband does to his wife," he barked at Susan. "Who are you?" he asked in a raised voice, "What's it your business what happens in this case?" "I'm a director of the Agunah organization," Susan answered. "No more questions!" he shouted, and scurried away.

Susan and Honey returned to the courtroom, but the proceedings had not yet resumed. Taking advantage of the lull, Susan approached the young black woman seated next to Joseph Zitrenbaum at the defense table and asked who she was, another defense attorney perhaps? "A minister," the woman replied. "I'm the chaplain at the prison across the street." "What denomination are you?" Susan inquired. "Pentecostal," she answered pleasantly. "Oh," Susan said, "are you going from courtroom to courtroom to observe the trials of various prisoners?" "No," she said, "I'm here because Mr. Zitrenbaum asked me to be with him during the trial." Susan could not help thinking it was a very odd twist for Zitrenbaum, a card-carrying Orthodox Chasidic Jew, to ask a Christian clergywoman to sit beside him as his advisor. Why not a rabbi? Did Zitrenbaum think the presence of a clergywoman would help him win some sympathy from the jurors? Who knows how a mind like Joseph Zitrenbaum's works?

The proceedings resumed with additional police testimony and the expert testimony of the surgeon who had saved Blima's life. Joseph Zitrenbaum sat passively through the medical testimony which described the grievous head wounds his wife had suffered. His only reaction was to turn around and, bizarrely, smile at those seated in the spectator gallery. Finally the judge called a recess for lunch and the courtroom emptied.

Susan and Honey set out to find a kosher eatery. The suburban roads were confusing, and they had to flag down a police car for directions. As soon as they mentioned the reason for their presence in Monsey to the police officer, a grimace of distress crossed his face. He sent them on their way toward the kosher shopping area. As they crossed the parking lot toward a bagel shop, Honey and Susan encountered two young, *sheitel* (religious wig) wearing women carrying their wig boxes into a beauty salon. Honey stopped them and asked, "Do you know that the Zitrenbaum trial is on today?" "Yes," they answered demurely. "We were surprised that no Orthodox women were in the courtroom," Honey said. They did not reply. Susan added, "It's important for the community to show the judge that they are up in arms over this terrible crime. The courtrooms were packed during other trials when the victim was an Orthodox Jew, like the Crown Heights riots." "You're right," the young women acknowledged, showing slight discomfort at this probing by women who didn't look or speak like them or the other pious women they were accustomed to. As they moved to continue on their way, Honey encouraged them to show up in court and bring other women with them.

Susan and Honey hurried into the bagel shop, anxious to grab a quick bite and return in time for the afternoon court session. As they waited for their order, Susan and Honey mentioned to another patron, who, like every other woman in the store, was clad in long sleeves and a *sheitel*, that they had just left the Zitrenbaum courtroom.

"Do you know that Blima is an *agunah*?" Susan and Honey asked the woman.

"So what else is new?" she responded.

"Don't you think the rabbis are remiss in not freeing this woman from this sick marriage?" Susan and Honey continued.

"The rabbis?" she scoffed.

"What?" Susan and Honey said. "Don't you think the rabbis are obliged to help Blima?"

"Don't tell me about rabbis," the woman responded. "I'm an *agunah* and they haven't lifted a finger to help me."

"You should be in the courtroom," Susan and Honey said.

"I'm going to be there later if my ride shows up," she replied.

Honey and Susan gave her the Agunah Inc. hotline number which she took but indicated she would probably not call as she had given up hope of ever being freed from her husband.

Susan and Honey ate quickly and waved goodbye to the *agunah* they had just met. She told them with regret that she wouldn't see them in court as she had received a phone call that her car ride had fallen through.

When they returned to the courtroom, Honey and Susan noticed some new faces. There was a middle-aged religious woman dressed in dark clothing and a head covering that covered all her hair and most of her forehead. Seated further down the bench was a broad shouldered, husky religious man. The young, bearded religious man and the middle-aged man who had shouted at Susan and run off were both back in their places. Several other people including a number of women, not identifiable as part of the pious Monsey Jewish community, were present.

The afternoon's first witness was another police official whose testimony was brief. There was a short break, and in walked the *agunah* whom Susan and Honey had met at the bagel store. Her ride must have come through after all. As she took her seat she pointed at the man who had shouted at Susan and whispered, "That's him, my husband." So now seated in the courtroom, attending a trial where the victim was an *agunah*, was another *agunah* and her recalcitrant husband. No wonder he had shouted at Susan and stormed off earlier in the day when Susan asked about the injustice of men withholding a *gett*.

Susan couldn't let this opportunity to demand a *gett* pass. Since the judge was not yet in the courtroom, she leaned toward the front bench where the recalcitrant was seated and said firmly, "Give your wife a *gett*." "Go to hell," was the reply. "You should be ashamed of yourself talking that way," Susan said sharply. He reached into his pocket, took out a matchbook, wrote on it and displayed it for Susan to see. It read, "Drop dead."

The judge entered and testimony began. The witness was Sheva Wagschul, whose testimony was described above. She seemed deeply agitated and upset as she described the horror of discovering her friend Blima and frantically trying to get help. The judge interrupted Sheva's testimony a number of times to admonish spectators not to gesture or smile at the witness. Honey and Susan were puzzled by this. Almost angry, the judge interrupted again and said that the courtroom had to be cleared, stating that the number of people present exceeded the small courtroom's legal occupancy rate.

Interested in hearing what another Chasidic man would have to say about the *agunah* issue, Susan approached the broad-shouldered Chasidic man who had turned up only for the afternoon session.

"Isn't it a shame that Blima Zitrenbaum and the other woman in the courtroom are *agunot*?" Susan began. "The rabbis should really find a *halakhic* way to free these women, don't you think?"

Unlike the first man who shouted at Susan and displayed the "Drop Dead" matchbook message, this man was pleasant enough in his demeanor but responded, "The Torah can't deal with bad people like men who won't give a *gett*. The Torah can only deal with good people."

Susan was frustrated at his acceptance of women's suffering and his apologetics as to why Jewish law does not protect *agunot*. She countered, "Only deal with good people? Torah law deals with the trial and punishment of murderers and thieves." He shrugged his shoulders and drifted away.

In the meantime, Honey had met another woman in the hall whom she now introduced to Susan as Valerie, a staff person from a battered women's shelter in the area. Valerie had probably had contact with Blima prior to the dreadful assault. After a few moments, the *agunah* from the eatery joined our little group. She had heard her husband tell Susan to go to hell and was nervous about Susan's challenging and criticizing her husband for withholding the *gett*. Susan responded that being a quiet, "good girl," was not going to secure her *gett*.

Valerie turned to Susan and warned her that she should be careful because these men can harm their wives. Susan inquired if the *agunah* feared physical violence from her husband. She said no, but Valerie persisted, saying that men can harm their wives in many ways. She was advocating no form of confrontation with these men, not even castigating such men as Susan had done in the courtroom.

The remarks of the woman from the shelter underlined the frightening situation of *agunot*, caught between their desperate desire for a *gett* and the fear that demanding a *gett* might provoke a violent response from their husbands.

The Zitrenbaum case was Exhibit "A," evidence of the fearful situation of *agunot* whose husbands have a history of violence. Other women can sever legal ties with their abusive husband, get a divorce in civil court and try to rebuild their lives. But *agunot* can never sever their marital bonds unless their abuser husbands consent.

The day in court came to an end. Honey and Susan returned for the next court session a few days later when Blima Zitrenbaum took the stand and identified Joseph as her assailant. Her speech was slow and halting, probably as a result of the injuries to her brain, but she described how a few seconds before the first blow she caught a glimpse of Joseph's face and was, therefore, able to identify him as her assailant. Joseph's attorney attempted to discredit Blima by getting her to admit that she too had at one time used cocaine like Joseph. But Joseph was found guilty of attempted murder, assault and robbery. He was sentenced to a long jail term. In an interview from jail he declared that he would never give Blima her *gett*, and Blima remained bound in marriage to her murderous husband.

It was the ultimate in perversity that this man who had almost succeeded in murdering his wife could still hold her hostage in their marriage. Susan, Honey and Rivka called a number of rabbis asking, demanding, that the right of a husband to control the marriage be abrogated when the husband has attempted to murder his wife. He should never hold any power over her ever again, they insisted. Clearly the marriage is over. "Give her freedom to pursue the rest of her life unchained from him. Promulgate a *takkanah* (amendment) that extreme violence severs the marriage bonds." Not a single rabbi considered it.

One evening, a few weeks after the sentencing, Irwin Haut received a telephone call from California. A male voice asked if Agunah Inc. wished to help Blima obtain her *gett*. "If the answer is yes," he said, "I know how to do it." "What's the plan?" Irwin inquired. "Let Agunah raise money for Joseph's appeal, get him a good lawyer to help get him out of jail and he will make a deal with you to give the *gett* in return." Irwin responded, "Agunah Inc. is not interested in getting Joseph back on the street before he serves his time." "Joseph did nothing wrong!" the caller exclaimed. "He was framed by Blima because she wanted out of the marriage, and Joseph wouldn't give a *gett*." The absurd accusation against Blima put an end to the conversation as Irwin hung up.

A short while later Susan heard a rumor that Joseph had hanged himself in prison, but she never heard any confirmation of that either directly or in the media. Nor did she hear that Blima had received her *gett*.

Naomi's and Blima's cases are horrifying, but they are not isolated examples of physical and sexual abuse. Agunah Inc.'s files contain many stories of black and blue bruises, broken limbs, fathers sexually abusing sons and daughters, women terrified of husbands who assault or threaten to assault them with knives and guns or household items like bookends or chairs.

Rabbis often advise women not to go to the police, warning them that any publicity will damage their children's marriage prospects. Worse than that, rabbis often advise women to return to such men, and they often place obstacles in the way of women seeking orders of protection. Not infrequently, rabbinic courts grant custody and unsupervised visitation to fathers who have admitted abusive behavior.

One of Agunah Inc.'s cases, being adjudicated by a Modern Orthodox *beit din*, involved a man who had broken his son's arm in a fit of temper. The *agunah* mentioned this uncontested fact to the rabbinic judges but did not get any response. In the end, she was awarded custody, but the *p'sak* (decision) had an unusual clause. The rabbis demanded, for religious reasons, that the woman remove all television sets from the house. Should she ever bring in a TV, the *p'sak* warned, the question of custody would be reopened. When we saw the *p'sak* we were outraged that the rabbis could subject this woman to such emotional turmoil by suggesting that she could ever lose custody to an abusive father. We called an official of the *beit din* who expressed strong disapproval and asked to see the *p'sak*. Very soon a new *p'sak* was issued without reference to TV or modification of custody.

In another case we worked on, a teenage girl reported that during her weekend visitation her father had slept in the same bed with her. Her mother, an *agunah* whose husband had been withholding a *gett* for years, complained to the *beit din* that she didn't want her daughter to have overnight visitation. The rabbis questioned the husband who admitted he slept in the same bed with his adolescent daughter because, he explained, he didn't have extra beds. He was not asked why he didn't sleep on the couch or let the girl use a sleeping bag on the floor. Instead of denying him overnight visitation, the *beit din* ruled that the father must provide a separate bed for each daughter.

The mother was beside herself and refused to allow the daughters any more overnight visitation. The father then complained to anyone in the community who would listen that his ex-wife was denying him visitation. Eventually, the mother was forced to relent since she did not wish to harm her daughters' reputations in the community by revealing the truth. Soon after, the older daughter had to be hospitalized for psychiatric treatment.

Sadly, we could tell many more such horror stories. Rabbis too often give men the benefit of the doubt and do not take the complaints of women and children seriously enough even in the face of incontrovertible evidence. In their effort to mollify the husbands and persuade them to give the *gett*, rabbis shield men from the consequences of their behavior and in so doing further victimize women and children.

# 10

# Conferences

In 1992, after years of working to help *agunot*, we decided that the time had come for a full-blown conference. We had demonstrated at other organizations' conventions and dinners and been out on the streets publicizing the plight of individual *agunot*, but these brief encounters with members of the Jewish community did not afford an adequate opportunity to fully convey the magnitude and urgency of the problem. We wanted others beyond the families and friends of *agunot* and the handful of rabbis directly involved in cases to understand the full measure of the injustice and suffering imposed on *agunot*. The conference was meant to provide *agunot* a platform to tell their stories and enable *agunah* activists to advocate for change. We hoped that this would build pressure on the Orthodox rabbinate to remedy the situation.

In planning our conference, we were helped by a wealthy philanthropic couple that was involved in helping *agunot*. They contributed generously to many Orthodox institutions and were on close terms with many prominent rabbis. The husband was insistent about getting rabbis to attend as he felt that educating the rabbinate about the extent of the problem was vital. He sent out his own personal invitations to hundreds of rabbis, many of whom he knew well, informing them of the conference, describing its importance, and urging them to attend. We felt that this personal invitation from such a prestigious contributor would assure that a good number of rabbis would attend. We were wrong.

We invited a number of rabbis to be on the program. Rabbi Kis of the Rabbinical Council of America (RCA) accepted our invitation as did Rabbi L. Landesman, a *dayyan* on the Monsey Kollel Harabbonim Beit Din. We also included some lawyers who would speak about civil law issues such as the New York State Gett Laws, prenuptial agreements and the like.

The day of the conference dawned, a bitterly cold day in New York City. We drove into Manhattan to find that the hall we had rented had a problem with its heating system. The indoor temperature was so low that for the entire day we all tried to keep warm by drinking hot coffee and tea and keeping our coats on. The chill in the air was a marked contrast to the heat generated in the room by strong differences of opinion boiling over, emotions expressed by *agunot* and by rabbis who attacked us and each other.

There was a turnout of about 150 people, including about 30 *agunot*. Most of the *agunot* sat together in the front rows, easily identifiable. It was soon apparent that Rabbi Kis was a no show. We placed a symbolic empty chair, with his name on it, at the speakers' dais to represent his absence as well as the absence of the large number of rabbis who had been personally invited. Only about 10 rabbis showed up despite the influential philanthropist's considerable efforts to have them attend.

We invited Dr. Norma Joseph, an *agunah* activist in Canada and our personal friend, to chair the conference. She opened the conference by introducing two *agunot*. One told of the physical and mental abuse she had suffered for years from a man to whom she was still *halakhically* married. The second told of her troubles, including a diabolical invitation she had received from her husband inviting her and their child to join him and his new wife in Europe. Although he was refusing to grant her a *gett*, he had remarried and continually taunted her. He had sent her a photograph of a mocked-up tombstone with her name on it. She bitterly asserted that despite his frequent and constant abuses she was still his "wife," and the many rabbis she had consulted all maintained that they could do nothing to help her.

As the *agunot* finished, the audience was hushed, upset by the stories they had heard, especially the cruel and eerie tombstone story. Suddenly Rabbi Yitzchak Sladowsky of the Va'ad Harabbanim (Rabbinic Council) of Queens stood up and began angrily berating the speakers and the audience. He accused all of us of "rabbi bashing" and said we were committing a *Hillul Hashem*, a desecration of God's name. We were shocked at his reaction. The *agunot* in the audience found their voices and responded to Sladowsky by defending the *agunot* who had spoken, getting up at their seats, one after another, and relating their own, similar, troubled stories. They all insisted that they were suffering while the rabbis did nothing to help and that Rabbi Sladowsky's accusations were unfair. After about a half an hour, we called a halt to this unexpected confrontation and continued with the next part of the program.

After hearing from Dennis Rapps of COLPA (*C*ommission *o*n *L*aw and *P*ublic *A*ffairs that dealt with legal issues of concern to the Jewish community), and other attorneys, who detailed the limited help that could be expected from civil law, we had a short lunch break.

During the break, a daughter of one of the *agunot* approached Rivka and said that her father, whom she feared because he had beaten her many times, had just arrived. She asked if we could have him ejected. Rivka felt compassion for the young girl, but explained that this conference was open to the public, and we could not eject a man if he did not cause trouble. However, Rivka told the girl that if her father bothered her we would call the police. The man did not misbehave and, indeed, he remained the entire day, speaking up several times, voicing the opinion of "the other side," trying to explain why a man who "loves his wife" would choose to withhold the *gett*. He identified himself by name and people who knew his wife were flabbergasted, as his physical appearance alone showed him to be a dysfunctional, even scary person, while his wife was an attractive, charming and intelligent woman. (The *gett* was finally given after about seven years and much turmoil.)

After lunch, the program continued with a panel of volunteers from the GET and Agunah Inc. organizations. Before the discussion began, Rivka was walking down an aisle when she was called over by Rabbi Sladowsky, who insisted that he had to make a statement. "We've already heard from you," Rivka told him, "we know what you have to say." He insisted that he had to leave early but really needed to speak to the entire group. He was given the floor and, to everyone's amazement, publicly apologized for his earlier scolding. He said that he had spent the hours after his previous remarks listening to the *agunot* and he heard their pain and was feeling it too. Rabbi Sladowsky acknowledged that the rabbis are guilty of ignoring the issue and he promised that he would try to help.

After that emotional episode, we commenced with the panel of activists. Deborah Eiferman of GET provided the audience with a sharp and detailed view of the problems facing *agunot* and the frustrations experienced by volunteers who try to help them. She stressed the short shrift given to them by rabbis and rabbinic organizations, studding her talk with examples and case histories. We of Agunah Inc. continued with our own *agunah* horror stories. Then, having noticed Rabbi Emanuel Rackman in the audience with his daughter-in-law Honey, we invited him to the podium to say a few words. (We were later to work closely with Rabbi Rackman; see Chapter 16.) Rabbi Rackman agreed that the situation was indeed as we had been depicting it and argued that the time had come for the organized rabbinate to find and implement *halakhic* solutions.

At this point, Rabbi Samuel Turk, one of the few rabbis in attendance, started to yell from his seat in the audience. We offered him the microphone and he proceeded to attack us, the conference organizers, and Rabbi Rackman. Turk delivered a blistering personal attack on Rackman. We tried to respond calmly to his invective, but the mood had turned ugly.

The last part of the program was a presentation by Rabbi Moshe Antelman, who had been ordained at Yeshiva University and then made *aliyah* to Israel. A chemist whose work brought him to Rhode Island periodically each year, Antelman had contacted us and asked to speak.

Antelman had a novel and creative approach toward freeing *agunot*. He used a *"gett al yedei zikkui"* (a *gett* as a benefit). Jewish law provides that a person may benefit another, even without the other's knowledge or consent. For example, suppose you are away from your home or business as the Passover holiday approaches. Without your permission, I can perform a reversible ritual sale of items you own that, according to *halakhah*, must be sold to a non-Jew for the duration of the Passover holiday. If the sale is not made, you will suffer a financial loss. My unauthorized sale on your behalf is valid because it is a benefit (*zikkui*) to you. In the case of divorce, the idea was that a *gett* could be issued without the consent of a recalcitrant spouse if the *gett* could be construed as a "benefit" to that unwilling spouse.

Historically, the *gett zikkui* was used to facilitate a *gett* being issued against the will of a wife whose husband wants to end their marriage. Though Talmudic law allows a husband to divorce a wife against her will, Rabbenu Gershom, a preeminent 10th century scholar, decreed that a *gett* is not valid unless the wife agrees to accept it. However, if a wife is refusing to accept a *gett* but is living with another man in an adulterous relationship, her husband can divorce her against her will on the grounds that the *gett* is a "benefit" for her. Better for her to be divorced/single and no longer guilty of the sin of adultery. The *beit din*, therefore, suspending Rabbenu Gershom's decree, allows the husband to bestow the "benefit" of a *gett* on the wife despite her refusal to accept. Of course, the husband is a winner here in that he succeeds in freeing himself of his wife against her will.

Turning this well-known use of the *gett zikkui* around, Antelman argued that a *gett zikkui* could be issued when men refuse to issue a *gett*. Antelman argued, quite logically, that when a *beit din* issues a *seruv* (contempt of court citation) against a man who refuses to give a *gett*, it is a black mark against the husband, just as adultery is a transgression that disgraces the wife. Removing this stain on the husband's reputation would clearly be a "benefit" to him. By issuing the *gett* despite the husband's refusal to cooperate, Antelman's *beit din* "benefits" the uncooperative husband by ending his disgraceful defiance of the *beit din*'s order to give the *gett*. Here the wife is the winner in gaining her freedom against her husband's will.

Antelman's use of the *gett al yedei zikkui* to help an *agunah* when there was a *seruv* against her husband was highly controversial as heretofore this method of freeing the spouse had been utilized by *batei din* only to help men end their marriages. It should be kept in mind that according to biblical and Talmudic law, a man may have more than one wife and can force a *gett* on his wife. Therefore, allowing the man to free himself by issuing a *gett zikkui* against the will of his wife is not a radical change but rather a return to the more ancient biblical law that permits a man to divorce his wife at will and have more than one wife. On the other hand, freeing an *agunah* against her husband's will through a *gett zikkui* is more innovative and not traceable to any biblical precedent.

Antelman's unique approach seemed to be what we had been looking for: a *halakhic* remedy for a *halakhic* problem. It didn't rely on shaky civil legal remedies or prenuptial agreements that would be difficult and expensive to enforce in civil court. It allowed rabbis to take the exclusive power to end the marriage out of the hands of the husband and could be used all over the world to help *agunot* wherever they might be. Antelman had gone beyond publishing learned papers—he was actually utilizing his approach and had already freed a number of Israeli agunot. He was now prepared to free *agunot* in the United States.

Antelman's *beit din*, The Supreme Beit Din of America, was composed of Orthodox rabbis who, like him, were employed in other areas and were not earning their living from the rabbinate. They were all Orthodox rabbis, ordained by well known Orthodox institutions. Neither Antelman nor any member of his *beit din* earned any money from freeing *agunot*. In fact, they insisted that their work was a *mitzvah* of the highest order and refused compensation. One member of Antelman's, *beit* din, Rabbi Friedman, appeared with Antelman. Friedman, a bearded man whose dress and manner testified to his Orthodoxy, stressed the *halakhic* legitimacy of Antelman's approach and his *beit din*.

Antelman claimed that there was *halakhic* precedent in prewar Europe for his approach of using a *gett al yedei zikkui* to help women. He had written a book describing his activities called *Lifdot Mechakei Get* (To Free/Redeem Those Who Wait for a Gett) and had sent us a copy before the conference. We read it and were impressed with his dedication to the cause of helping *agunot*. We were pleased to offer him a platform to espouse his views.

Antelman's talk presented his approach to freeing *agunot* in great detail, outlining its *halakhic* underpinnings and historic precedents. While most of the *agunot* and the rest of the audience were clearly not following the intricacies of his discussion, which was lengthy and complicated, and came at the end of a long and tiring day, they all understood that finally here was a rabbi who claimed he could, and would, help free them. The audience turned receptive faces toward him, and he offered his address and phone numbers, encouraging them to contact him. We could see that many people were writing down his contact information.

Antelman's trail blazing remedy was clearly controversial, but he provided a sliver of hope. The conference ended, therefore, on a note of great excitement. Some of the few rabbis present were noticeably skeptical, but the *agunot* and their supporters were cheered.

## Conference Results I

The conference did not accomplish all we had hoped for. The sparse turnout of rabbis was a serious disappointment, for it impeded our efforts to educate the rabbinate about the problem. The conference did receive publicity in the Jewish media, not all of it positive. Rabbi Turk wrote a review in his regular column in *The Jewish Press*, where he misrepresented some things and presented others in the worst possible light. But, on the whole, the media coverage was accurate and positive. Rabbi Sladowsky was true to his word. He was instrumental in setting up a *beit din*, connected to the Va'ad Harabbanim (The Rabbinic Council) of Queens, where he was director. Over the years we referred women to this honest and sincere *beit din* though even in this well intended *beit din*, *agunot* suffered delays, extortion and other injustices as the price of their *gett*.

Most exciting, Antelman's solution got a full hearing, and the number of *agunot* called him and met with him. One of the *agunot* he spoke with at the conference was freed by him, the first *agunah* he freed in the United States. He later freed more American women.

## One Conference Begets Another Conference

One unexpected result of Agunah Inc.'s conference was that it served as the impetus for another day-long conference devoted to the *agunah* issue. An *agunah* who attended the first conference happened to be an active member of Amit Women (a large Orthodox, Zionist women's organization). She spoke to the leadership of Amit and convinced them to sponsor a similar conference in Queens, her home community. It was to be held in the auditorium of a well-known synagogue.

While the conference was under the sponsorship of Amit, we were asked to take charge of the programming, a task we welcomed. Still overly optimistic, we believed that now that a major mainstream Orthodox women's organization was dealing with the *agunah* issue in a serious way, people would flock to attend, and that the opportunity to educate the typical Orthodox Jew interested in Jewish causes had finally arrived.

The *agunah* who had undertaken the organization of the conference worked very hard. Hundreds of invitations were sent out. The pre-conference publicity was excellent. We expected a large turnout and came prepared with hundreds of flyers and voluminous educational material. We arrived early to help set up. Very few people were in the synagogue auditorium. Soon, the time arrived to begin, yet the attendance remained sparse. There were only a handful of Amit women. To our surprise and disappointment, we had to acknowledge to each other that rank and file Amit women were simply not going to appear. Almost everyone in the audience was already quite involved with the *agunah* issue. It seemed like we would be preaching to the choir.

Indeed, this conference was a mirror image of Agunah Inc.'s first conference. Our first conference was well attended by lay people but few rabbis. This Amit conference was attended by a sizeable number of rabbis, but very few lay people. Despite our initial discouragement at the low turnout, we realized that the compact, focused group represented an excellent opportunity for those in the field to interact and engage in serious discussions about the issues, where they agreed and where they differed.

The day opened the same way as the first Agunah Inc. conference did, with *agunot* presenting their case histories. The audience had ample opportunity to question the women. Some media people were present who asked sharp questions, and that part of the day went very well. We then moved to a different issue, an airing of a controversial and important matter of extreme interest to all the assembled, the second New York State Gett Law that had recently been passed in the Albany legislature.

In the summer of 1992, about a half year before this conference, the second New York State Gett Law, known as the amendment to the equitable distribution act, was signed by Gov. Mario Cuomo. If invoked, the law allowed a judge to award a wife a better financial settlement when her husband was withholding the *gett*. Passions, both in support of and opposition to this law, were at a peak. While we had come prepared with flyers explaining the benefits of the new law, others had distributed literature blasting the law, claiming it would result in *gittin* that were not kosher.

Rabbi Chaim Malinowitz, a member of the Beit Din Kollel Harabbonim of Monsey, New York, had come to present his view, opposing the new law. He maintained that the new law represented coercion of the husband, improperly forcing him to grant a *gett* to stave off a financial penalty. In Malinowitz's view, this financial pressure was a form of coercion on a husband that is prohibited by Jewish law. A man is required to grant a *gett* willingly, and a *gett* procured by coercion is not a kosher *gett*.

While he spoke, Malinowitz never looked at his audience. He stood at the podium, a bearded man in a business suit, looking down, his eyes glued to the floor as he spoke. During his talk, several people, mostly women, tried to interpose questions, but he continually said that he would entertain questions only after he had finished.

Malinowitz ended his prepared talk and then announced that all questions must be written down and handed to him. He would not accept any questions asked aloud; he would only read them if submitted in writing. We protested, thinking that this tactic would enable him to pick and choose from among the questions and only respond to those he wished to respond to. He assured us that he would read aloud and deal with every question asked.

Suddenly, it dawned on us that he might be trying to avoid hearing the women's voices, and that was probably the reason behind his puzzling request. Though we all knew about the laws concerning women's singing voices being sensual and forbidden by some, his refusal to look at his audience and to listen to spoken questions struck people as inappropriate. We could not help wondering how he dealt with *agunot* coming before his *beit din*. He undoubtedly had to listen to their voices, but in this public gathering these were the rules. He read and answered all the questions that were posed to him.

Malinowitz exhibited uncompromising adherence to a strict reading of *halakhah*, and some felt his replies did not demonstrate any sense of compassion for the *agunot*. His insistence on repeal of the new New York Gett Law, which had already proven to be a boon to one *agunah*, without offering any other solution in its place, was seen by some as a sign of insufficient desire to remedy the situation. One elderly woman could not contain herself. Despite Malinowitz's refusal to hear women's voices, this woman, mother of a young *agunah*, jumped up from her seat and raised her voice: "I can't stand your attitude. You are treating the *agunah* problem as though it's a chulent [Sabbath stew] recipe. Throw in this law, take out that law. My daughter is not chopped liver!" she exclaimed. There was a stunned silence, and then the sounds of hands clapping.

Next, Rabbi Simcha Krauss, rabbi of the Young Israel of Hillcrest, spoke in favor of the new law. He defended its *halakhic* legitimacy. We were pleasantly surprised to discover an ally we had not known about.

Another surprise was the totally unexpected remarks of the late Rabbi Louis Bernstein, former President of the RCA. We had prior occasion to make Rabbi Bernstein's acquaintance because of his and our involvement in another issue: Orthodox women's prayer groups. Bernstein had commissioned the notorious REITS Five Responsum, a document drafted and signed by five Yeshiva University rabbis, forbidding women's prayer groups. We were actively involved in the then nascent women's prayer group movement and considered Bernstein to be a staunch adversary, yet there he was suddenly delivering an impassioned speech on behalf of *agunot*, recognizing and detailing their struggles and suffering, denouncing, in public, the *beit din* system and advising all to stay away from *batei din*, including, he added, "his own" RCA Beit Din!

Bernstein explained that his niece, living in Israel, was an *agunah* and, in his efforts to help her, he had become acquainted with the facts of life for *agunot*. He expressed remorse that during his presidency of the RCA he had not become involved in this issue, but he said he was unaware at that time of the magnitude of the problem. Now he knew and was saddened and wanted to help.

Bernstein's emotional and obviously sincere words affected us profoundly. His public acknowledgment of the realities of the *agunah* situation and lack of rabbinic responsiveness was both startling and poignant.

Rabbi Emanuel Rackman, also in the audience, then asked for the floor. He agreed with Bernstein's remarks and discussed the remedies and solutions that Antelman had discussed at the previous conference, the *gett al yedei zikkui*. Rackman urged women to begin using the Antelman *gett* in order to induce the organized Orthodox rabbinate to recognize its validity. He suggested women beyond childbearing age be the first ones to apply for the Antelman solution because there would be no problem of *mamzerut*, illegitimate children being born. Rackman stated that he would perform wedding ceremonies for women who obtain the *gett* from Antelman. (He subsequently did so.)

Before the day ended we heard from a panel of volunteers from various organizations dealing with the problem of Jewish divorce. In addition to Agunah Inc. and GET, we heard from Rabbi Yehuda Levin of Get Free and Isaac Skolnik of Kayama. Levin, clearly annoyed by some of the statements we and others had made during the course of the day, attacked us as being "high pitched" and "strident." In keeping with his own strategy of "helping" *agunot*, he advised *agunot* to make concessions in return for their *gett*, to make deals, and thereby to end their struggles and obtain their *gittin*.

Isaac Skolnik of Kayama, a Brooklyn based organization that educates about the need for a *gett* and attempts to facilitate the process, described his great success in teaching Reform Jews about the need for a *gett*. He said they readily agreed to grant a *gett* once they understand the importance to their children's future. Susan reacted sharply to the irony that was emerging from his talk, namely, that many Orthodox Jews readily use the *gett* for extortion while non-Orthodox Jews seem to be more ethical in this regard. She engaged in a lively dialogue with Skolnik about whether it was advisable to make Reform Jews feel that a *gett* was essential, given that Rabbi Moshe Feinstein had written that Reform marriages are not binding and do not require a *gett*. "If Reform marriages do not chain wives to their husbands and, therefore, do not require a *gett*, why make Reform Jews feel that a *gett* is necessary and risk spreading *gett* extortion to the Reform community?" Susan asked. Better to leave Feinstein's sweeping ruling as the sole solution, she said, though Skolnick strongly objected.

## *Conference Results II*

This second conference ended with a feeling of accomplishment. Though disappointed with the low turnout of lay people—perhaps 15 Amit women showed up during the day—we were elated with the totally unexpected networking that took place among the *gett* activists who were in attendance.

A real dialogue between experts had occurred, an airing of issues and elucidation of positions—for and against the new New York State Gett Law, and regarding different attitudes and approaches of *batei din* and rabbis. Also we had discovered two new allies—Rabbis Louis Bernstein and Simcha Krauss.

A few weeks after the Amit conference, Rivka was at home on Christmas Eve when her phone rang. To her amazement, it was Rabbi Louis Bernstein, whom she had personally argued with in the past about women's prayer groups. When she expressed surprise at hearing from him, he immediately said that he had called not to discuss "those issues we don't agree about but to talk about what we do agree about." Bernstein said that he was very moved by the *agunot* who spoke at the conference and asked what, if anything, he could do to help. He said that he was going to England in a few weeks. It so happened that one of the *agunot* we were working with had mentioned that her husband was living there and that the rabbis in England were extremely uncooperative. Bernstein thought that perhaps he could use his influence with the rabbis and motivate them to pressure the husband. Rivka put him in contact with the *agunah* and, indeed, Bernstein was true to his word and tried to help, though unsuccessfully.

Bernstein's eagerness, to involve himself in helping *agunot*, had potential to become a major step toward remedying the problem. He was well respected among his rabbinic colleagues and had much influence, and he truly wanted to make a difference. But alas, his good intentions could not be brought to fruition. Somewhat later, when we tried to call him to ask for his help in a particular matter, his wife told us that he was out of town, undergoing treatment for a brain tumor. He died not long after.

As for Rabbi Simcha Krauss, we will meet him again in later chapters.

Taken together the two conferences did not turn out to be the catalyst for change that we had envisioned. They did not produce the powerful grass-roots outcry that we had anticipated, nor was there a major breakthrough in dealing with the issue.

Nevertheless, the conferences served several useful and important functions. They brought *agunot* together, women in the same predicament who otherwise might never have met. These woman were able to give each other strength and also share strategies and knowledge of rabbis and *batei din*. The conferences educated some people, although not nearly enough, and focused media attention on the problem. They served to inform *agunot* about the remedies available to them and to identify rabbis who might be of help. These were useful but small gains. However, no comprehensive, widely accepted solution had emerged, which meant that we still had countless grim cases ahead of us.

# 11

# Child Brides

## Kiddushei Ketanah—*Betrothal of Minor Daughters*

In 1993–95, the Orthodox Jewish world was stunned when two fathers revived the ancient practice of betrothal of minor daughters. These fathers testified, one of them in the presence of a *beit din*, that they had betrothed their young daughters to men whose identity they refused to disclose, thereby turning the girls into *agunot*, chained to unknown husbands.

Under Jewish law, a betrothal is more than what we today describe as "engaged." It is similar to marriage, for though the couple does not cohabit, the betrothal bond can be dissolved only with a *gett* or death of either spouse. Though not yet a wife, a woman who violates betrothal is considered an adulteress.

In 1993, the betrothal of minor daughters was no longer practiced in any Jewish community. The relevant laws are discussed in the pages of the Talmud and centuries old rabbinic literature, but the practice had long been viewed as unacceptable and incompatible with modern life. (The practice could still be found in some Middle Eastern Jewish communities until the mid–20th century.) In 1993, a few recalcitrant husbands latched on to this archaic, dead letter law as a tool to further torture their wives by making their young daughters *agunot*. When this happened, some rabbis initially pronounced it to be a chimera, and advised ignoring it. Some rabbis, however, insisted that, indeed, an ancient practice had been resurrected, was still binding and could not be dismissed unless a formal *halakhic* solution was found to free the girls.

## The Child Brides

The cases of American and Canadian Jewish child brides of 1993–95 were a weird, aberrant phenomenon that was squelched relatively quickly, but the episode is still an important chapter in the *agunah* saga because it illustrates the initial disarray of the Orthodox rabbinate in the face of immoral acts that seem to comply with *halakhah*. When the phenomenon of child brides, child *agunot*, surfaced and attained widespread publicity in both the Jewish and secular media, rabbinic leaders were at a loss for what to do. Besieged by the press, rabbis said they were powerless to help the little girls. "It's immoral and disgusting, but it's *halakhic*," said one rabbi. Only the posthumously discovered ruling by a recently deceased rabbi enabled the Orthodox rabbinate to rule against this travesty.

The girls were ultimately rescued from *aginut* (the state of being an *agunah*) by the deceased rabbi when reports surfaced that this respected rabbinic authority had issued a pivotal decision before his death, freeing the girls. The decision had never been written down or publicized and came to light many months after the rabbi's death, but it carried the day, and rabbi after rabbi declared the girls free. The rabbis found a way to free child *agunot* but still left a question unanswered: When will the Orthodox rabbinate finally rally around a rabbi who declares that *halakhah* can free adult *agunot*?

## *Halakhic Background*

At what age did the rabbis of the Talmud consider a girl to be a *ketanah* (a minor), subject to her father's authority to betroth and marry her off even without her consent? The Talmud categorizes a girl as a *ketanah* when she is younger than 12 years and a day. Signs of puberty also play a role in determining when a girl is no longer a minor and transitions into adulthood. For our purposes, it is sufficient to say that once a girl is twelve and a half years old she is considered an adult and can no longer be betrothed to anyone without her consent.

In the Torah there is no clear statement relating to child marriage or a minimum age for marriage. Nor is there a clear statement relating to a father's right to give his daughter away in marriage. But a father's controlling interest in his daughter's sexual status is inferred by the rabbis from the Torah's rule that if a man rapes a virgin who is still in her father's household, not yet betrothed or married to anyone, the rapist must pay monetary damages to her father (Deuteronomy 22:29), rather than to her, the actual victim. In other words, the father has a monetary interest in the virginity of his daughter. Virgin brides warrant a higher bride price.

The rabbis also derived the right of a father to marry off his minor daughter from another Torah text, Deuteronomy 22:16, which deals with a husband who accuses his new wife of not being a virgin. If her parents can produce proof of her virginity (blood on the sheets of the marital bed) the father states to the elders, the judicial authorities: "*I gave* my daughter to this man. But he despises her...."

Emphasizing the words "*I gave*," the Midrash on Deuteronomy teaches: "From here we learn that a father is permitted to betroth (*give*) his minor daughter." As for sons, there is nothing comparable. Fathers cannot betroth their minor sons.

There is an important limitation on the father's right to betroth his daughter: he can do this only once. This rule is stated in Mishnah *Yevamot* 13:6, "...a minor daughter whose father married her off and [then] she was divorced, is like an orphan whose father still lives." What this text is saying is that though the girl's father is still alive, and she is still a minor, his right to betroth her or marry her off again is terminated. The intention here, as understood by the commentaries, is to prevent an unscrupulous father from prostituting his young daughter for financial gain through serial marriages which would bring him multiple bride prices.

While betrothal and marriage of minor daughters is deemed abusive by us today, in the past there may have been benevolent reasons for it. Indeed, a poignant *Tosafot* (medieval Talmud commentary), in BT Tractate Kiddushin page 41a, reflecting the reality of Jewish communities in 12th century France and Germany, states that "now we are accustomed to betroth even our young daughters because every day the *galut* (exile) oppresses us, and if a man has an opportunity to give his daughter a dowry now, [he should do so] because he may not be able to do so later, and his daughter will remain like an *agunah* forever."

The medieval Jewish communities of France and Germany had been put to the sword and pillaged by Crusaders. The *Tosafot* scholars, though clearly uncomfortable with a father marrying off his young daughter, felt that given the vicissitudes of Jewish life, a father should seize the opportunity to ensure a match for his daughter whenever he had sufficient funds for a dowry. After all, she would in all likelihood outlive her father, and single women lacking the protection of a father or husband were regarded as pitiful and vulnerable. The use of the term *agunah* to describe the misfortune of a girl who might remain a spinster because of her father's poverty indicates how tragic the rabbis felt was the fate both of *agunot* and unattached women.

As with many other disturbing rabbinic laws and concepts, there are counter perspectives within the rabbinic tradition that express disapproval of the betrothal of minor daughters.

Early condemnation can be found in Avot D'Rabbi Natan (an explication of the Mishnaic Tractate Avot, probably compiled between 700 and 900 CE) 48: Rabbi Shimon compared a father who does *kiddushei ketanah* to a murderer.

Strong disapproval is also found in BT Tractate Sanhedrin, page 76a, where the verse in Leviticus 19:29 "Do not degrade your daughter, make her into a harlot" is interpreted, according to Rabbi Mani, as referring "to a man who marries off his daughter to an old man." In BT Tractate Kiddushin, page 41a, we find: "A man is forbidden to betroth his daughter when she is a *ketanah* until she matures and says; 'I want this man.'"

So while *kiddushei ketanah* was theoretically *halakhic* and apparently practiced in Jewish communities at certain historical times, it came to be viewed as a last resort, motivated by a father's prudent concern for securing his daughter's future during turbulent times. These *halakhic* and historic principles became important factors in the nullification of the modern *kiddushei ketanah* situations we will describe in the next section.

It is of interest to note that in non–Western cultures the betrothal and marriage of young girls is still widely practiced. For example, in September 2013, CNN spotlighted a case of an eight-year-old Yemeni girl who died a few days after being married to a 40-year-old man. On May 6, 2014, the *Wall Street Journal* reported on an 11-year-old girl in Pakistan being married off to a man three times her age to settle a crime her uncle committed. Samira Khan, a women's rights activist, is quoted as saying that this case is just the tip of the iceberg. In June 2014 England passed a law criminalizing forced marriage. The majority of known cases in England involved girls in families originating from Pakistan, India and Bangladesh. These cases, in contrast to the aberrant *kiddushei ketanah* cases we are about to discuss, involve the actual consummation of the marriage, sometimes with fatal consequences for the child bride.

## *Contemporary Cases*

In 1993, Israel Goldstein, a 39-year-old man from Montreal (who had moved to New York though his family remained in Montreal), exercised the *halakhic* power of fathers to betroth their minor daughters. Goldstein was a recalcitrant husband who had been withholding a *gett* from his wife Gita, a teacher in Bais Yaakov of Montreal, for four years. He decided to tighten the thumbscrews on Gita by using his *halakhic* power to turn his 11-year-old daughter into an *agunah* as well.

He went to a *beit din* headed by Rabbi Yossef Taussig and betrothed his daughter. Goldstein, not unexpectedly, refused to reveal the name of the girl's "husband." If deemed *halakhically* effective, this betrothal would have an immediate effect: the young girl would become an *agunah*, who could be freed from this betrothal in only two ways: the death of her anonymous "husband" or his granting her a *gett*.

Goldstein justified his cruel act by stating that he feared violence would be used against him to force him to grant a *gett* to his wife. This betrothal was his "insurance policy," he said. So long as he kept the identity of his daughter's "husband" secret, he would not be killed, as the identity of the secret husband was essential if the child was ever to be freed from her *agunah* status.

Goldstein also reportedly complained about the custody and visitation terms of his divorce. He was quoted as saying, " The court says that fathers have no right to their children, but the Torah says they do."

Gita, the desperate mother, as was reported in the *New York Times*, was going all over the world, seeking rabbis to annul the betrothal.

Two years later, in 1995, another case of *kiddushei ketanah* surfaced. The father in this case, Yossi Shereshevsky, was a despised figure in his Borough Park community. He was thought to be a drug dealer, whose dealings had apparently harmed many people financially and otherwise. He was also withholding a *gett* from his wife.

A document that was widely circulated in his neighborhood stated: "Yossi Shereshevsky ... has refused to give a gett to his wife Suri for five years. He does not pay child support for their five children.... It is public knowledge and public record that he has served time in jail on criminal and federal charges. He has sworn in front of witnesses that he will never give a get." It was signed "The Community."

The Shereshevsky case had the hallmarks of a typical *agunah* situation. A number of demonstrations had been held outside the home of Shereshevsky's mother, with whom he was living at the time. The house was a large one, surrounded on all sides by a wide porch. Many people came to join the demonstrations, hundreds, demanding that a *gett* be granted. One sunny Sunday afternoon, we decided to attend the demonstration. We stood in the crowd and watched Shereshevsky emerge from the house, wearing a white T-shirt (unusual in Borough Park where Orthodox men always wore white dress shirts and black jackets), surrounded by two burly security guards. He railed at the crowd like a flamboyant wrestler before withdrawing into the home.

It was during this period that Shereshevsky, like Goldstein, managed to increase the harm he inflicted upon his wife by betrothing one of the couple's minor daughters.

This cruelty perpetrated upon his own child further incensed the community, and the demonstrations became even larger and angrier.

Suddenly, the demonstrations were stopped. What had happened was that a local Gadol (prominent rabbinic authority), head of a well-known Brooklyn yeshivah, issued a statement forbidding any more demonstrations. The rabbi declared that as Shereshevsky's mother was a Holocaust survivor, she had experienced enough suffering, and the demonstrations were too difficult for her to bear. Therefore, he decreed that they had to stop. He did not demand that Shereshevsky grant a *gett* to his wife.

"What about the *agunah*'s parents' suffering? They too are Holocaust survivors. Why doesn't the rabbi care about them?" friends of the *agunah* asked with bitterness.

Despite the fury of the community directed at Shereshevsky, now compounded by his cruelty towards his child, people obeyed the rabbi and ceased all public actions to help the *agunah*. Obedience to rabbinic authority short-circuited the community's efforts to help Shereshevsky's wife.

During this time, Rivka was doing her weekly shopping in a local grocery when an elderly woman approached her and asked "Are you Rivka Haut?" "Yes," Rivka replied. "I am a neighbor of the little Shereshevsky girl whose father Yossi betrothed her," said the woman. She pointed to a group of girls standing and chatting in the next aisle. "See the girl with the blue sweater? She's the one. She doesn't know she is betrothed, and her mother doesn't know who she is betrothed to. Her father is threatening to betroth another daughter." As unobtrusively as she could, Rivka looked and spotted a little girl in a blue sweater, a sweet looking child. The elderly woman explained that all the children knew what their father did. It was all over the newspapers and the entire neighborhood was talking about it. However, she said, the girls in the family had not been told which daughter was the one betrothed.

When the actions of Goldstein and Shereshevsky became widely known, the Orthodox Jewish community was greatly shamed. Jewish newspapers all over the world reported the story. It soon made its way into the secular media, and many well-known newspapers and magazines highlighted these events. This form of child abuse, made possible only if rabbis said that it is *halakhically* binding, made religious Jews and religious law look primitive and cruel. However, the same communities that were fairly passive about the enduring *agunah* disgrace reacted strongly to child *agunot*. The stigma attached to divorce in the religious world (What is wrong with the wife? Why can't she get along with her husband, hold the family together?), could not be applied to innocent children. The religious laity demanded redress from their rabbis.

If *kiddushei ketanah* was not bad enough, around this time a group of men formed the Shalom Bayis (Peace in the Home) Organization and publicly endorsed *kiddushei ketanah*, suggesting that more fathers act similarly. In addition, they advised men to withhold *gittin* for at least five years and advocated that husbands take concubines in the meantime. As you, the reader, can imagine, all this was quickly picked up by the news media, both Jewish and secular, American and Israeli. *The New York Times*, women's magazines, and many other papers ran articles about the crazy goings-on in the Orthodox community. The matter was out of control.

The community watched and waited for its rabbinic authorities to provide guidance. Eventually, they did. Though hesitating at first, finally they acted decisively, grabbing the lifeline that had been extended from the grave and finally putting an end to the deeply disquieting episode.

## *First Rabbinic Reactions-Paralysis*

The immediate questions asked by everyone were: Is *kiddushei ketanah* valid today? Can a father really do this to his daughter? Does the child actually need a *gett*? Is she really betrothed? What are the rabbis doing about this?

Nobody seemed able to answer. The rabbis appeared paralyzed in the face of this travesty of Jewish law. They offered no remedy for unjust and immoral treatment of women that was allegedly legal under *halakhah*.

Honey Rackman, speaking in another context about the suffering of *agunot*, contrasted the rabbis' passivity in *agunah* cases to their speedy responses when kosher food issues arose. She said (*New York Post* May 27, 1997) that a question once arose about whether milk from steroid treated cows is kosher. "They got together in three days, and managed to resolve the issue. It's sad when a Jewish woman isn't as important as a cow."

Here's what several rabbis, considered to be an outstanding authorities, had to say when they were asked to comment on *kiddushei ketanah*:

Rabbi Gedalia Dov Schwartz, then the head of the Rabbinical Council of America (RCA), was quoted in the *New York Times*: " I'm not a computer that can press a button. All I can say is the matter is definitely going to be taken up and discussed."

The RCA issued a statement: *Kiddushei ketanah* "is abhorrent and contrary to the teachings of the Torah and *halakhah*.... It is a transgression for which such individuals should be ostracized and shunned from the Jewish community." No comment about whether the girls were actually betrothed or not.

From Rabbi Kenneth Auman, chair of the Flatbush Rabbinical Council: "I'm just one rabbi; I can't do anything about it myself. A solution has to come from the big rabbis."

Rabbi Solomon Herbst, head of the Beit Din Tzedek Ein Sof in Brooklyn, said, "The rabbis are very upset and we haven't decided how to react to it. It is so painful that I cannot even talk about it."

Rabbi David Zweibel, of Agudath Israel of America, stated that it was "a tragedy of the highest order. I've heard rabbanim describe people who do this as evil. I prefer the term maniac." When challenged by a reporter with Rivka's demand that every rabbinic organization should declare *kiddushei ketanah* to be null and void and announce that all their rabbis will perform weddings for these girls when the time comes, Zweibel responded: "*Halakhah* cannot be so easily manipulated."

Rabbi Chaim Malinowitz, a Monsey, New York, *dayyan* (see Chapters 4 and 10), said the rabbis were discussing what to do about it.

The hesitancy of the rabbinic community to unequivocally declare the betrothals null and void under Jewish law served to encourage the Shalom Bayis Organization. Their outrageous statements and flyers appeared all over neighborhood streets, strongly advocating *kiddushei ketanah*, encouraging more fathers to use this *halakhic* tool when necessary.

We knew only of the two cases discussed above, but, according to the *New York Times* and other media, there were 20 other actual or threatened cases. The *New York Magazine* of June 5, 1995, stated: "As many as 20 girls have been similarly married off within the last year or two, according to a man named Yossi." Yossi was associated with the Shalom Bayis group and claimed that the group was financially supporting fathers who had done *kiddushei ketanah*.

In the normative Orthodox community, however, Goldstein and Shereshevsky were considered pariahs. It was clear that both were acting out of malicious motives. Both were trying to gain financially by imprisoning their young daughters in phantom marriages as leverage to extort money from their wives. Both refused to name the "husbands" they chose for their daughters.

As these events unfolded, with no remedy put forward by the Orthodox rabbinate, Orthodox lay leaders stepped into the breach left by the inaction of the rabbis. Sheldon Silver, Speaker of the New York Assembly and an Orthodox Jew, stated that until a *halakhic* solution was found he wanted to pass a law declaring it a felony to do *kiddushei ketanah*, including making witnesses liable to the felony charge. The National Jewish Commission on Law and Public Affairs (COLPA) was also looking into civil law remedies to the situation.

(Silver and COLPA had teamed up earlier to draft and pass the 1992 New York State Get Law to help *agunot* (see Chapter 14).

Another attempt to use civil law to resolve the problem was that of the late attorney David Stern, who was known as an advocate for *agunot*. Stern was reportedly looking into applying laws concerning the endangerment of minors, extortion and inflicting emotional distress. Stern sought to file criminal charges against Goldstein, who, in response, filed an "angry affidavit" against Stern. Sadly, Mr. Stern's life was cut short when he became the lone fatality of a New Jersey Transit train crash.

However, Rabbi J. David Bleich, a prolific writer on *halakhic* issues, objected to involving civil law. He noted that *halakhic* betrothals are meaningless under civil law. After all, he pointed out, the girls are not actually being forced to live with their "husbands," which would be statutory rape. Bleich warned against the danger of harnessing the power of the state to religious law. He did not want civil courts to examine the issue of whether the girls' marriage prospects are harmed. Bleich had a record of opposition to mobilizing civil law to deal with issues regarding *halakhic* marriage and divorce. He was highly critical of the 1992 New York State Gett Law that had been engineered by Silver and COLPA. Bleich condemned the father but said the girl could not marry unless she received a *gett* or the death of the unknown husband was proven. He called for a "communal ban" on this practice, meaning that going forward the practice would have no binding effect. But the rabbis did not take up his call, and even had they done so, it would not have helped little girls betrothed by their fathers before such a ban was implemented.

Some began to fear an epidemic of *kiddushei ketanah*. We heard from some *agunot* that more husbands were threatening their wives that they too would betroth their young daughters if they were angered or displeased. Wives in abusive marriages were afraid to leave their husbands. One *agunah* we were working with, a victim of domestic violence, told us she decided to remain in her marriage rather than risk her daughter's future. Could the rabbis continue to ignore what was happening as their constituents urgently demanded something be done?

## *A Solution*

Finally, in 1995, a solution was found, though unearthed might be a better word.

The Goldstein *kiddushei ketanah* had taken place in 1993. Rabbi Shlomo

Zalman Auerbach, a major Israeli rabbinic authority widely accepted by the right-wing Orthodox world, died on February 20, 1995. A few months after his death, a decision of his was discovered that ruled that the Goldstein daughter was not married and did not require a *gett* because her father did not produce witnesses to his *kiddushei ketanah*.

This posthumous oral, unwritten ruling was articulated by Rav Eliahu Rominek of Far Rockaway, Queens.

## *Media Accounts of Auerbach's Ruling*

### THE JEWISH PRESS

In *The Jewish Press* of June 30, 1995, a front page headline declared: "Rabbi S. Z. Auerbach Nullified the Betrothal of a Minor Daughter."

The article stated that Rabbi Auerbach rendered the decision in response to a "detailed written analysis of Jewish law" (a *teshuvah*) that was prepared by Rabbi Eliahu Rominek in response to the Goldstein *kiddushei ketanah*.

While the Rominek's *teshuvah* dealt with the Goldstein case, an addendum noted that the Shereshevsky case was also covered under the ruling. Furthermore it was reported that several rabbis felt that the Shereshevsky case could more easily be dismissed because Yossi Shereshevsky, unlike Goldstein, did not have his betrothal act validated by a *beit din*.

What apparently occurred is as follows. Rabbi Rominek, after being approached by Gita Goldstein about her daughter's plight, had written to Rabbi Auerbach in Israel about the case, and included his (Rominek's) *teshuvah*, which concluded that the girl was not actually betrothed. Although Rominek never received a reply from Auerbach, witnesses from Rabbi Auerbach's family attested that Auerbach had accepted Rominek's *halakhic* reasoning and had requested that Rominek publicize the decision in the young girl's Montreal community.

Auerbach reportedly made his decision on August 7, 1994. Rominek, in a personal interview, said that Auerbach's decision, while unwritten, was attested to by Auerbach's son Rabbi Baruch Auerbach and his secretary. It was then supported by separate treatises written by Rabbi Zalman Nehemia Goldberg, Auerbach's son-in-law (whom we will meet again later in this book) in addition to another son-in-law and a *dayyan* of the Jerusalem *beit din*, and also by Rabbi Moshe Sternbuch, of the devout *Edah Hacharedis* of Jerusalem. All these *Haredi* (ultra–Orthodox) rabbis agreed that the Goldstein girl may marry and does not require a *gett*.

In other words, they did not accept the *halakhic* validity of the betrothals. *The Jewish Press* reported: "Rabbi Auerbach's decision was received with acclaim and joy by world Jewry...."

## The *Jewish Telegraphic Agency*

Deborah Nussbaum Cohen, in a June 30, 1995, article for the *Jewish Telegraphic Agency* (JTA), provided a timeline of the events in the Goldstein case that filled in a few more details. According to Cohen, Gita Goldstein contacted two Canadian rabbis about her daughter's situation, who then turned to Eliahu Rominek. In May 1994, Rominek wrote a *teshuvah* that denied the legitimacy of the betrothal. In order to have his *teshuvah* accepted more widely in the religious world, he sent it to Israeli rabbinic authorities, asking for their agreement.

Rominek said that on August 7, 1994, Auerbach told him by phone that the *kiddushei ketanah* was not valid and the girl was free. Auerbach asked Rominek to inform the Montreal community about his ruling. Auerbach said that if the rabbis wished, they could call him to discuss it. Rominek told the Canadian rabbis, but they did not follow up; they did not call Auerbach and did not announce it to their community. Auerbach died a half a year later, and Rominek remained silent.

Cohen noted that in May 1995, the JTA ran a story about *kiddushei ketanah*. Rominek again looked into the matter and learned that Auerbach didn't write anything down, nor had he ever signed Rominek's *teshuvah*. Convinced that Auerbach had nevertheless ruled, Rominek discovered witnesses to attest to Auerbach's ruling. Consistent with what had been reported in *The Jewish Press*, Rominek found Auerbach's secretary Rabbi Elimelech Cooperman and Auerbach's son Rabbi Baruch Auerbach, who both confirmed that Auerbach ruled that way. Then two other accepted authorities said they agreed with Auerbach's ruling and wrote their own concurring rulings: Rabbi Zalman Nechemia Goldberg, Auerbach's son-in-law, and a *Haredi* rabbi, Moshe Sternbuch.

## *Rabbinic Reaction in the Wake of the Posthumous Ruling*

The reports of this ruling by the deceased Torah authority helped the rabbinate find its voice. Rabbis began to publicly endorse Auerbach's ruling freeing the Goldstein and Shereshevsky girls, but opinion was divided with regard to whether *kiddushei ketanah* could be binding in other cases. The

Orthodox rabbinate did not absolutely rule out the possibility of betrothing minor daughters even today.

Rabbi Sholom Klass, publisher of *The Jewish Press*, which long advocated for justice for *agunot*, published an early and courageous article in which he declared that *kiddushei ketanah* is not binding in today's Orthodox communities. Writing in *The Jewish Press* on June 2, 1995, several weeks before the newspaper publicized the Auerbach ruling, Klass ruled that Jews do not accept *kiddushei ketanah* for minor girls because such a marriage is illegal, and Jews are obliged to comply with the law of the land of their residence. Klass quoted the well-known Jewish legal precept *"dina d'malchuta dina,"* the law of the land in which Jews reside is the law. Further, Klass stated that if a daughter doesn't live with her father and is estranged from him, he has no jurisdiction over her. She is considered an orphan. If she was unaware of his action, she can ignore it completely "under the appropriate circumstances...."

In a second column, published the following week, Klass supplied numerous additional *halakhic* sources in support of his position. Among other sources, he referred to the *Tosafot* from page 41a of Tractate Kiddushin, cited above, in which the *Tosafot* puts *kiddushei ketanah* into the context of a father seeking to protect his daughter from future poverty and vulnerability, but not to spitefully try to harm her.

After the June 30, 1995, news of Auerbach's ruling, it was as if a dam broke—rabbis started going on record in support of Auerbach.

In July 1995, Gedalia Dov Schwartz announced that the RCA accepts Auerbach's ruling. The BDA (RCA) called a meeting of twenty rabbis, from nine different *batei din*. They relied on Auerbach's ruling, accepting the statements of the various witnesses, all rabbis themselves. They said the Goldstein betrothal and all such cases of *kiddushei ketanah*, including future cases, are nullified, because a father who would do this is a *rasha* (wicked) and not to be believed, since he did not produce witnesses. Should the father, however, produce witnesses, the cases might have to be re-examined. Schwartz said he was proud of the RCA for calling together such a group of rabbis and *batei din*.

Rabbi Yisroel Belsky called *kiddushei ketanah* a "cancerous growth." A group of independent rabbis, numbering almost a dozen, disparaged the rabbis who supported *kiddushei ketanah*. Among the few rabbis reported to be supportive of *kiddushei ketanah* were Menashe Klein, known as the Ungvarer Rov, and Shlomo Blumenkrantz.

Aguda's Council of Torah Sages expressed outrage about the practice of *kiddushei ketanah*, but did not declare the practice null and void. Aguda's David Zweibel said the council does not issue *halakhic* rulings.

Rabbi Marvin Antelman (see Chapter 10), head of the Supreme Rabbinic Court of America (founded in 1974), formed a *Sanhedrin Ketanah* (small Sanhedrin) to deal with all *kiddushei ketanah* cases. In their proclamation, published in the *Jerusalem Post*, August 19, 1995, signed by 21 rabbis and filled with *halakhic* citations, Antelman's group declared that Goldstein and Shereshevsky are condemned to death. They compared *kiddushei ketanah* to kidnapping, and ruled that though they cannot carry out the requisite death penalty, the men are "*halakhically* dead." Therefore their wives are free to remarry and may even marry a Kohen because they are now *halakhically* widows.

Antelman's declaration also named another recalcitrant, who had a *seruv* against him for withholding a *gett*, and said that he should be castrated, but since this cannot be done, they declare his wife to be free.

Rabbi Shmuel Tuvia Stern, writing in *The Jewish Press* on July 14, 1995, declared that *kiddushei ketanah* is meant only to improve a daughter's status, not to hurt her. As for the conclave some rabbis called for to deal with *kiddushei ketanah*, Stern opined that such a meeting may never happen, and he, therefore, calls on every *beit din* to rule that these marriages are null and void.

## *Skepticism About Auerbach's Ruling*

Rabbi Abraham Hecht, of the Rabbinical Alliance of America, raised a host of questions about the Auerbach ruling. Why did the ruling come out only after Auerbach's death? Why wasn't it written?

Rabbi Chaim Malinowitz, of Monsey, also expressed doubt about accepting a posthumously discovered unwritten ruling. He, therefore, presented his own analysis and ruling in the *Journal of Halachah and Contemporary Society*, Fall 1995.

In a mocking tone, Malinowitz wrote "a deceased *posek* (*halakhic* decisor) has 'nullified' the *kiddushin*." He also commented on newspaper reports that the RCA has nullified the *kiddushei ketanah*, saying that as he hadn't seen a written *teshuvah* from them he could not accept it.

Malinowitz pointed out that a father's testimony is decisive for *kiddushei ketanah*. The whole case rested on whether or not the father is believed. Usually two witnesses are required to substantiate a fact, but in the case of a father doing *kiddushei ketanah*, the Torah speaks (Deuteronomy 22:16) in singular language, "*I gave*." The father's testimony alone is, therefore, determinate in this case. Everything hinges on whether we believe this father or not.

Malinowitz labeled Goldstein, whom he referred to as "G," "wicked." "G" told the *beit din* that he was blackmailing his wife by doing *kiddushei ketanah*. But Malinowitz still wasn't ready to rule that alone is grounds for deeming him to be wicked. After all, Malinowitz observed, "the fact (*kiddushei ketanah*) can hardly be termed 'wicked' inasmuch as it is one sanctioned by the Torah." Moreover, Malinowitz added "G" was trying to force his wife out of civil court into a *beit din*, which in itself was a good thing.

In the end, Malinowitz concluded that the father had limited credibility. Since the father refused to name the husband or the witnesses to the betrothal, why believe him, especially as the context is a bitter divorce battle. Therefore, we don't have to believe him. Malinowitz said we could apply this reasoning to all future cases and refuse to believe the father. He ruled that the girl was not married.

He concluded his article by defending the laws of *kiddushei ketanah*, putting a positive spin on it, saying the Torah gave fathers ability to provide for their daughters.

With the unrecorded words of the late Rabbi Auerbach providing legitimacy, the Orthodox rabbinate managed to free the Goldstein and Shereshevsky girls, though several prominent rabbis left open the possibility that, according to the letter of the law, fathers could, even today, "give" their minor daughters away into a binding betrothal. The use of *halakhah* to abuse little girls was nullified and has not resurfaced, but the rabbis have yet to find a *halakhic* solution to free adult *agunot*.

# 12

# The *Beit Din* That Couldn't

Our involvement in one of our most unsettling cases began in a most unlikely place, at the eastern end of Long Island in a luxurious Hamptons vacation home. We had been invited to a dinner meeting to brainstorm solutions to the *agunah* problem. Our dinner companions were our hosts, a wealthy philanthropic couple, and two rabbis.

Wine flowed and course after course was served by the household staff as we detailed the suffering of *agunot* and the dismal state of *batei din*. The rabbis acknowledged that change was necessary, that the *beit din* system was not functioning adequately. As dessert was being served, one of the rabbis suggested that what was needed was an educational program to inform the community about the importance of settling all disputes—communal, business and marital—in a *beit din*. Divorcing couples should submit all issues to the *batei din* for binding arbitration. If *batei din* had more stature and power, they could deal more effectively with the *agunah* problem. The other rabbi expressed his agreement.

We exchanged glances across the table throughout the rabbi's presentation, amazed at how out of touch he was with the realities of the *agunah* problem. When it was our turn to comment, we expressed our doubts about his proposal. We explained that it was our experience that the more power the rabbis had over marital issues, the more the *agunah* and her children were at risk of being victims of extortion. Our position was, in fact, that *batei din* should be limited to overseeing the *gett*. All other issues should settled in civil court or through mediation, if possible. We also explained that husbands can game the *beit din* system by refusing to go to a particular *beit din* and then hold up the whole process by choosing a disreputable *beit din* or engaging in an endless process of putting together a *zabla beit din*. We described several cases in which *agunot* were held up for years by such machinations and reduced to poverty by their husbands' extortion demands in a *zabla beit din*.

Suddenly, one of the rabbis, Rabbi Fox, interjected sharply and surprisingly that men are not always to blame in *gett* cases. As he spoke, he seemed to be in such deep emotional distress that our hosts inquired if he was feeling all right. He surprised us all by becoming personal, revealing that he was suffering because of a *gett* situation in his family.

His son was embroiled in a contentious divorce with dreadful charges and countercharges being hurled back and forth in civil court. He said that his son's *gett* case was before the Chasidei Morozov *beit din*. "Why the Chasidei Morozov *beit din*?" everyone exclaimed simultaneously. We were all astonished that Rabbi Fox, a Modern Orthodox rabbi, would turn to a Chasidic *beit din*, whose rabbis are anti–Zionist and oppose secular education, the antithesis of Modern Orthodoxy. In response, Rabbi Fox explained that he had chosen Chasidei Morozov because he wanted a *beit din* that would be perceived as unbiased, not susceptible to being influenced by his stature in the Modern Orthodox rabbinate.

We returned from this personal digression to the subject of the new *beit din*. The evening wore on, and we were getting nowhere. The meeting ended on a pessimistic note. We told the rabbis that effectively helping *agunot* would require moving decisively, breaking new ground, and risking some criticism from the right. We were in touch with the sordid reality and urgent needs of *agunot*, and we tried to arouse the same sense of urgency in them. The rabbis, sitting in their rabbinic ivory towers, had proposed a plan that was out of touch with the reality of the world of *agunot* and *batei din*.

As we said our goodbyes in the foyer and walked toward our car, Rabbi Fox was quietly whispering, almost talking to himself, some vague remarks about his distressing situation. We couldn't grasp what he was saying, but we sympathized with his pain and parted company. Thus began a bizarre case with strange midnight phone calls and a bogus *gett* from the Morozov *beit din*, chosen by Fox, apparently, because it would cooperate with his schemes.

During the drive home, we talked about the familiar pattern that emerged at the meeting: rabbis proposing inadequate policies regarding *agunot* and then having no reply when we pointed out the shortcomings of what they were proposing. We were disturbed that large sums might be poured into this dead end solution. We wondered about the nature of Rabbi Fox's family problem and felt badly for him.

Our idle speculation vanished quickly, as we unexpectedly and unavoidably became embroiled in the Fox family problem.

Late that very night, around midnight, Susan's phone rang. It was Rabbi Fox. Susan was surprised that he had her personal phone number and that he called her at home in the middle of the night. He opened the conversation by expressing sympathy for Susan regarding her personal difficulties. Susan assumed he was referring to her being divorced but, again, was taken aback at his knowledge of her personal life since she had never met him before. He then described to her in great detail his son Asher's difficulties in having his wife accept a *gett*. Susan said that she hoped the situation would be resolved quickly and tried to cut the conversation short. It was after midnight, Rabbi Fox's son could give a *gett* anytime he pleased so there didn't seem to be any reason for Agunah Inc. to be involved. Rabbi Fox persisted, insisting that his family's *gett* problem would in no way interfere with his role in working on improving the *beit din* system. Susan listened, wished him well and said good night.

We were both puzzled by Rabbi Fox's late night call. We assumed that now that he had gotten this off his chest, we would not hear from him again. After all, if his daughter-in-law was refusing to accept a *gett*, his son could deposit a *gett* for her in the *beit din* and be granted a *heter me'ah rabbanim*, a rabbinic waiver that would permit him to remarry despite his wife's refusal to accept a *gett*.

A *heter me'ah rabbanim*, literally "permission of a hundred rabbis," permits a man whose wife refuses to accept a *gett* to remarry anyway, to take an "additional" wife. The rabbis found this "additional" wife *halakhically* acceptable because, as readers of the Bible know, the patriarchs Abraham and Jacob in Genesis were polygamous. It was not until around 1000 CE that a rabbinic prohibition against polygamy was enacted, by Rabbenu Gershom (Gershom Ben Judah Me'or Ha-Golah, 960–1028). As polygamy is biblically permitted, and only rabbinically prohibited, the rabbis devised a way for a man to bypass Rabbenu Gershom's prohibition under certain circumstances, for example, when the wife is unwilling or unable to accept a *gett*. In such cases, the rabbis suppress the prohibition of Rabbenu Gershom, permitting the husband to marry another woman. The husband must, however, issue a *gett* for the first wife, which is held by a *beit din* for her to accept at any time. Meanwhile, the husband is free to remarry.

We assumed that Rabbi Fox's son would avail himself of this *halakhic* tool and his problem would thereby be solved.

Within a week Rabbi Fox called Susan again. This time he opened the conversation by informing Susan that Asher had a civil court date coming up and that, in her court papers, Asher's wife had mentioned that she had spent time in a battered women's shelter sponsored by UJA/Federation, a New York umbrella organization of Jewish charities. Rabbi Fox said that he knew Susan was active in UJA and asked her if she knew a certain social worker who was scheduled to testify on his daughter-in-law's behalf.

Once again Susan was surprised at his knowledge of her personal life, as Rabbi Fox was a complete stranger to her. Seemingly anxious to persuade Susan of the correctness of his son's behavior, Rabbi Fox urged her to call the Chasidei Morozov *beit din* and confirm that a *gett* was deposited for his daughter-in-law Tirza. Susan did as he asked and, upon calling the *beit din*, she was informed that, indeed, a *gett* for Tirza had been written and deposited. There appeared to be no problem, and we could not understand Rabbi Fox's concern.

Shortly after these events, Rivka began receiving phone calls from various individuals asking for Agunah Inc.'s help on behalf of Tirza. The callers kept bringing up the heated civil court battle, but Rivka constantly repeated that Agunah Inc. deals only with *gett* problems. Once the *gett* is given and can no longer be used as leverage for extortion, the other issues in the case are the domain of judges, lawyers, arbitrators and mediators, not Agunah Inc. As far as we knew, Tirza could pick up her *gett* at the Morozov *beit din* whenever she wanted so Agunah Inc. had no role to play in this case.

One caller urging that Agunah Inc. become involved stuck in Rivka's mind—Izzy, a businessman who had become involved in helping Tirza and other *agunot*. Izzy and Rivka's husband Irwin knew each other as children growing up in Williamsburg, Brooklyn. Izzy was waging an all-out battle on Tirza's behalf. His raspy voice and plain speaking style became very familiar to us over the next few months as he called to give us updates.

Not long after hearing from Izzy, Tirza herself called Rivka. She confirmed that she and her husband Asher were in the midst of a bitter divorce but recounted a different version of events regarding the *gett*. She said that when she attempted to pick up her *gett* at the Morozov *beit din*, she found out that the *gett* wasn't kosher. Tirza had asked Rabbi Kaplan, the head of a another New York area *beit din*, to accompany her when she went to pick up her *gett*. Rabbi Kaplan advised her not to accept the *gett* that was on deposit as, in his opinion, it was not a valid *gett*. Tirza explained to Rivka that the *gett* identified her by several of her English names and nicknames but omitted her given Hebrew name, an omission which invalidated the document. She felt the omission was deliberate since her ex husband, like all Orthodox husbands, had used her given Hebrew name numerous times in various ceremonial blessings, and that was the name which appeared in her *ketubah*, her marriage contract.

## 12. The Beit Din *That Couldn't*

After speaking with Tirza, we felt we could not ignore her plea for help. What at first appeared to us to be nasty civil divorce proceedings, outside our purview, now seemed to be an *agunah* problem. Our initial step in dealing with the case was to contact Rabbi Fox, because we didn't know how to reach Asher.

We called Rabbi Fox's home, and his wife answered. As soon as we identified ourselves as directors of Agunah Inc., she said, "I can't believe Agunah is calling me. Tirza is not an *agunah*!" We tried to focus the conversation on the *gett* problem, but Rebbetzin Fox kept injecting other aspects of the thorny civil divorce proceedings. Each time Rebbetzin Fox raised these matters, Rivka said "We can't get involved in side issues. Our only area of expertise is the *gett*." We asked Rebbetzin Fox for Asher's number in order to speak to him directly, but she refused to give it to us. She told us to call the Morozov *beit din* regarding the validity of the *gett*. We dialed the number immediately, but nobody answered.

Eleven-thirty that same night, Rabbi Fox called Susan, expressed concern about our involvement and gave her Asher's number. We began to feel that Rabbi's Fox's repeatedly contacting Susan, gathering information about her personal life and attempting to establish a rapport with her was connected to his sense that Tirza would eventually turn to Agunah Inc. for help. Indeed, by the time Tirza reached us, he had already managed to tell his side of the story.

We spent the entire next day researching the case, trying to learn the truth about what was going on. Was the *gett* on deposit at the Morozov *beit din* valid or not? We finally managed to reach Rabbi Daitch at the *beit din*. He refused to answer most of our questions but conceded that the *gett* Asher had deposited was faulty and a new one had to be written. He also acknowledged that the *beit din* had issued a *heter me'ah rabbanim* for Asher, permitting him to date and remarry, while Tirza was unable to proceed with a social life until she received a proper *gett*. We challenged the *beit din*'s conduct in this matter since a *heter* requires that a kosher *gett* be in escrow at the *beit din*, ready for the wife to pick up at any time. Rabbi Daitch closed the door on any further discussion of the *heter* by saying, "I won't discuss *halakhah* with women." Despite our differences, Rabbi Daitch agreed that a new *gett* was necessary. We pressed him to set an appointment for a new *gett* to be written and granted. He refused, declaring that the *beit din* couldn't because there was no available *sofer* (scribe, pl. *sofrim*).

We were incredulous. A *beit din* without a *sofer* is like a restaurant without food. We suggested that the *beit din* find a *sofer* immediately and offered to call other *sofrim*. Rabbi Daitch said that his *beit din* only uses a particular *sofer*, and he gave us the *sofer*'s number, urging us to call him. After numerous attempts to reach the *sofer*, we spoke to his wife who had him call us back. He gave us several dates that he would be available but added that if the *beit din* didn't set a definite appointment soon, his calendar might get full.

That same day we also reached Rabbi Kaplan, who confirmed Tirza's account of the *gett* not being kosher. "Isn't it true that a kosher *gett* must be deposited with the *beit din* when there is a *heter me'ah rabbanim*?" we asked. We pointed out the inequity which permitted Asher to date other women while Tirza was unable to have any social life. We also wanted to know why the *beit din* insisted that Tirza come in person to accept the new *gett* rather than delivering the *gett* to her through an agent, sparing her an unpleasant direct encounter with her former spouse. Rabbi Kaplan responded that these were good questions that he could not answer. But he said that he felt the *beit din* was now proceeding properly.

The *beit din*'s alleged inability to schedule a session for the writing of a new *gett* was maddening. Since both parties appeared to be willing to cooperate in the writing and receiving of the *gett*, it was unnecessary to call Asher. In our view, the fault lay with the *beit din* and not with the parties. However, the delaying tactics of the *beit din* were clearly working for the husband. Asher was free and Tirza was not.

As our efforts proceeded, Tirza's champion, Izzy, was busy conducting his own campaign. He posted flyers in Rabbi Fox's neighborhood. He left stacks of flyers in Rabbi Fox's synagogue. Kosher eateries and grocery stores were blanketed with Izzy's flyers, which detailed Tirza's plight. He even took out an ad in a widely read Jewish newspaper, further publicizing the situation.

As the days passed, Rivka received a number of phone calls from people who lived in her Flatbush neighborhood, whom she knew only casually. The callers tried to pressure her to leave this case alone. One caller was a former teacher of one of Rivka's daughters. Another was a yeshivah student, unknown to Rivka, but who claimed to know her and her husband. Two years after this case was closed, a good friend of Rivka's revealed that she too had been called by the Foxes and had been asked to influence Rivka to back off. This woman felt that Agunah Inc. knew its business and never made the requested call.

Near midnight one Sunday night, Rabbi Fox called Susan again. Not having the ability to make a three way phone conversation, Susan told him she would drive immediately to Rivka's house and would call back together with Rivka. The conversation that followed lasted close to four hours, until the wee hours of the morning. In the first few minutes of the conversation, Rabbi Fox asked Susan, "Isn't your daughter a student in my friend Rabbi Wasserman's class?" This was another instance of the Foxes' digging around in our personal lives, which we found very unsettling. We had never experienced anything like this before.

Again and again we told Rabbi Fox that the Morozov *beit din* was not functioning properly. It's a well known rabbinic principle that when the parties are agreeable, the giving of the *gett* should never be delayed. We repeatedly asked why the *gett* had to be given in the Morozov *beit din*, which claimed it couldn't procure the services of a *sofer*. We offered to make arrangements with another *beit din* to conduct the *gett* proceeding and be done with it. Fox cited all kinds of obstacles to ending the matter, none of them convincing. We were going around in circles, making no progress towards a resolution. It was very late and we were exhausted.

Suddenly, more than two hours into the conversation, the tone turned nasty. Fox angrily inquired if we had any role in Izzy's flyer campaign. We said, "No," and explained that Izzy was acting on his own. Finally at about three a.m., Fox, probably realizing we would stick with Tirza until she got her *gett* and that we might publicize his *beit din* machinations, agreed that if a new *gett* was not written within the next two weeks, he would consider using another *beit din*.

Midnight phone calls, contacting our children's teachers and our friends— this case was intruding too deeply into our personal lives. The next morning, as Rivka was going about her errands, she was so preoccupied by the Foxes' disturbing tactics that she began to reevaluate Agunah Inc.'s future. We could not continue to absorb these obsessive phone calls and invasions of our private lives. She decided, the first of many such never acted upon decisions, to stop dealing with *agunah* cases once this was over. Immersed in these thoughts, Rivka took a wrong turn and painstakingly walked six icy blocks before realizing she was going the wrong way.

Arriving home after the unintended detour, Rivka ran to pick up a ringing telephone. Rabbi Fox's voice jarred her out of her thoughts. He said that his family was angry about Agunah Inc.'s involvement in the case, but, nevertheless, he had good news. "*The beit din* has just set a date for the giving of the *gett*," Rabbi Fox said. "If Tirza can make it, the *gett* will be given on Wednesday." We called the *beit din* to confirm the time and asked if Tirza had been notified. They said "No," and, to our surprise, asked that we call her, which we did.

Tirza couldn't believe the *gett* was imminent. Although she had work obligations on that day, she immediately jumped at the opportunity to finally gain her freedom. She asked us to accompany her. We assured her we would be there in accordance with our longstanding policy of advising women to bring another woman along to avoid the discomfort of being the only woman in a roomful of men. We called the *beit din* to tell them that Tirza would appear, and they cavalierly informed us that they had changed the time and again asked us to notify Tirza, which we did.

A light-hearted moment occurred when Susan called the *beit din* to confirm the appointment for the *gett*. The elderly *beit din* secretary answered when Susan called, and he told her that in addition to his *beit di*n work he had a sideline, he was also a *shadchan* (matchmaker). Susan kidded him saying he was ideally situated for picking up newly single clients in search of spouses. He carried on, saying, "How about you?" She replied with a chuckle, "The men you deal with are much too religious for me." Undaunted, he replied, "I have all kinds of men I could introduce you to. What kind of man are you looking for?" It wasn't easy to discourage this tenacious matchmaker, but Susan finally convinced him that she wasn't interested in a matchmaker's services.

Tirza was very worried about something going wrong at the *gett* proceeding and so were we. After all, a non-kosher *gett* had been proffered once. The *beit din*'s behavior since then did little to inspire confidence in their integrity. We did not feel knowledgeable enough about the Morozov *beit din*'s procedures to pick up on any irregularities. Tirza needed a rabbi she trusted to be there. She began making calls to various rabbis who knew her and her family. To her bitter disappointment, none of the rabbis she called would agree to accompany her. It seemed that everyone was afraid to tangle with Fox. Shloimy Eisen, who had brought us our first case, somehow knew what was going on, and he called us and warned us, "Be on the lookout for tricks. Otherwise, if Tirza ever tries to remarry, Fox just might say that her *gett* is not kosher, and she will be back at square one." When we asked Shloimy if he would accompany Tirza to the *beit din*, the usually intrepid Shloimy replied, "Get on Fox's bad side? I'm not crazy!"

It was increasingly clear to us that Tirza needed to bring a rabbi who would look out for her interests. Finally, a relative of hers found a young rabbi who agreed to come. His presence turned out to be crucial in reassuring Tirza when things took a strange turn at *beit din* on the day of the *gett*.

The morning of the giving of the *gett* was one of the coldest New York City had experienced in years. We had trouble scraping the ice off the car windshield and navigating the slippery roads we traversed. We shivered as we opened our windows asking passersby for the exact location of the *beit din*. Fearful of being late, we had allowed so much time for the ride that we arrived an hour early. We searched for a kosher restaurant where we could get hot coffee. As we walked we noticed a Chasidic man with a small child trailing behind him staring at us. Without *sheitels* and long skirts, we look out of place, we thought. Indeed, the Chasid soon approached us to ask if we were lost. Hearing that we were seeking a coffee shop, he surprised us with an offer to drive us. We accepted the ride with thanks but kept the unhappy reason for our presence in his neighborhood to ourselves.

Fortified with hot coffee, we retraced our steps to the Morozov *beit din*. When we arrived at the run-down, nondescript building, Izzy poked his head out his van window and yelled out a "Hello!" "What are you doing sitting out here in this freezing cold?" we asked him. "They won't let me in," he replied. "But I won't go away until I know Tirza has her *gett*." We steeled ourselves for similar treatment. When we entered the dark and narrow *beit din* hallway, we were immediately told to leave. We explained that for reasons of *tsniut* (modesty) we had to be there because it was uncomfortable for a lone woman to be in a room full of men. At that point, Tirza walked into the hallway and insisted that we stay. After some discussion we were permitted to stay and directed to a side room.

Seated at a long table was a young man who, by his dress and clean shaven face, was obviously not a Morozov Chasid. He was intensely focused on a religious volume he held. We realized that he must be Asher. We were enveloped in grief, sensing the tragedy and emotional upheavals that beset this young pair. We also felt the loss sustained by the Jewish community at the dissolution of yet another young marriage. Neither of us broke the silence. After a short while, someone came upstairs from the basement chambers of the *beit din* and summoned Asher down.

We were surprised that Tirza, her family members and the rabbi she brought with her were not permitted to be present in the *beit din* chambers while the *gett* was being written. Rabbi Kaplan, who had earlier contacted the *beit din* on Tirza's behalf, was, however, invited downstairs. After two hours, Rabbi Kaplan came up to escort Tirza down to receive the newly written *gett*. Tirza immediately inquired if her given name, the omission of which had caused the problem with the first *gett*, was included in the newly written *gett*. To everyone's astonishment, Rabbi Kaplan said, "No." We all became upset. Some of Tirza's male relatives began protesting loudly. There were some side discussions, after which the men quieted down. Rabbi Kaplan repeatedly instructed Tirza to accept the new *gett* "*b'lev shalem*," "wholeheartedly." At this point some of her male relatives encouraged her to accept the *gett*. Tirza, distraught and conflicted, with tears in her eyes, ran to call her brother, a rabbi living in France, to ask for advice.

We had remained quiet while all this transpired. While Tirza was frantically trying to reach her brother, we were taken aside by one of the rabbis who whispered to us that there were to be two *gittin* written that day, one after the other. Tirza had to accept the first *b'lev shalem*, despite the omission of her name again, before being informed that yet another *gett* would be written immediately afterward that would include her Hebrew name. Everyone but Tirza now knew the plan. We were upset at the *inui ha'din* (suffering due to the postponement of justice) that Tirza was undergoing, but could do nothing. She was in a quandary because she was unable to reach her brother. We took her aside and advised her to accept the *gett*. After several more moments of anguish, she was persuaded by the young rabbi her family had recruited just a few days ago to accept the *gett b'lev shalem* and then to point out the omission of her given name to the rabbis.

When she finally returned she told us what had happened downstairs. She had accepted the *gett* and felt relieved. After she accepted it, they revealed to her that another *gett* would now be written containing her given Hebrew name. She felt her ordeal was finally almost over.

At the time Tirza had been trying to phone her brother, a disturbing event took place. The *sofer* suddenly bounded up the stairs and asked for the women he had spoken to from the Agunah organization. We identified ourselves and were shocked when he began badmouthing Tirza for her hesitation in accepting the *gett*. "You see she really doesn't want a *gett*," he yelled, "or else she wouldn't be making a problem." We expressed our disapproval of this strange, slanderous talk and refused to listen.

Tirza's rabbi was permitted to accompany her downstairs while the second *gett* was being written, but we were told to remain upstairs. After the second *gett* of the day, which was actually the third of this whole bizarre case, was given to Tirza along with the *p'tur* (a document indicating that a *gett* has been granted and received), she was visibly relieved. We hugged her and gave her a *brachah*, a blessing, for future happiness.

Upon leaving the building, we asked Rabbi Kaplan why two *gittin* had to be written that day rather than including Tirza's given name in the first. He had no explanation. We asked him if he had ever seen this before and he said, "No." The entire episode remains enigmatic in our minds.

As we were putting on our coats the *beit din*'s secretary, who all this time had been sitting quietly at a small desk in the corner of the waiting room, approached us and asked which of us was Susan. He renewed the offer he had made on the phone to find her a *shidduch*, a match. She thanked him with a smile but declined his enthusiastic offer.

Five hours after entering the building, we exited, and found ourselves again plunged into the frigid winter weather. Still sitting faithfully in his van was Izzy. He yelled out, "Did she get the *gett*?" "Two of 'em," Susan quipped. "It's all over," Susan added when she saw the puzzled look on Izzy's face. "Now I can go home," Izzy sighed. He offered us a ride, but we explained that we had come with our own car. We arrived home exhausted but convinced that our efforts had been worthwhile. We had thwarted an attempt to keep an *agunah* in chains through the subterfuge of an invalid *gett* and the outlandish claim that the *beit din* couldn't find a *sofer*. Yes, we had outfoxed them!

# 13

# A Success Story

Lena was the youngest *agunah* to approach us for help and turned out to be one of the rare success stories in which an *agunah* obtained her *gett* relatively quickly through public pressure rather than giving in to extortion.

When we met Lena she was 22 and had been an *agunah* for a year. Graceful and attractive, she looked like a high school girl. Her marriage to Rafi had lasted only six months. Her father had wanted her to sign a prenuptial agreement before the wedding, but Rafi resisted, and Lena acceded to his wishes.

The couple had no children and very few assets. Lena said that she had been physically abused by Rafi. One night his violence reached such a pitch that neighbors heard the row and called police, who put Rafi in jail overnight. Lena feared Rafi was going to kill her. She filed criminal charges against him and secured an order of protection.

Lena was willing to drop the criminal charges and to relinquish all marital assets if only Rafi would grant her a *gett*. But nothing she offered could sway him. He seemed bent on torturing Lena, who had dared to leave him. Rafi and his family had a strategy to keep Lena an *agunah*. They were well-to-do and money meant nothing to them. They mounted a successful harassment campaign to deter her witnesses from testifying on her behalf in the criminal case against Rafi.

Rafi's refusal to give the *gett* didn't stop him from going on with his life. He was seen regularly with a young woman on his arm. Rumor had it that he was on the verge of getting engaged.

Lena's family became completely absorbed by the effort to free her. They were reeling from their discovery that the *halakhic* system, in which they had believed all their lives, now entrapped their daughter who was innocent of any wrongdoing.

Lena, a yeshivah student for 12 years, was deeply disappointed when she turned to the rabbis who had been her teachers for help. All but one said they were too busy to see her, and the one who did give her some time threw his hands up in the air and said he could do nothing to help her.

Fortunately for Lena, the *beit din* she turned to issued a *seruv* against Rafi fairly quickly. She began to publicize the *seruv*, sending it to the rabbis of the three synagogues where Rafi and his family prayed. Rabbis from the *beit din* called the synagogue rabbis and asked that the *seruv* be honored, but the synagogue rabbis ignored it. Rafi's affluent family were major contributors to all three synagogues. Rafi and his father continued to be counted in the *minyan* and given ritual honors such as being called up to the Torah.

Lena now realized that even the *beit din*'s best efforts would not secure a *gett*. She began civil proceedings for a divorce. It took about a year, and the civil divorce was finalized. Yet she was still imprisoned in a dead marriage. At this point, Lena's mother, deeply distressed about her daughter's future, called us for an appointment. A few seconds into Lena's story, her mother began crying uncontrollably. Lena's father took over the conversation. We discussed the option of appealing for community support and suggested they attend and observe a demonstration for another *agunah*.

Lena and her parents came to that demonstration, standing quietly on the sidelines. From that time on and until Lena received her *gett*, they attended every demonstration and public event that we held. We always thanked them for coming but found it increasingly difficult to speak to them because their pain was so palpable.

At one demonstration, our picketing of the Ezras Torah dinner (see Chapter 8), Lena took a more active role. She held up a sign saying, "I AM AN AGUNAH FOR TWO YEARS." She attracted a great deal of attention because of her youthful appearance. Many people approached her to talk and were visibly moved by her story.

Meanwhile Rafi's behavior became even more brazen. He began appearing in synagogues with his steady girlfriend. Though many congregants disapproved, the synagogue rabbis' reactions varied. Rafi was thrown out of one synagogue at the rabbi's insistence. At another synagogue, Rivka's son-in-law Seth recognized Rafi in shul at *minchah* time. Seth whispered to the rabbi that a *mesarev* (one in contempt of a *beit din*) was participating in the *minyan* and should be asked to leave. Nothing was done and Rafi was permitted to remain until the end of the service.

Lena's parents called us frequently. They sensed that Lena was nearing a crossroad in her life. She would either remain within the Orthodox world, unable to date, marry and have children, or she would begin to date non–Orthodox Jews, some of whom had already asked her out. One of her uncles, distraught at the thought of her leaving Orthodox Judaism, begged her to wait a year during which time he would dedicate all his energy to obtaining her *gett*. He began visiting other communities, telling his niece's story and imploring everyone to get involved. At this time, we received a phone call from Gail, a philanthropist long interested in *agunah* problems, who asked to be assigned a case to work on. We put her in touch with Lena and her uncle. In the course of their conversations, Lena's uncle discovered that Gail's family was a major supporter of the yeshivah where Rabbi Ploni, one of Rafi's rabbis, taught. Rabbi Ploni's shul was one of those where Rafi was still welcomed despite the *seruv* against him. Gail was outraged that Rabbi Ploni was permitted to remain on the faculty of the yeshivah, and she began making a series of phone calls to the heads of the yeshivah demanding that Ploni be fired.

Lena's uncle was working on all fronts. He began organizing a demonstration and asked us for guidance. He had placards and flyers made up. He called upon the rabbi of the shul where Lena and her parents prayed and mobilized that congregation to attend the demonstration. Many of Lena's young friends, who were outraged at the entire situation, got involved in the plans. They hired buses to take people from the various neighborhoods to the demonstration site.

The day of the demonstration arrived. People had been told to assemble in front of the home where Rafi and his parents lived. It was in a quiet neighborhood of large, private houses, on a tree-lined street. Soon there was a sizable crowd, men and women, young and old, holding large oak tag placards demanding that a *gett* be granted and flyers containing copies of the *seruv*. The serenity of the neighborhood was disturbed as the group began to circle around, loudly chanting: "Rafi, Rafi, give your wife a *gett*!" Cars coming down the small street slowed or stopped, and drivers hung their heads out of windows to ask what was going on. They were handed flyers and asked to help persuade Rafi to give the *gett*.

After an hour or so, we decided to attend afternoon services, *minchah*, at two of the shuls where Rafi and his family prayed. We broke up into two groups, one led by Rivka and one by Susan, and each headed for one of the shuls.

Rivka's group walked to a large building whose doors were locked. The group waited for someone to come, knowing that afternoon services had to start soon. Some people needed a bathroom, but the shul was in a residential area, with no public facilities. An elderly man appeared and yelled at the group for making a ruckus and airing Jewish problems in public. He did not want to open the doors of the shul. Finally, one of the demonstrators asked him what he would do if Lena was his daughter. "She would have no problem," he replied, "because she would be a widow by now." After articulating those feelings, the justice of Lena's cause apparently sank in, and he quietly proceeded to take out his keys and open the shul.

The group entered the shul and engaged some of the worshipers in conversation. They all knew why the group was there. Some showed compassion for Lena, but most seemed to feel that the entire matter was none of their business. The prayers proceeded normally, and the services ended. The group left flyers around, and went to find the other group.

Susan's group, taking Lena with them, made its way to Rabbi Ploni's shul, about a quarter of a mile away. This was a smaller shul and *minchah* was held in a small study hall (*beit midrash*) with no space partitioned off for women. The men in Susan's group filed in and joined the shul regulars for services in the crowded room. The women, including Lena, asked the men to hand them *siddurim* (prayer books) and stood in the hallway for services.

At the conclusion of the services, Susan stepped into the room and said, "This is Lena. She is 25 years old and has been an *agunah* for three years." Some of the congregants began to mutter and tried to shout Susan down, but Rabbi Ploni interrupted them, saying, "Let her speak." Susan continued, "She could be your daughter," then after looking around and noting the advanced age of the congregants she added, "or your granddaughter. I'd like you to listen to what she has to say."

Susan had asked Lena earlier if she felt able to speak publicly about her situation, and she had assented. But when the moment came, Lena hung back and was hesitant. Susan took her by the hand and brought her to the center of the room. Lena spoke briefly but movingly. She said, "I have been waiting for my *gett* for three years. The best years of my life are slipping by. All of you know Rafi. I am appealing to you for help." The men had trouble maintaining eye contact with Lena. Many cast their eyes down to the floor. Their formerly gruff and confrontational demeanor melted away in the face of Lena's poignant plea. The group withdrew from the room leaving behind total silence.

The two groups reassembled near the buses and did a quick assessment. Everyone felt we had made headway and changed some community members' minds by telling Lena's side of the story. We all agreed to a repeat performance in two weeks if the *gett* was not given by then.

During the next week rumors abounded. One had it that Rafi's girlfriend had been driving around in a car observing the demonstration and had given him an ultimatum, either give the *gett* or she would break off the relationship. She was embarrassed to see some of her own friends on the picket line. Another rumor was that a group of Rabbi Ploni's students stopped him on the grounds of the yeshivah and demanded that he help Lena. We had also heard that administrators of the yeshivah were feeling the pressure from Gail, who had taken up Lena's cause.

The following *Shabbat*, a week before the next demonstration was scheduled, Rafi and his father were visiting a different community and attended synagogue services there. Rafi was called up to the Torah when suddenly somebody recognized him and started protesting, "He has a *seruv* against him. He can't *daven* here and have an *aliyah* (be called to the Torah)." The honor was rescinded. Saturday night immediately after *Shabbat*, Rafi called Lena and said he would give the *gett* the next day.

Lena called us with the news. She asked if she should cancel the demonstration which was still a week away. We told her to wait until she had the *gett* in hand. She could always cancel the demonstration on Monday. Sure enough, that Sunday a *beit din* was hurriedly convened for the giving of the *gett*. Lena's rabbi accompanied her. She was finally free.

We were elated. Lena's uncle had made good on his pledge. She had her *gett* before the year was out.

Lena's decision to go public was the key to Rafi's capitulation. The public embarrassment affected his socially prominent family and girlfriend. Rabbi Ploni, who had been one of his supporters, also came under pressure and was withdrawing his backing. The young people who were demonstrating made it clear that they would be back for as long as it took. Lena's rabbi mobilized his congregation to support her. A few rabbis and laypeople refused to pray with Rafi in their midst. Lena's uncle's tireless dedication and our efforts kept the campaign focused and energized.

A year and a half later, we happened to meet Lena's mother in the supermarket. She looked years younger and the light had returned to her eyes. She told us that Lena was happily remarried to a wonderful man. We shared her joy, but she said that she had to tell us an incredible postscript to the story. Several weeks before her second marriage, Lena approached her shul rabbi, who had been so involved in her struggle for the *gett*, and asked him to perform her wedding ceremony, to which he happily agreed. Lena asked him for a prenuptial agreement which would offer some protection against her husband's withholding a *gett*. The rabbi replied, "What do you need it for?"

## 14

# Civil Remedies: The New York State Gett Laws, or, Less Than Meets the Eye

Inevitably, *gett* conflicts have spilled into the civil courts of the United States and other countries with sizeable Jewish communities. Women have turned to civil courts to reject inequitable *beit din* arbitration awards regarding alimony and marital assets and to sue for damages on the grounds that withholding a *gett* is intentional infliction of emotional distress. Recalcitrant husbands, on the other hand, have objected to civil courts intervening to modify *beit din* monetary rulings that favored them and allowed them to extract concessions in return for the *gett*. The verdicts and implications of individual court cases have been discussed in detail in other books and articles. This chapter will not deal with individual civil court cases but rather with general civil legislation dealing with *agunot*, specifically the two "Gett Laws" passed by the New York State legislature. The history of these two "Gett Laws" will reveal that civil legislation provides only limited relief to *agunot*, and that this limited relief may open a dangerous door for patriarchal religious law to seep into the civil court system.

New York State, the place that has the largest concentration of Jews and *agunot* outside of Israel, has two laws on the books designed to help *agunot*. The first, which we call Gett Law I, was enacted in 1983 (NYS, Domestic Relations Law, Section 253). The second, Gett Law II, was enacted in 1992 as an amendment to NYS's equitable distribution laws (NYS, DRL, Section 236 (B)(5)(h) and (B)(6)(d)). Both the 1983 and 1992 laws address the *agunah* problem by creating incentives for the recalcitrant husband to grant the *gett*.

Tiptoeing around the American separation of church and state issue, both laws call for "removing barriers to remarriage" rather than using the obviously religious terminology of "giving a *gett*." Given the husband's controlling role in *sharia*, these two New York State laws are relevant to the Muslim population of New York as well.

## *Gett Law I*

Gett Law I was passed by the New York State legislature with broad support from the Orthodox rabbinate in New York, including the right-wing Agudath Israel of America, also known as Aguda. As the *agunah* issue garnered increasing public exposure, pressure increased on rabbis to show that they were doing something to help *agunot*. Sheldon Silver, an Orthodox Jew and member of the New York State Assembly, was the law's sponsor. Gett Law I basically provides that when a civil divorce is sought in New York State, the plaintiff, the party initiating the divorce, must file an affidavit stating that "to the best of his or her knowledge, he or she has ... taken all steps solely within his or her power to remove all barriers to the other party's remarriage."

For an *agunah*, what the law means is that if her husband initiates divorce proceedings, he cannot obtain the civil divorce while withholding a *gett*. The fundamental, structural problem with Gett Law I is that in almost every *agunah* case, it is not the husband, but the wife who is the plaintiff, anxious for a civil divorce to secure her financial future and for a *gett* so that she can seek a new partner in life. The recalcitrant husband, on the other hand, is probably quite happy that there be neither a civil divorce nor a *gett*. If there is no civil divorce, the recalcitrant husband can avoid dividing marital assets that he may be dissipating or attempting to hide. If there is no *gett*, he can continue to torment his wife. Gett Law I, therefore, has no leverage against the typical recalcitrant husband. The defendant/husband cannot prevent the court from awarding a civil divorce decree to his plaintiff/wife, who has indeed done all in her (non-) power to remove the "barriers to remarriage," but Gett Law I provides no incentive for him, the defendant, to give the *gett*.

We found that even in those few cases in which the husband was the plaintiff, and Gett Law I should have been efficacious, judges granted civil divorces to husbands who continued to withhold the *gett* either because the wife or her attorney had overlooked the law or because those judges regard the law as a violation of separation of church and state and, therefore, refrain from taking any initiative to enforce it. This discomfort with the way that the *gett* law may be infringing on separation of church and state has also limited the impact of the more promising Gett Law II as we shall see.

## A Court Fails to Enforce Gett Law I

Several years after Gett Law I was passed, Agunah Inc. was involved in a case in which, despite the law, a plaintiff husband obtained a civil divorce without granting a *gett*. He was able to remarry civilly, and he did. He attended synagogue with his second wife and was permitted to remain despite the fact that the first wife, the *agunah* we will call Linda, spoke to the rabbi and explained the situation.

Linda was a young woman, who was well connected in the Orthodox world through her family. She was a determined woman who felt that her situation was terribly unjust. She decided to go on with her life just as her former husband had, and she soon became engaged. Despite not obtaining a *gett*, Linda made marriage plans and set a wedding date. She made many calls, informing people in the Orthodox community that she was to be married on a particular date, with or without a *gett*.

As the wedding day approached, Linda's family redoubled its efforts to persuade her husband to release her. With the prospect of increasingly humiliating public exposure, the husband finally acceded and granted the *gett*. Her husband's vaunted control of her ultimately became a source of embarrassment to him as it became apparent that he could not stop his "wife" from remarrying. Perhaps the rabbis exerted more pressure on him rather than see a woman set an example of openly defying *halakhah*.

In Linda's case, it was her boldness which carried the day, not the law which she, her lawyers and the judge had overlooked. Some years later, a similar case came to Rivka's attention, but with different results. Cases in which Gett Law I comes into play are few and far between because, as noted above, it is rare that a husband who is withholding a *gett* is the plaintiff in the civil divorce. But, in Eva's case, which follows, the law helped her obtain a *gett* in a rather unusual way.

## A False Affidavit Temporarily Defeats Gett Law I

In 1998, not long after Rivka had joined the GET organization as a caseworker, she received a call from Eva, asking for help. Eva had left her husband, Aaron, a pulpit rabbi, 15 years earlier in 1983, walking out on him because of abuse. She never attempted to obtain a financial settlement for herself and her son and somehow managed, on limited resources, to raise her child and go on with her life. She received neither a *gett* nor a civil divorce.

Suddenly, in December 1997, Eva was served with divorce papers. Not knowing about Gett Law I or II, and not having the financial resources to hire legal help, she did nothing and the divorce went through uncontested by Eva. No *gett* was forthcoming despite the fact that, as required by the law, Aaron, the plaintiff, had signed an affidavit stating that he had "removed all barriers to remarriage." The court was not obliged to verify the truth of Aaron's affidavit, and the divorce slipped through the system.

In July 1998, Eva attended a public discussion of the *agunah* issue, and she learned about the *gett* laws. Realizing that her husband, who was the plaintiff, was obliged to give her a *gett* under the terms of Gett Law I, she called the GET organization and was referred to Rivka. Speaking to Eva, Rivka expressed surprise that Eva had not applied to the civil courts for relief of any kind. Eva responded that she felt Aaron, in her words "a wealthy man," would strongly resist ever granting the *gett* and providing support. Eva said she had a consultation with a divorce attorney shortly after leaving Aaron, but the attorney asked for a $15,000 retainer; Eva couldn't afford to risk a protracted, expensive lawsuit so she resigned herself to managing without a civil divorce, alimony and child support and without a *gett*. She understood that after 15 years of separation, Aaron had suddenly filed for a civil divorce in 1997 because he was getting older, thinking about the future and didn't want her to inherit his money, which she would have, had they not been divorced. Eva was not interested in trying to claim any of Aaron's money, but she wanted her *gett*.

When Rivka heard Eva's story, she called her husband Irwin, an attorney, and asked if it was possible to remedy the situation retroactively when a person managed to unlawfully evade Gett Law I's requirement to remove all barriers to remarriage. Irwin called Aaron and asked how he could have signed the affidavit when he hadn't given a *gett*. When Eva delivered a copy of the affidavit to Irwin, he mailed it immediately to Aaron. After a few days, Irwin called Aaron and informed him that, unless Aaron issued a *gett*, the civil divorce could be overturned and Eva would still be his wife and his legal heir. Irwin also called the law firm that had handled Aaron's divorce and informed them that Aaron had not removed all barriers to remarriage, as he had claimed in his affidavit.

Within days of Aaron receiving a copy of the affidavit he had falsely signed, Eva received a call from a *beit din* that she should come to their office to pick up her *gett*.

Eva's case is the exception that proves the rule that only when the husband wants a civil divorce does Gett Law I help. Because, unlike Aaron, most men who withhold a *gett* are not the plaintiffs, Gett Law I exerts no influence whatsoever over them. Moreover, there are *agunot* who, though they had a *halakhic* marriage ceremony, never married civilly. Should these women become *agunot*, Gett Law I may never come into play because their husbands never married them civilly and, therefore will not seek a civil divorce at all.

Passage of the 1983 Gett Law I provided the Orthodox rabbinate an opportunity to claim that they had acted to alleviate the *agunah* problem. Aguda trumpeted the law as a major accomplishment. The reality was that the law helped *agunot* only rarely, but all the hype around the law misled many into believing that a major stride had been taken in dealing with the *agunah* problem. What the Aguda had actually done was to lobby for a civil law that reflected the dominant role given to men in *halakhic* marriage. Just as a man must give a *gett* of his own free will, so the 1983 *Gett* Law I exerted pressure on a man to give the *gett* only when it was he who wanted the civil divorce. If the husband was not the plaintiff, he was immune to Gett Law I. Behind the smokescreen of the Gett Law I, the *agunah* problem continued unabated.

## Gett Law II

In 1992, a second effort, this one more significant, was made to supply a civil remedy. A new law, Gett Law II, was passed in the form of an amendment to New York's Equitable Distribution Law. This law opens the way for a judge to take into account an *agunah*'s inability to remarry when deciding the amount of financial support and marital assets to be awarded to her. As an *agunah* is barred from improving her financial situation through remarriage, the judge may decide that it is equitable to award a higher amount to the wife. Thus, "the failure to remove a barrier to remarriage," in the religiously neutral language of the law, may result in significant financial costs for the husband whether he is the plaintiff or the defendant, making *gett* extortion a losing proposition.

This time, unlike Gett Law I, the Orthodox rabbinate was not united behind the law. Indeed, Aguda and other Orthodox rabbinic leaders sought and continue to seek to have the law repealed.

Gett Law II grew out of an important and highly publicized case, *Naomi Schwartz v. Yehuda Schwartz*. Naomi, now Naomi Mauer, is the daughter of the late Rabbi Sholom Klass, founder and publisher of *The Jewish Press*, a major

New York Jewish weekly. She was married to Yehuda Schwartz, who wrote for the paper. When their marriage broke up, Yehuda withheld a *gett* while demanding a large ownership share of *The Jewish Press*—a highly valuable asset.

This divorce became a topic of much debate and speculation in the Orthodox community. After years of anguish and civil litigation, Naomi finally was granted her *gett*. In the civil court, Justice William Rigler ruled that withholding a *gett* could be taken into consideration by a judge when dividing marital assets. If a husband withholds a *gett*, he doesn't enter the litigation over the financial aspects of the divorce with "clean hands." Rigler held that a judge may decide to award the wife a larger share of the marital assets if a *gett* is being denied to her since she cannot remarry and build financial security with a new partner. Therefore, instead of granting her 50 percent of the marital assets, as might be expected, a judge might give her 80 percent, or even 100 percent. Similarly, if a judge thought a man should ordinarily pay his wife $500 per week support for three years, a judge might award the wife $700 per week with no cutoff date, with the possibility of review should the parties' circumstances change, i.e., if the *gett* is granted.

Rigler's precedent setting ruling provided legal reasoning that afforded protection to *agunot* from husbands seeking to extort marital assets in return for the *gett*. Rigler's ruling made law when the New York State Legislature unanimously passed Gett Law II in the summer of 1992. It is important to note that only in "equitable distribution" states like New York does the law give divorce judges such discretionary leeway on financial matters. In "communal property" states like California, marital assets are divided 50/50, with the judge having no discretion and hence no ability to take "barriers to remarriage" into account.

As Gett Law II was making its way toward Gov. Cuomo's desk for signature, we were kept updated about the progress of the law in the Albany legislature by one of its supporters. We were asked to make some phone calls in support of the law. The legislation, supported once again by Orthodox Assemblyman Sheldon Silver, was quietly pushed through the two houses of the Albany legislature during the summer when many rabbis were vacationing upstate, escaping from the New York City heat and away from their communal synagogues and organizations. Aguda's well-oiled lobbying network was in vacation mode on the assumption that no significant legislation would be passed in the waning days of the legislative session. Many Modern Orthodox rabbis worked to pass the law. The Young Israel movement and the Orthodox Union strongly supported it.

Aguda was taken by surprise by passage of the law and was up-in-arms when they found out. Almost immediately, an uproar arose. Aguda declared the law violated *halakhah* by exerting unacceptable financial coercion on the husband who must give the *gett* of his own free will. They asserted that *gittin* granted under the influence of the law were invalid, which broadly interpreted might mean that all *gittin* granted in New York State were now of questionable validity, for who could know whether fear of this new Gett Law II was lurking coercively somewhere in the back of a husband's mind when he granted a *gett*.

Articles pro and con were written, and debate raged within the Orthodox community. Supporters of the law, mostly Modern Orthodox, argued that financial pressure of this type does not represent unacceptable coercion under *halakhah*. Some maintained that *halakhah* forbids physical coercion, not financial pressure, and the law does not therefore create *halakhic* problems. Marvin Jacobs, an attorney and advocate for the law, argued forcefully on its behalf. *The Jewish Press*, of course, was a strong supporter. But many Orthodox rabbis were among the law's detractors. Rabbi J.D. Bleich, for example, echoed Aguda's position, declaring that every *gett* given in New York State is under a cloud of doubt because the husband may have felt coerced by the law to give the *gett* even if the law was never explicitly mentioned by anyone involved.

In the summer days following the enactment of the law, much activity and negotiation took place amongst the interested parties. Meetings were held, and a committee was formed by Assemblyman Silver to facilitate discussion and understanding among the various factions for and against the law. The *agunot* themselves, the ones affected by the law, were not included in the discussions. As Agunah Inc. had counseled and represented hundreds of *agunot*, we requested a seat at the table to provide women a voice on this issue.

Securing an audience with Assemblyman Silver, by then Majority Leader of the New York State Assembly, was not easy, but we managed to see him in his New York City office. We told him we believed that the law was a major step forward in dealing with the *agunah* problem and requested to be included in the committee meetings being held to discuss it. We were not well received and were told that this was business for rabbis and men and that women would be well taken care of without our help. Before we could raise any questions, we were quickly and gruffly hustled out of the office by one of Silver's aides.

Very shortly after Gett Law II was put on the books it proved its worth. Within weeks of the passage of the law, one of our clients received her *gett* from her husband, Barry, a lawyer who was stubbornly withholding the *gett* but caved when his wife's attorney mentioned the new Gett Law. As a lawyer, Barry understood that he was at risk to take a financial hit with regard to weekly maintenance for his wife if he continued to withhold the *gett*. This case put into clear relief the difference between Gett Law I and Gett Law II. Since Barry was not the plaintiff Gett Law I was ineffectual against him, but Gett Law II was a threat. It is impossible to calculate how many women have been helped by Gett Law II because, as Rabbi Bleich opined, we can never know how many men who considered withholding a *gett* quietly relented when they learned about the new law.

Gett Law II's limitations, however, should be noted. The law only has teeth if the recalcitrant husband has a substantial, declared income and/or there are significant marital assets which can be awarded to the *agunah* at the discretion of the judge. Unfortunately, recalcitrant husbands are very often poor providers or shirkers who deliberately leave their jobs, cut their incomes, work off the books and conceal their assets, leaving the judge with nothing to award to the *agunah*. Furthermore, some judges are averse to invoking the Gett Laws, viewing them as unconstitutional, which brings us to a landmark case in which the constitutionality of both Gett Law I and Gett Law II came under attack.

## Becher v. Becher: *A Landmark Case Though the Jury Is Still Out on Gett Law II*

In 1997, in the case of *Becher v. Becher*, Yehuda Becher argued that both New York Gett Laws violated his religious freedom as an Orthodox Jew by forcing him to commit a religious act, the giving of the *gett*, and that the very giving of the *gett* under the circumstances was against *halakhah* because a coerced *gett* is a *halakhically* invalid. He challenged the constitutionality of the two laws and argued for their repeal.

Mina Becher, an *agunah*, found her herself in an unenviable position. She was a private person, an Orthodox housewife and mother, who wanted a civil divorce and *gett* in order to quietly go on with her life. Instead, she found herself thrust into the center of a public battlefield. A demonstration was held outside Yehuda's place of work on a busy Manhattan street. Dozens of women circled the entrance to the building with placards, but to no avail. Yehuda refused to give a *gett*, and his challenge to the Gett Laws went forward under an intense spotlight of public interest. Every twist and turn in the litigation was documented in secular media, such as the *New York State Law Journal*, as well as Jewish media.

The judge in the Becher case was William Rigler, whose ruling in *Schwartz v. Schwartz* was the template for Gett Law II. Rigler, as expected, ruled against challenges to the law, upholding the possibility that Mina Becher might get a better financial settlement if Yehuda persisted in withholding the *gett*. Aguda filed an amicus brief in support of Yehuda Becher's challenge to Gett Law II. Aguda maintained that the threat of financial loss for withholding the *gett* was so coercive that it negated the husband's free will and made it *halakhically* impossible for Yehuda to give a kosher *gett*. Aguda claimed that no *beit din* would allow Yehuda to give a *gett* under the circumstances. Putting an ironic twist on it, Aguda argued that Gett Law II, rather than helping a woman obtain a *gett*, made it impossible for her to obtain one in New York State since one must assume that all men who give a *gett* in New York have been improperly coerced. On the other side of the issue were the prominent attorneys Nathan Lewin of Washington, D.C., and Dennis Rapps of New York City. Lewin and Rapps filed an amicus brief on behalf of Assemblyman Sheldon Silver, in which they defended the constitutionality of Gett Laws I and II, both of which Silver had help shepherd through the Albany legislature. This clash over the constitutionality of the Gett Laws took place in the Appellate Division of the New York State Supreme Court.

Somewhere along the line in these protracted divorce proceedings, Mina waived her financial rights in return for the *gett*. Since she did so, the Appellate Court judges ruled that Yehuda Becher's challenge to the constitutionality of Gett Law II was moot, and the court never addressed the challenge. It looked like Aguda and Yehuda Becher were prepared to go all the way to the U.S. Supreme Court on this issue, but Mina just wanted her *gett*, which could have been delayed for years as the case wended its way through the courts, perhaps all the way up to the Supreme Court. As of this writing both *gett* laws are still standing, but a new challenge may arise at any time and their status, when examined in light of the failed attempts to pass similar laws in other states, is precarious.

## *Objections to Sharia Law Put the Spotlight on Gett Laws and Rabbinical Courts in the U.S.*

*Gett* laws have been considered in other states, but have only passed in New York. Sponsors in the Maryland legislature made two attempts to pass a law similar to New York Gett Law I. Aguda was behind the first effort, but it failed as Maryland legislators questioned its constitutionality. Efforts to pass *gett* legislation to help *agunot* have failed in New Jersey, Florida and Connecticut.

The future of *gett* laws in the U.S. will be further clouded by a wave of "anti–foreign law" legislation passed in numerous states, including North Carolina, Arizona, Kansas, Louisiana, South Dakota and Tennessee. These laws aim to prevent "foreign laws, legal codes or systems" from playing any role in the courts of these states. Opposition to the influence of *sharia* law gave rise to these state laws, but these laws clearly have implications for the status of rabbinical courts and *gett* laws. In Florida, which has a large Orthodox Jewish community, "anti-foreign law" bills have been introduced to the legislature numerous times but have not made it into law. Jewish organizations, concerned about preserving the status of rabbinical courts, found themselves allied with Muslim leaders in opposing the Florida law. Increased focus on the issue of barring "foreign laws, legal codes or systems" from playing any role in American courts might pave the way for a renewed challenge to the two New York State Gett Laws.

Outside of the United States, Canada has the most powerful *gett* law on the books. It allows the courts to dismiss any divorce application and strike out any pleadings filed by the party that fails to remove religious barriers to remarriage. If you don't cooperate regarding the *gett*, you are deemed to be lacking "clean hands," to request anything from the Canadian civil divorce courts. Yet in Ontario in 2005, objections to giving any official recognition to *sharia* law led to the passage of a "one law for all Ontarians" law, eroding the respected status that rabbinical courts had long enjoyed in Canada. England, Wales and South Africa all have "clean hands" *gett* laws, but they are similar to the weak New York State Gett Law I. In England and Australia, courts have awarded alimony to women when their husbands refused to deliver a *gett*. In France, courts have been awarding damages to women whose husbands cause them harm by refusing to deliver a *gett*. In Canada, an appeals court upheld a decision to award damages for breach of contract when a husband refused to fulfill his written obligation to give his wife a *gett*.

While civil legislation has added a weapon to the meager arsenal available for helping *agunot*, it is clear that the only systemic solution is a *halakhic* one. Civil legislation and case law provide financial and other incentives for recalcitrant husbands to deliver *getts* to their wives, but in countless cases these laws and rulings are of no help. Men with little income or assets, missing and incapacitated husbands, men with no social conscience are impervious to the financial pressures that civil courts can impose. Furthermore, rabbis and *batei din* increasingly pressure women to stay out of civil court and litigate all matters in a *beit din*, which deprives the women of the limited protections afforded by civil *gett* legislation. In a reversal of the BDA's 1980s recommendation that couples resolve all matters in civil court before coming to the BDA for the *gett*, Rabbi Mordechai Willig, the Vice-Chair of the BDA, wrote in 1996 that "resolutions of marital property disputes are within the jurisdiction of the *bet din*, unless *bet din* permits the parties to resolve them in court."

As new *agunah* cases pour in before the old cases are resolved, civil *gett* legislation and creative judicial decisions are like a Band-aid on a hemorrhaging wound. Ultimately it is the Orthodox Jewish community that must find effective remedies within the corpus of *halakhah* in order to deliver justice to *agunot*.

# 15

# Prenuptial Agreements

The story of the role of prenuptials (prenups) in contemporary Orthodox marriage follows the same pattern that repeats itself throughout this book—Orthodox rabbis doing far too little, far too late to help *agunot*. Being in denial about the magnitude and severity of the *agunah* problem, the Orthodox rabbinic establishment dragged its feet in formulating and adopting a prenup to forestall *aginut* (the state of being an *agunah*). It took spontaneous grassroots action, activists' untiring demands for acknowledging the *agunah* problem and the proliferation of various versions of Orthodox prenups created by individual scholars and rabbis to finally push the Rabbinical Council of America (RCA) and Beth Din of America (BDA), Modern Orthodox institutions, to develop and promote a prenup agreement. This chapter will recount and analyze the history of RCA/BDA prenups. The more right-wing, ultra–Orthodox rabbinic leadership has not adopted any prenup at all.

The first RCA prenup, created by Rabbi Abner Weiss in the early 1980s, empowered the *agunah* to sue for financial damages in civil court if her husband withheld the *gett*. But this prenup had a serious flaw: the husband was not liable for damages for withholding the *gett* as long as the civil divorce was not finalized. The problem with linkage between the *gett* and the civil divorce was that a husband could delay the *gett* by deliberately prolonging the civil divorce proceedings, as will be illustrated by cases presented later in this chapter.

In 1992, Rabbi Mordechai Willig introduced a new prenup which became known as the RCA (or BDA) prenup. This RCA prenup eliminated the problematic linkage between the *gett* and the civil divorce, but a new drawback was introduced—the *agunah* can sue in civil court for a delayed *gett* only if the *beit din* has issued an arbitration decision awarding her money. The ten year history of the Willig/RCA prenup indicates that, for reasons which remain unclear, the BDA is disinclined to award any money to *agunot*.

## Jewish Prenuptials Are Different

Attorneys practicing family law often advise a spouse who is entering marriage with significant assets to sign a prenuptial agreement. Prudence dictates using a prenuptial to protect assets acquired before the marriage from unfair claims should the marriage end in divorce.

Orthodox Jewish prenuptial agreements are different. They aim to protect something more precious than financial assets—the basic human right of freedom to marry and build a family within the Orthodox Jewish community. Every Orthodox woman, no matter what her financial status, risks the possibility that should her husband refuse to issue a *gett*, she will become an *agunah*, chained to a dead marriage, forbidden to remarry and bear children.

"Danger: Enter at Your Own Risk" is the warning that should be given to every woman who intends to marry under Orthodox auspices. The prenup is an attempt to protect women from this danger though we will argue that it is flawed. Note that the primary focus of Orthodox prenuptials is on protecting women, not men, because under Orthodox *halakhah* it is the freedom of women, not men, that is in serious jeopardy.

While it is true that a wife can also impede the religious dissolution of an Orthodox marriage by refusing to accept a *gett*, such cases are relatively rare and have much less dire consequences for the husband. As we have explained in the pages of this book, a wife who remarries without a *gett* from her previous husband is branded an adulteress, and any children she bears by other men are stigmatized as *mamzerim*, barred from marrying other Jews save another *mamzer* or a convert. However, in the case of a man whose wife refuses to accept a *gett*, the man can partner with a new woman (so long as she is not legally attached to another man) despite his wife's intransigence. He need not marry his new partner in order for his new children to be legitimate and eligible to marry any Jew.

Some men are even able to secure a *heter*, rabbinic dispensation, to formally marry their new partner, even though the first wife has blocked a divorce by refusing to accept a *gett*. This is because under both Biblical and Talmudic law, men are technically permitted to have more than one wife. Think Abraham with Sarah and Hagar, Jacob with Rachel, Leah, Bilhah and Zilpah, Elkanah with Hannah and Peninah.

Given women's vulnerability to being held hostage to a dead marriage, even as their recalcitrant husbands go on with their lives, contemporary Orthodox prenuptials aim to secure a legally enforceable financial incentive for the husbands to cooperate in the giving of the *gett*.

## *Talmudic Prenuptial Aimed to Protect Women from Divorce*

Prenuptial agreements are nothing new to Judaism. In fact, the history of Jewish religious prenups goes back two thousand years to Talmudic times. At that time, however, the rabbis felt that women needed protection from the husband's unchecked power to *give* a *gett*, not his power to withhold one. In the eyes of the rabbis of the Talmud the major risk facing a woman was that her husband would divorce her against her will, precisely the opposite of today's problem of a man refusing to divorce his wife. The sages of the Talmud viewed divorce as a sorry fate for women. They felt that divorcees and widows were disadvantaged economically, socially and psychologically. Accordingly, the scholars of the Babylonian Talmud devised the *ketubah*, the Jewish marriage contract, to act as type of prenup that would make divorcing a faithful wife costly by requiring the husband to pay a hefty lump sum divorce settlement to his wife. In the language of the Talmud, the *ketubah* was instituted "so that he shall not regard it as easy (inexpensive) to divorce her."

To be sure the rabbis of the Talmud were aware of the opposite problem, a husband refusing a wife's demand for a *gett*, but they felt they had tools other than a prenup to deal with recalcitrant husbands. Insufferable husbands who refused to divorce their wives could be physically coerced (*kofin oto*, we force him) or otherwise effectively pressured to give a *gett* despite the competing Talmudic idea that the husband must grant the *gett* of his own free will. Maimonides, the towering 12th century Sephardic Torah scholar, endorsed flogging a husband until he agreed to give a *gett*. Maimonides reconciled the use of force with the requirement that the husband grant the *gett* of his own free will as follows: Deep inside, the husband's will is to comply with Jewish law and give the *gett* as the rabbis have ordered him to do. The beating just puts the husband in touch with his true inner will.

As for *agunot* whose husbands disappeared in war and during travel, leaving their wives without a *gett*, the Talmudic sages relaxed the rules of evidence necessary to prove a man's death. They accepted the testimony of a lone witness, women, and non-Jews, all normally considered ineligible witnesses, in order to release *agunot* by establishing that they were widows who would then be free to remarry.

As the centuries wore on, using corporal punishment or other coercive means to secure a *gett* became *halakhically* controversial. The rabbis became unwilling to force recalcitrant husbands into giving a *gett*. Orthodox rabbis began to give primacy to the position of Rabbenu Tam, a 12th century French/Ashkenazi *halakhist*, who, in contrast to Maimonides, held that because the husband must give the *gett* willingly, there are limits on the forms of pressures that can be applied. For Tam, social ostracism and denying a recalcitrant husband synagogue honors are permitted forms, but physical coercion is forbidden. Moreover, it became illegal for rabbis to use physical coercion in most countries where Jews resided. This left *agunot* stranded when their husbands adamantly refused their demands for a divorce.

In Israel some forms of coercing a recalcitrant husband have been revived and passed into legislation by Israel's parliament, the Knesset. Israeli *batei din* are empowered to jail a recalcitrant and to suspend his driver's license, professional license, right to vote and credit cards. But these sanctions are invoked relatively infrequently, with some rabbis of the Israeli *beit din* system refusing to apply these sanctions against recalcitrant husbands in line with Rabbenu Tam's view that such coercion may render a *gett* invalid. Furthermore, even applying the extreme sanction of jailing a man may be ineffective. There have been cases where men prefer to stay in jail for years rather than grant the *gett*. In one well-known case in Israel a man died in jail after decades of imprisonment rather than grant his wife a *gett*. As of this writing, there is one man who has opted to remain in jail for twelve years rather than agree to a *gett*.

In the rare publicized cases in recent decades in the U.S., where physical coercion was employed against a husband, the coercion either failed to secure the *gett* (see Chapter 4), or the *gett* was challenged as invalid because of *halakhically* unacceptable coercion of the husband. In 2013, Rabbi Mendel Epstein and others were arrested in New York and New Jersey for running a kidnapping and torture ring to extract a *gittin* from recalcitrant husbands. Bottom line: Whether rabbis stand with Maimonides in allowing the flogging of recalcitrant husbands or with Rabbenu Tam in prohibiting it, violence is no solution to the *agunah* tragedy.

Given the challenges to the *halakhic* validity of various forms of coercion, the practical limits to its use and communal resistance to endorsing violence in the name of *halakhah*, prenups came to the fore as a possible preventive measure to guard against future *aginut*.

## 1953—Amending the Ketubah to Help Women Obtain a Divorce

In 1953, the late Rabbi Shaul Lieberman, a scholar and revered Professor of Talmud at the Conservative Jewish Theological Seminary in New York, proposed a solution that became known as the Lieberman Clause, an amendment to the ancient, traditional prenup, the *ketubah*. The late Rabbi J.B. Soloveitchik, a venerated Modern Orthodox leader, at first joined hands with Lieberman in his proposal to amend the *ketubah*, which meant that both Conservative and Orthodox women might be helped. Such open cooperation between the Orthodox and Conservative movements was rare; Soloveitchik, however, later withdrew his support.

The Talmudic *ketubah* offered no help in compelling recalcitrant husbands to give a *gett* as the *ketubah* had been crafted to have the opposite effect—to deter husbands from giving a *gett*. Lieberman decided to amend the traditional *ketubah* so that it could deal with the modern reality that women needed help attaining their *gett* rather than protection from an unwanted *gett*. The Lieberman Clause simply obligated the bride and the groom to bring their marital disputes to a specified *beit din* for arbitration.

Lieberman and Soloveitchik agreed to recommend the clause to their respective movements, but at the last minute the Orthodox RCA balked. Rabbi Emanuel Rackman, a leading Modern Orthodox rabbi at that time, told Susan that copies of the Lieberman Clause were printed up and ready to be mailed to the RCA membership. Rackman attributed the RCA's withdrawal to interdenominational rabbinic politics, Orthodox reluctance to associate with the Conservative rabbinate despite the urgency of the *agunah* matter. Rabbi Avi Weiss has written that the reason that the Lieberman clause was rejected by the Orthodox rabbinate was that it did not precisely delineate the financial consequences that would result from the husband not cooperating in the *gett* process. According to some rabbis, not stipulating a specific sum would make the agreement *halakhic*ally invalid. In 1998, at the second JOFA Conference, Rabbi Shlomo Riskin publicly described the RCA withdrawal as a disgrace.

Lieberman went ahead on his own, and the Conservative movement integrated the Lieberman Clause into their *ketubah*. In the end, however, Lieberman's approach turned out to be inadequate. A key weakness of the Lieberman Clause was that enforcing it required protracted and expensive litigation in civil court, which included defending the clause against allegations that it violated the second amendment to the U.S. Constitution—freedom of religion and the separation of church and state. *Avitzur v. Avitzur* was one such protracted New York State case. The New York courts ruled in favor of enforcing the Lieberman clause despite the husband's protesting that civil intervention in the matter represented a violation of his religious freedom. But the case dragged all the way up to the U.S. Supreme court, and Mrs. Avitzur eventually dropped the financially draining litigation. Since then, the Conservative movement, in contrast to Orthodox Judaism, has adopted the use of annulments when husbands withhold the *gett*, thereby eliminating the *agunah* problem for its members.

## *The Modern Orthodox Grass Roots Takes the Lead on Prenups*

After rejecting the Lieberman Clause, the Orthodox rabbinate took no meaningful action with regard to prenups for decades. However, by the 1980s a variety of Orthodox prenuptials, drafted by individual scholars, began springing up. In 1983, an RCA Commission on *Agunot*/Divorce headed by Rabbi Abner Weiss of California produced a prenup that secured Rabbi Soloveitchik's approval. This prenup stipulated that the *gett* must be given after a civil decree of divorce and that failure to cooperate regarding the *gett* after the civil divorce would obligate the recalcitrant party to pay per diem damages to the other party of $250, indexed to inflation as measured by the CPI, for each day of delay. The RCA did little to promote this prenup, nor did it offer guidance as to which of the other crop of prenups might have advantageous clauses.

Despite the Orthodox rabbinate's half-hearted effort regarding prenups, prenups slowly began to find their way into Orthodox wedding ceremonies. Lay people rather than rabbis led the way. Young Orthodox couples, in a gesture of commitment to justice for *agunot* and equity in Jewish marriage, sometimes made a point of informing their wedding guests that a religious prenuptial had been signed prior to their wedding, often mentioning it in wedding programs handed out to their guests. Some made it part of the "*Hoson*'s [groom's] or *Kallah*'s [bride's] *tish*," the more intimate celebratory prelude just prior to the actual wedding ceremony.

We advised young couples to sign a prenup that in some way anticipated and ameliorated the risk of *aginut*. Rivka's husband Irwin, a *halakhic* scholar and lawyer, often provided his own prenup, drafted together with Rabbi Judah Dick, or edited various prenuptials to improve them for couples who asked his advice. Some people suggested that married couples sign post-nuptial agreements with the same provisions that a newly marrying couple would sign.

This would protect women who were already married, and make signing a prenup more routine, less freighted with the negative specter of possible divorce.

However, as the years passed *agunot* who signed the Abner Weiss/RCA prenup began to turn up on Agunah Inc.'s doorstep, disappointed and disillusioned that they were trapped in a dead marriage despite having signed the prenup.

## *Marrying with a Prenuptial: The Dangerous Illusion*

In 1991, Melanie, an *agunah* with the Abner Weiss/RCA prenuptial, turned to us for help. She was upset and disillusioned because the prenup was of no help to her. Even worse, the prenup was actually cited by her rabbi and recalcitrant husband to justify delaying the *gett*.

Melanie had been struggling for two years and had sought help from the rabbis of both her synagogue and her recalcitrant husband's synagogue. She told us that her rabbi felt that she should not be considered an *agunah* because she didn't have a civil divorce yet, and without a civil divorce she couldn't remarry anyway. Furthermore, her rabbi added that the Abner Weiss prenuptial that she had signed stated that the husband does not have to give the *gett* until after the civil dissolution of the marriage. Melanie was also upset because her rabbi had begun canvassing people in the synagogue, including her brother-in-law, asking if they considered her an *agunah*. Adding insult to injury, Melanie's rabbi accused her of "using" the *gett*. He quoted her husband who had said that if he gave Melanie the *gett*, she would stretch out the civil proceedings. The truth, however, was the opposite—that it was he who was delaying the civil divorce in order to avoid giving the *gett*.

We called Melanie's rabbi and pointed out that it was unfair for Melanie's husband to hold the *gett* over her head to pressure her during the civil proceedings. Civil proceedings can be long and complex, even longer if one party deliberately delays the civil divorce. Today, general society pays little mind to the social conduct of men and women during the civil divorce proceedings. But if Melanie's *gett* was held hostage to civil proceedings, she could not resume dating and seeking a new partner in her community.

Furthermore, Melanie had no guarantee her husband would give the *gett* after the civil divorce. She might find herself back in another lengthy civil court proceeding to enforce the prenup and win her *gett*, with doubtful results as in the Avitzur case. We asked the rabbi, "Given that the marriage is broken beyond repair, what possible reason could Melanie's husband have for holding back the *gett* except to torment her or pressure her to make concessions in the civil proceedings?"

The rabbi had no answer to our question, but replied by praising the Abner Weiss prenup. We countered that the Weiss prenuptial was also depriving Melanie of the protection of the 1992 NYS "barrier to remarriage" law. Melanie's husband could claim he only had to remove the "barrier to remarriage" (i.e., give the *gett*), after the civil divorce was finalized. At this point, Melanie's rabbi became testy. "I'm ending this conversation," he said and hung up on us. Our conversations with the other rabbis involved were equally unsatisfactory, and the Weiss prenup remained a hindrance rather than a help to Melanie.

Ilana, another woman who had signed the Weiss prenuptial, turned to *Agunah* Inc. shortly after Melanie. Ilana lived in the Midwest and was the daughter of wealthy parents. She had turned to numerous rabbis, but none provided any help. Her husband was trying to extort money for the *gett* and had been bringing one motion after another in the civil court, delaying the civil divorce for years. Her husband had forgotten about the prenup, and we warned her not to mention it in court or to any rabbis. She would be better off if everyone forgot about the Weiss prenup because it would provide the rabbis with a justification for not helping her until the civil proceedings were complete as in Melanie's case.

Furthermore her husband, who was living in a friend's apartment and working for cash off the books, had no traceable income or assets, so that even if he continued to withhold the *gett* after the civil divorce, Ilana would have no way of collecting any of the compensation for damages that the prenup imposed once the civil divorce was finalized. This case had an additional potential pitfall. The husband was an immigrant to the United States and threatened to leave the country and disappear, leaving Ilana an abandoned *agunah*. The prenuptial would be of no help if the husband disappeared. In the end Ilana paid off her husband in order to obtain her *gett*. Her Weiss prenuptial turned out to be useless.

These two cases illustrate how ineffectual the Abner Weiss/RCA prenup was. This prenup, by making the *gett* contingent on the civil divorce, proved to be at best useless to women and, at worst, harmful to them. It was clear that the *gett* had to be completely severed from the civil divorce process and that Weiss and the RCA needed to go back to the drawing board and to advise the community not to use this prenup. To our knowledge, neither Weiss nor the RCA warned people against using this prenup.

As the 1990s wore on, however, the Modern Orthodox rabbinate began to coalesce around a new prenuptial formulated by Rabbi Mordechai Willig. This prenuptial became known as the RCA or BDA prenuptial. And it is to the history of this second RCA/BDA prenuptial that we now turn.

## The Willig Prenuptial—The RCA's Second Try

In 1992, now forty years after the RCA's rejection of the Lieberman Clause, Rabbi Mordechai Willig, a member of the RCA and Beth Din of America (BDA), formulated a new prenup, which became known as the RCA (or BDA) prenup. It was widely touted as finally providing effective protection from *aginut*. There were three key changes in Willig's new RCA prenup as compared to the Abner Weiss prenup. First, the Willig prenup stipulated that the husband is liable for a per diem payment for withholding the *gett* beginning from the day the couple is no longer living together rather than from the day the civil divorce is finalized. Second, under the Willig prenup, the *agunah* can sue to collect the per diem money in civil court only if the *beit din* issues an arbitration award to her while under the Weiss prenup the *agunah* could sue for the money without any authorization from the *beit din*. Third, the Willig prenup structured the per diem payment that resulted from withholding the *gett* in the form of the husband's pledge to support his wife at the rate of $100 per diem (indexed to the CPI, $150 by 2014) rather than the Weiss approach of structuring the per diem payments as damages for withholding the *gett*. Structuring the payments as damages may raise *halakhic* problems, but husbands are clearly permitted under *halakhah* to undertake a pledge to pay a specific amount of spousal support. The implications of these changes are best understood from the cases that follow.

The RCA trumpeted the new Willig prenup as a dramatic step forward though the rabbis acknowledged that the Willig prenup could not help *agunot* who had married in the past or married in the future without it. Rabbis took to comparing the risks of Orthodox marriage to exposure to the polio virus. "It's like polio," several rabbis said. Polio's a dangerous disease, but there's a vaccine. If you don't get vaccinated, you risk paralysis. Similarly, Orthodox marriage is dangerous for women. If women marry without a prenup, they risk becoming *agunot*.

But the rabbis glossed over the remaining weaknesses of the new RCA prenup. Like the Abner Weiss prenup, the new one would be ineffective in cases where the husband had no traceable income or assets or disappeared since there would be nothing or no one against which to enforce the prenup.

To enforce the per diem payments the *agunah* would have to go to civil court, which could lead to lengthy and complex litigation. Furthermore, the Willig prenup gave the *beit din*, not the *agunah*, sole control over the decision to demand or waive the per diem support payments. Notwithstanding these major limitations, the RCA and BDA declared that a vaccine was now available to protect women from the paralytic danger inherent in Orthodox marriage.

Gradually Orthodox rabbis began to advocate that couples sign prenups. In 1993 the RCA adopted a resolution stating that "every member of the RCA will utilize prenuptial agreements," but it did not, and still doesn't, categorically require that member rabbis use it. This resolution was reaffirmed by the RCA in 1994. In 1996, Rabbis Basil Herring and Kenneth Auman published an anthology containing the Willig prenup along with articles and approbations from about twenty RCA and Israeli rabbis. By 1998 the Orthodox Caucus, a group formed to deal with contemporary Jewish problems, made the claim that half of the weddings performed by RCA rabbis in the preceding three years included a prenuptial. In early 2014 we were told by an official of the BDA that approximately 70 percent of RCA rabbis use prenups.

Despite the fanfare surrounding the new RCA prenup, within a few years of the RCA prenup's introduction, *agunot* who had signed it began to seek our help. Sharon and Ira had been married two years, but holding the marriage together had been a struggle from the beginning because Ira had serious emotional problems, which Sharon had been unaware of when she wed. The two of them attended therapy sessions together, but Sharon was becoming frightened of Ira because he was becoming violent. She decided that she had to end the marriage. Afraid that Ira might injure her or himself when she told him of her decision, Sharon told Ira's parents of her plans and asked them to invite her and Ira over for dinner one evening so that she could break the news to Ira when they were all together.

On the appointed evening, Sharon went straight from work to her in-laws' house, but no one was home. She was worried that something might have happened to Ira so she rushed home. When she opened the door to her apartment, she found that in her absence it had been emptied of all its furnishings. She called her brother-in-law Leon, an attorney, who told her he would set up an escrow account the next day so that Sharon could transfer the couple's $10,000 of financial assets into the escrow account pending the final divorce settlement. Leon counseled her that although it appeared that Ira and his parents had absconded with the couple's home furnishings, Sharon should do the right thing and deposit the couple's money in escrow until a court decided how the $10,000 should be divided. Sharon followed Leon's advice.

By the time Sharon sought our help, she had been working with the BDA for several months. When we heard that she had signed the RCA prenup, we told her that she was in a good position to take advantage of the provisions of the prenup because, assuming that Ira was entitled to a share of the $10,000 in escrow, she could enforce the per diem support payment of $100+ CPI against Ira's share. Sharon grasped what we said about the prenup as did her brother-in-law Leon. But the BDA kept putting Leon and Sharon off, saying that they were trying to persuade Ira to give a *gett* and didn't want to rile him up by mentioning the prenup and the per diem payments.

The BDA got nowhere with Ira. In one instance, Ira indicated that he might give the *gett* if the BDA convened a special session in New York. With great effort on the part of several rabbis and Sharon and Leon, the session was convened, but when Ira saw that things weren't going his way, he suddenly jumped to his feet and stalked out. The presiding rabbi immediately declared the session over, and Sharon was left devastated and in tears.

Leon, acting as Sharon's attorney, traveled back home and filed a motion in civil court to enforce the RCA prenuptial which he thought would result in an award of $100+ per day to Sharon from the day she and Ira parted. But the court told Leon that the RCA prenup was not enforceable in civil court. The judge explained that if the BDA, which was arbitrating the Jewish divorce, issued an arbitration award granting the money to Sharon, the civil court could enforce it as a binding arbitration decision. But as a standalone prenup, it was unenforceable. Leon and Sharon contacted the BDA and explained the situation, but the BDA still refused to issue the necessary arbitration award. Sharon and Leon were puzzled and frustrated since Sharon even had the escrow money against which to enforce her claim. It appeared that the BDA was uncomfortable imposing any financial costs on the husband. The RCA prenup, therefore, turned out to be worthless for Sharon. Several more months went by. Sharon and Leon concluded that the prenup and the BDA would do nothing to help her. She capitulated to Ira's demand for the full $10,000 and all the couple's home furnishings and received her *gett* in return.

Rita, was another *agunah* for whom the prenup failed. For months her husband Jonah was playing cat and mouse with her and the BDA, promising to give the *gett* one day and then backing out the next. Rita asked the BDA to issue a decision awarding her the accumulated per diem money owed to her under the terms of her RCA prenup, but the BDA kept counseling her to hold off each time Jonah made another one of his empty promises to give the *gett*. Ultimately Jonah did give the *gett* but not until he had tormented Rita for about a year. Under the terms of the prenup, Jonah owed Rita thousands of dollars. She got not one red cent, and the BDA offered her no guidance or support in pursuing that claim. They just kept stringing the husband along, appeasing him, rather than invoking the financial provisions of the prenup. When it was all over, Rita drew this conclusion about the value of the prenup. "My husband drove me crazy and got off scot free: The prenup's not worth the paper it's written on," she said.

Following these cases in which the BDA failed to deploy the per diem support clause of the prenup, Susan became curious as to how many *agunot* had actually received payment under the terms of the prenup. Susan had two conversations on this topic with Rabbi Yona Reiss, then the administrator of the BDA. Rabbi Reiss praised the efficacy of the prenup but said that he knew of no *agunah* who had received payment. Reiss added that the prenup per diem money should be understood more as a bargaining chip to be traded for the *gett* rather than as a predetermined support award owed to the wife when she is chained to the marriage after the couple has separated. He went on to explain that once the husband has withheld the *gett* and now owes the wife money, the money can be waived in return for the *gett*. To Susan, this seemed like another incarnation of *gett* extortion. After all, the *agunah*'s financial claim against her recalcitrant husband is an asset, perhaps one that may be hard to collect, but an asset nonetheless. What Reiss outlined was another version of the same old story—counseling an *agunah* who has suffered *gett* abuse to give up what was hers—in this case her per diem support claims in the event of separation. When Rabbi Weissmann took over Reiss's job in 2008, Susan queried him as well. He likewise said that he knew of no *agunah* who had collected any money under the terms of the RCA prenup.

## *An* Agunah *Receives Payment Under the RCA Prenup Despite the RCA's Failure to Deploy the Prenup*

Molly was an immigrant from Venezuela who had come to the United States with her husband and daughter to escape the political and economic turmoil and rising anti-semitism in her home country. After living in the United States for a while, she became a *ba'alat teshuvah*, a Jew who turns away from a less observant way of life to embrace Orthodox Judaism. She enrolled her daughter in an Orthodox school and became active in her local Orthodox community.

The stresses of starting over in the United States and her adoption of the Orthodox way of life put a strain on her marriage as her husband was not similarly inclined toward Orthodoxy. She and her husband divorced; a *gett* was arranged without a hitch. A few years went by, and Molly met Yoram, an Israeli transplant to New York. Molly and Yoram dated for a while and decided to marry.

Shortly after marrying Yoram, Molly realized that he had serious problems. She tried to help him, but it became clear that would not be possible. Molly confided her situation to Rabbi Katz, her local rabbi. Katz counseled Molly to try again to salvage the marriage. She tried but to no avail. When she told Yoram that the marriage was doomed, Yoram became incensed and said he would never give her a *gett*. Molly moved out and stayed with a friend while looking for her own apartment.

After a few more weeks of trying to persuade Yoram to give the *gett*, Rabbi Katz contacted the BDA and together with Rabbi Reiss tried numerous times to get Yoram to agree to give the *gett*. But Yoram kept procrastinating and raising one issue after another that he wanted resolved before he gave the *gett*. After a while, Rabbi Katz began blaming Molly for the problems with the *gett*. She should be more patient, he said, and not ask the *beit din* to call Yoram so often, because it was stirring Yoram's temper up. Molly was getting a "blame the victim" treatment from her rabbi.

As more doubts arose in her mind about Rabbis Katz and Reiss, Molly turned to another rabbi in her neighborhood. The rabbi asked her how much she was willing to pay Yoram for the *gett*. Unfamiliar with the extortion associated with Orthodox divorce, Molly was baffled by the rabbi's question and asked him to explain what he was saying to her to be sure she hadn't misunderstood as her English wasn't perfect. She hadn't misunderstood, but she didn't know what to make of what the rabbi was telling her.

Molly began to worry about how the situation would affect her daughter. She was concerned that her daughter might be alienated from Orthodoxy when she saw how little the rabbis were doing to help, even blaming her mother for her predicament. Molly fretted that after such a short and contentious second marriage, her daughter might find it harder to find a match in their circles.

Somewhere along the way, someone gave Molly Susan's name as someone to turn to for help. Molly handed Susan a bulky folder filled with financial papers, forms for a civil divorce, a civil prenup, lists of items that Molly and Yoram were squabbling over, her *ketubah* and, to Susan's astonishment, a copy of the RCA prenup which Molly and Yoram had signed. "You signed a Jewish prenup!" Susan exclaimed. "Yoram has a job and he is liable for $125 per day for refusing to come the BDA to issue a *gett*. Every day that he continues to withhold the *gett* will cost him."

Molly didn't understand how the prenup worked so Susan explained it to her. Susan asked if Rabbi Reiss knew that there was a prenup. Molly said she had given copies of all the documents to Rabbi Reiss, but he never mentioned anything about the prenup to her or to Yoram as far as she knew. Susan told Molly that she would call Reiss the next day to find out why he hadn't invoked the prenup in order to expedite the *gett*.

Susan reached Reiss the next day and asked if he knew that there was a prenup. He did. Then why hadn't he invoked the prenup to pressure Yoram to give the *gett*, Susan inquired. Reiss replied that each time he spoke to Yoram he thought that the matter would be resolved soon and that Yoram would come in and give the *gett*. Susan expressed her surprise that Reiss hadn't deployed the prenup to induce Yoram to give the *gett* without delay. She reported the results of the discussion with Reiss to Molly and told her to call Yoram right away and tell him that he owed thousands of dollars for delaying the *gett* after they had separated and that the clock was still ticking.

Yoram argued with Molly and said that he was going to challenge her claim for payment. But he also made arrangements for the *gett* to be written immediately. Within a few days, the *gett* was given, but Yoram demanded a *din torah* to dispute his obligation to pay Molly.

The *din torah* was scheduled and a single *dayyan*, Rabbi Hamber, was appointed to hear the case. Susan accompanied Molly to the *din torah*, and Yoram brought his cousin, who was a lawyer, to advise him. When the hearing began, Yoram demanded that Susan be ejected from the room. Hamber noted that Yoram was within his rights since the parties have a right to have a lawyer present, but no one else. Susan said that she understood the technical rule but that making her leave the room would prolong the session as Molly would have to step out frequently to consult, and there would probably be time consuming shuttling back and forth to clarify Molly's questions and Susan's advice. In the end Yoram's cousin persuaded him to allow Susan to stay.

Each party was permitted to make opening statements. Susan reeled off the history of the case, the numerous phone calls and requests from Molly, Rabbi Katz, Rabbi Reiss and other rabbis asking Yoram to give the *gett*. Yoram interjected that he had been willing to give the *gett*; he had just wanted the financial and property matters settled first. Susan countered that recalcitrant spouses typically say that they "just" want this or another thing settled while the *agunah* waits anxiously for her *gett*. Susan cited the prenup which stipulated that from the time the couple lives separately, the husband must pay the per diem support unless the wife refuses to appear in the *beit din* for the *gett*. But Molly had clearly been anxious to go to the *beit din* for her *gett*. She had called Rabbi Reiss countless times and mobilized a raft of rabbis to help her attain her *gett*. "The kind of delaying and bargaining that Yoram admitted to is exactly the kind of behavior that the prenup was designed to prevent," Susan said.

Yoram protested that he had many conversations with Rabbi Reiss about various aspects of the case, including property and financial matters, but Rabbi Reiss never mentioned the prenup and the per diem charges Yoram was exposed to. Yoram, increasingly frustrated with the drift of the exchanges, requested to call Reiss as a witness. Reiss corroborated that he had spoken to both parties many times as the months elapsed but could say no more than that. Both sides offered summations and the *dayyan*, rabbinical judge, allowed several weeks for the submission of final statements. Shortly after that, Hamber issued his ruling, holding that Yoram owed Molly $11,000, which she received.

Why did Molly get this rare prenup monetary award, the first and only prenup payment that Susan knew of at that time? After hearing Rabbi Reiss's perspective on the prenup, that the husband's debt to the wife builds and then can be traded away for the *gett*, Susan concluded that Molly was just lucky that Yoram was as unfamiliar with the prenup and *gett* machination tactics as she was. Had Yoram protested *before* giving the *gett* that he was unaware that he was incurring the financial charges as the months elapsed, Susan felt it was likely that the BDA would have turned to Molly and said, "He's ready to give the *gett*. Which do you want, the money or the *gett*?" And with the choice presented to her in that way, Molly would have ended up waiving the money. After all, Reiss had told Susan explicitly that he viewed the money owed to the *agunah* under the prenup as a bargaining chip to be traded away for the *gett*.

As it turned out, Yoram rushed to give the *gett* to stop the per diem clock and only after that challenged the financial terms of the prenup. Molly was lucky that she received her *gett* before she could be pressured to waive the cash. Susan felt that Molly was also fortunate that Hamber was not one of the *dayyanim* listed as a member of the BDA, but an outsider that the BDA recruited from time to time.

Not long after Molly was awarded the $11,000, Susan was browsing the BDA website and noticed that the BDA had changed the language of the prenup, adding that the wife must make a reasonable attempt to notify her husband, via a notarized document, that she actually intends to exercise her right under the terms of the prenup to collect the per diem money. This meant that the per diem payments would no longer automatically commence from the day the couple began to live apart. When Susan saw this change on the BDA website she became concerned that, like Molly, many women would rely on rabbis and *batei din* to guide them, and these rabbis would fail to advise the woman about the newly required notarized notification just as Reiss had failed to invoke the prenup in Molly's case. If the women failed to send the notarized letter, the prenup would not be activated.

Susan called Reiss to ask about why the BDA had added the requirement of a notarized notification letter as a trigger for the per diem payments. Reiss reminded Susan of Yoram and Molly's case and said that he felt Yoram wasn't a really bad guy like some recalcitrants. After Yoram and Molly's case, the BDA decided they wanted to protect husbands from inadvertently running up per diem debt by requiring wives to inform their husbands in writing that they intended to invoke the prenup. Susan responded that in light of Molly's ignorance of how the prenup worked, it would be a good idea to draft and attach a form letter to the prenup with instructions to wives on how to use it to provide the required notification.

Susan was struck by how quickly the BDA moved to protect husbands by requiring a notarized letter of notification from the wife. She checked the prenup section on the BDA website from time to time but couldn't find the suggested notification letter. When Susan called the BDA to follow up, a BDA staffer told her that a suggested notification letter had been added to the BDA website but not in the prenup section. Neither Susan nor the BDA staffer was able to find the notification letter on the website. The staffer called Susan back an hour later and told her to look in a section labeled "Section VII Notification Language." When Susan asked why the letter wasn't in the prenup section where it belonged, the BDA staffer expressed the concern that if men saw the letter it might be more difficult to persuade them to sign the prenup.

## *A 2014 Progress Report—Which Do You Want, the* Gett *or the Money?*

Over the years, the RCA and BDA continued to promote the RCA prenup as a highly effective "vaccine," the word they favored, to protect women against the dangers of Orthodox marriage. They declared that in cases where there is an RCA prenup, the *gett* is assured, but they provided no details. Were women receiving the per diem support money that accrued in their favor during the time that the husband withheld the *gett* or were women being held hostage and then being deprived of the per diem payments? We had no way of knowing how *agunot* were being treated since the BDA published no data about how long *agunot* had to wait for their *gett* and how many women received the per diem payments due them.

An article published by Rabbi Willig in the Spring 2012 inaugural issue of the *Journal of the Beth Din of America*, stunned us because it revealed that an *agunah*'s rights under his RCA prenup were even more tenuous than we suspected. Willig outlined the *halakhic* bases for a *beit din* to exempt the husband from the daily payments notwithstanding the plain language of the prenup obligating him to pay. He made it clear that the *beit din* alone had the power to decide whether the per diem money would be pursued, not the *agunah*. If the *beit din* decided not to award the per diem money to the *agunah*, she had no legal recourse.

*Agunah* activists and many others were heretofore unaware that the husband paying the per diem was at the sole discretion of the BDA. At a 2013 *agunah* program held at his synagogue, Rabbi Haskel Lookstein thought that Susan was mistaken when she explained to the audience that the BDA controlled the *agunah*'s ability to enforce the per diem payments. Likewise, when Susan was contacted by a Long Island synagogue that was organizing an *agunah* program, the program chair was skeptical when Susan explained this to her. One attorney, highly knowledgeable about the *agunah* issue, was irate when she learned the truth and called the BDA prenup a fraud.

In response to the concerns Willig's article raised, we together with Estelle Freilich, a director at *Agunah* Int'l. since 1998, organized a group of *agunah* activists and rabbis to attend a meeting with Rabbi Shlomo Weissmann, who had replaced Reiss as administrator of the BDA. At Rabbi Weissmann's request, it was agreed that everything said at the meeting would be held confidential so no report of the discussion can be provided. Shortly after the meeting, Susan and Rivka published an article in *The New York Jewish Week* (hereafter *The Jewish Week*) criticizing the fact that the BDA routinely traded away the accrued per diem payments in return for the *gett*. Reacting to our article, Allen Fagin, an attorney on the board of the BDA, invited Susan, Rivka and Estelle to a meeting at his law firm in November 2012. Fagin and Weissmann requested once again that what was said at the meeting be held confidential. Susan objected, saying that the issues to be discussed were of vital importance to the community, and shouldn't be kept under wraps. Fagin and Weissmann agreed to proceed without a confidentiality agreement.

Fagin began by saying that he had called the meeting because he felt that we were all on the same side and should confer about problems rather than exchange salvos in the columns of newspapers. Susan said she was happy he had scheduled this meeting but she differed with him about being on the same side, pointing out that *beit din* rabbis are "on the side" of securing the *gett* even at the cost of treating women and children unfairly, whereas we activists are on the side of a *gett* with justice for *agunot* and their children. Susan continued that "siding" with the *gett* underlies the BDA's routinely rewarding husbands for finally giving the *gett* by making the per diem money and the *gett* an either or situation. Instead the BDA should award the support money to the *agunah* and let her decide how to proceed. If the *agunah* at some point wishes to trade the money awarded to her for the *gett*, that would be up to her. She might retain some or all of the money and still receive her *gett* as there would be pressure on the husband to stop the clock as in Yoram and Molly's case.

Fagin seemed to agree with our suggestions for giving the woman, rather than the BDA, full control over the decision whether to waive the per diem money in return for the *gett*. Rivka mentioned a suggestion that had come up at the earlier meeting, having the husband put money in escrow every month to cover the accumulated daily payments so that the financial pinch of withholding the *gett* became real. Fagin seemed supportive of that as well, but Weissmann seemed uncomfortable with these ideas. He wouldn't agree that the *beit din* should give up its control over whether the per diem support payments should be waived. Fagin continued to probe Weissmann as to why these changes couldn't be made, but the discussion went nowhere. At the close of the meeting, it was agreed that our suggestions would be brought back to the BDA for consideration. In several subsequent conversations, Weissmann said he would report shortly to us on the BDA's response. We never received a response.

Not long after these two meetings a precedent-setting case with regard to the BDA prenuptial was adjudicated in the Connecticut state courts: the case of Rachel Light. The lower court and the appellate court upheld Rachel's claim for per diem payments under the terms of her BDA prenuptial, and Rachel collected a substantial amount of money and received her *gett*. Susan had an opportunity to discuss the case with Weissmann. She told him that she thought that the Light case was a terrific precedent that would benefit other *agunot*. Susan felt that Weissmann seemed less than enthusiastic about Rachel's success, and her curiosity was aroused. She asked him about what role the BDA had played in this case considering their habit of trading away the per diem money in return for a belated *gett*. Weissmann told Susan that the Lights had signed the earliest version of the BDA prenup, which was divided into two parts. The couple had signed only the husband's pledge to make the per diem payments but had omitted signing the second part of the prenup that designated the BDA as the arbitrator over the implementation of the prenup. As a result the BDA had no control over the per diem payments. Rachel, the *agunah*, was in control, and she collected the money due her. She got both support money for the time she was held hostage in the marriage and her *gett*.

In a November 2013 article in the *Jewish Forward*, Rabbi Weissmann stated that in almost every case the payments that have accrued to the benefit of the *agunah* are waived once the husband agrees to give the *gett*. Following this article, Susan and Rivka had several conversations with Weissmann about the prenup. Weissmann said that the BDA dealt with about five or six cases per year in which the husband was troublesome enough that the BDA had to invoke the prenup to pressure him. He pointed out that there are probably additional cases where the prenup helps, but the BDA never becomes aware of it because the *gett* is given with minimal delay. He said that, regrettably, the BDA was not keeping track of which divorcing couples had a prenup.

Weissmann said the average wait for the *gett* in cases where the prenup is invoked is a few months, and in the worst cases, as much as six months. He described the process as follows. The *agunah* calls the BDA for help, and the BDA typically has a series of phone calls or even a meeting with the husband pointing out to him the financial consequences of withholding the *gett*. As this process progresses, Weissmann keeps reminding the husband that if he doesn't give the *gett*, he will have to pay. Weissmann made no mention of the requirement that the *agunah* send her husband notarized notice of her intention to collect the per diem money.

When the husband softens up and agrees to give the *gett*, Weissmann recounted, the BDA turns to the *agunah* and asks if she wants the money or the *gett*. Weissmann said he also points out to the *agunah* that a *beit din* arbitration session to award her the per diem support and enforcement of this award in the civil court could be a long, expensive and risky process.

It is understandable that in light of the horror stories of women remaining without a *gett* for years and the risky litigation required to collect the per diem money, *agunot*, when prompted by the *beit din* to forfeit the money, do so. And while six months of waiting can be an eternity for an *agunah*, it's a relatively short time compared to other notorious cases. However, six months of per diem payments equals $27,000. We don't know what would happen if the BDA demanded that the money be put in escrow or paid to the *agunah* each month. Perhaps this would speed up the process as parting with $4,500 for a month of delay might motivate swift action. Nor do we know what would transpire if instead of prompting the *agunah* to waive the money, the BDA said to the husband, "So far you owe her $27,000. If you pay up and give the *gett* now, you'll stop the clock." Like Molly and Rachel Light, other *agunot* are entitled to the per diem support payments promised them as well as the *gett*. If the BDA made this clear, perhaps delays of even six months might no longer occur.

Weissmann also glossed over a case, which Rivka and Susan knew about, where a *gett* had been withheld for more than two years, and the BDA waived the per diem money. Weissmann referred to it as "that awful case." While such a protracted case may be rare when there is a prenup, this case highlights the BDA's predisposition to waive the per diem money, at the risk of eventually undermining the effectiveness of the prenup. Husbands may learn that they can wait as long as they want to give the *gett*, knowing that the *beit din* will waive the debt in the end.

Awarding the support money to the *agunot* is also more in keeping with *halakhic* rules which originally justified the prenup per diem payments as spousal support that *halakhah* allows men to undertake. By routinely implementing this waiver of the spousal support, the BDA is ironically linking the support payments to the *gett* in a way that undermines the *halakhic* vitality of the prenup. In this vein, Rabbi Jeremy Stern, of the Organization for the Resolution of Agunot (ORA), has frequently said that *agunot* are not entitled to receive the per diem support money when they obtain their *gett*. To use his word, the prenup is not meant to "enrich" the woman. Stern's approach also seems to be at odds with the *halakhic* justification of the per diem payments as spousal support which the husband undertook and to which the *agunah* is *halakhic*ally entitled.

In sum, the BDA prenup is better than nothing but still only a partial solution to the *agunah* calamity. It does give the BDA leverage in pressuring husbands to give the *gett*. All but two recalcitrants, however, have escaped without paying anything because of the routine waiver of the debt. Husbands who have little or no money or assets, whether in truth or by design, are immune from the requirement to pay the per diem money or may be unable to pay anything beyond the support already ordered by the civil court. The prenup is of no avail when men flee to foreign countries and escape enforcement. Furthermore, as Rabbi Weissmann tells *agunot*, enforcing the prenup in civil court could be costly and complicated.

Finally, the BDA prenup obviously does nothing to protect women who marry without the prenup "vaccine" against the dangers of Orthodox marriage. This group of women at risk includes women married before the prenup existed and all women in the ultra–Orthodox communities where a prenup is not used at all. Furthermore, as of 2014, as many as 30 percent of Modern Orthodox RCA rabbis do not use the prenup. The RCA has announced that they have embarked on research to determine why so many of their members refrain from using the prenup when officiating at marriages.

## Look But Don't Touch

In 2004 a new prenup was proposed that revived three well known but much criticized *halakhic* strategies to solve the *agunah* problem. The three strategies were (1) conditional marriage, which would result in the nullification of the marriage should the husband violate the condition of granting a timely *gett*; (2) the husband's irrevocable appointment, at the time of marriage, of an agent to grant the *gett* in the event he does not do so for whatever reason; and (3) empowering rabbinical courts to declare a marriage dissolved. Each of these systemic solutions, which would have completely done away with the husband's unilateral control of the marriage, provoked intense rabbinic debate and criticism at the time they were first proposed. For the details of these debates, which are beyond the scope of this book, we refer to the books listed in the preface and bibliography of this volume. Suffice it to say that none of these systemic solutions was ever widely adopted by the Orthodox rabbinate. Hence the thousands of chained women around the world.

Still, in 2004, Rabbi Michael Broyde, before his 2013–2014 resignations from the BDA and RCA under difficult circumstances, proposed what he titled a Tripartite Agreement, which was a prenup that combined and elaborated all three of these long-debated solutions. Shortly after that Susan Weiss, Director of the Center for Women's Justice (CWJ) in Jerusalem, edited and condensed Broyde's agreement and made it available on her Center's website. After the publication of the Tripartite Agreement, copies of it circulated for a while with explanatory material appended. Broyde labeled his Tripartite prenup as *Shelo le-Halakah*, which means the document was for theoretical legal discussion only, that it was emphatically not for actual use. Look but don't touch!

For years, Broyde's tripartite prenup seemed to be off the Orthodox rabbinate's radar. In June 2013, however, at an Agunah Summit convened at NYU by the Tikvah Center and JOFA, several rabbis called for considering the implementation of Broyde's Tripartite. In addition, a rabbi from the more progressive wing of Modern Orthodoxy was said to be working on an amendment that would enhance the Tripartite. If widely used and accepted the Tripartite prenup would offer superior protection to brides as the husband's cooperation in dissolving the marriage would no longer be required at all though women would still be dependent on an all male *beit din* to declare them free. Unfortunately, as of the writing of this book, not a single Orthodox rabbi has made any effort to promote widespread use of the Tripartite. Every day of delay leaves additional women exposed to the danger of *aginut*.

# 16

# The Rackman *Beit Din*: A Watershed

When we began our work as directors of Agunah Inc., we naïvely believed that in the course of advocating for individual *agunot*, we would inform *beit din* rabbis of the systemic problems we discovered, and they would then work with us on *halakhic* solutions to these problems and put an end to recalcitrant husbands using the system to abuse their wives and children.

Years of case work, along with in depth interviews of *batei din* in the New York metropolitan area, opened our eyes to the fact that *batei din* were not part of the solution to *agunah* agony, but actually a central part of the problem. Case-by-case advocacy, mobilizing pressure on individual husbands, would not solve the problem. For while in each case the husband was a villain, the *batei din* and the rabbis were enablers, empowering the husband to perpetrate his villainy.

Time and again *batei din* pressured women to make unconscionable concessions in return for the *gett*. At best, a handful of Orthodox rabbis acknowledged the sorry state of Orthodox *batei din* but did nothing to rectify the situation. At worst, many Orthodox rabbis defended *batei din* as dispensing decisions that were *halakhically* proper notwithstanding the complaints of critics.

After more than a decade of frustration, we felt like Sisyphus. We would never finish our task. No matter how many cases we resolved, usually with the *agunot* paying a high price for their freedom, there would always be more cases just around the corner. Countless new *agunot* were being ground into submission with the cooperation of *batei din* faster than we could close even one case. If the *batei din* didn't start applying the available *halakhic* tools for freeing *agunot*, the *agunah* catastrophe would never end.

Often we were emotionally exhausted. Susan sometimes joked, half seriously, that perhaps we should disband Agunah Inc. and issue a press release explaining that it was hopeless for *agunot* to seek justice in the Orthodox *beit din* system. However, the voices of desperate *agunot* on the phone and tales of children at risk kept us involved. Finally in 1996, some real hope emerged.

The year 1996 was a watershed year for Agunah Inc. because of the establishment of a new *beit din* specializing in the problems of *agunot* and guided by a *halakhic* approach that provided justice for these women. This new *beit din* was initiated by Rabbi Moshe Morgenstern, who, though ordained as a rabbi, earned his living as an accountant. Rabbi Emanuel Rackman, who would head the new *beit din*, and Rivka's husband Rabbi Irwin Haut, an attorney with expertise in Jewish divorce, joined Morgenstern in signing *teshuvot* (responsa/rulings) that freed the first three *agunot* whose cases were adjudicated by the *beit din*. Rabbi Sholom Klass of *The Jewish Press* newspaper later signed on several rulings as well.

Morgenstern approached Agunah Inc. in late 1996. He told us that for more than 30 years, he had been a student of the late, revered Rabbi Moshe Feinstein, who was known as a trailblazer in helping *agunot*. Morgenstern claimed to have witnessed Feinstein nullifying many more marriages than Feinstein had written about in his *teshuvot*. Honey Rackman, Rabbi Rackman's daughter-in-law and a director of Agunah Inc., insisted that we all speak to Morgenstern together. We decided to meet him.

An opportunity for a meeting presented itself in early 1997 when on a Sunday evening in January, Morgenstern called Rivka's home and said that he was at a client's house in Brooklyn and had time for a meeting. Rivka called Susan and Honey to come over. Morgenstern walked into the Haut residence, weighed down by a large document case which contained his client's accounting files as well as some *halakhic* material. After a lengthy discussion, in which Morgenstern cited many *teshuvot* of the late Rabbi Feinstein, Irwin said that Morgenstern's "lamdoos" (scholarliness) was exceptional. "Gevaldig!" (Terrific!) Irwin exclaimed in Yiddish as Morgenstern laid out his *halakhic* approach. We were all impressed with Morgenstern's knowledge of the issue.

As Morgenstern was packing up, Irwin was excited about a strange coincidence. None of us had ever met Morgenstern or even heard of him until a year ago. But going back a few years, Irwin had written a novel, unpublished, about a rabbi in Poland who frees an *agunah*. The name of the rabbi in the novel? Moshe Morgenstern!

## The Rackman-Morgenstern Beit Din Begins Taking Cases

Agunah Inc. began referring *agunot* to Morgenstern. He interviewed them and took notes on their cases. Morgenstern wrote a *teshuvah* (responsum/ruling) for *agunah* no. 1. He invalidated her marriage on the grounds of *kiddushei ta'ut*, a marriage under false pretenses. This woman had documentation that her husband had lied on their marriage application, stating that he had never been married when in fact he was divorced from at least one previous wife. It seemed that he had swindled his first wife out of money just as he had swindled *agunah* no. 1. Morgenstern found other grounds as well: her life was endangered by his serious violence, and the witnesses to the marriage were not *halakhically* qualified.

After *agunah* no. 1 had been freed, she informed us that there was a chance that her former husband might now give her a *gett*. We had felt all along that in many cases husbands would give a *gett* after a Morgenstern *p'tur* (release). Upon learning their wives were free, husbands would lose hope of extorting concessions and would no longer have the sadistic thrill of controlling their wives' lives. Two well-known New York area Sephardic rabbis concurred with *agunah* no. 1's release, but a *gett* would still be welcome because it would be accepted across the board by all rabbis. We, therefore, advised her to cooperate in arranging for the *gett* to be given. As it turned out, the husband made several appointments to give the *gett* but never showed up.

Morgenstern gathered enough information to release *agunah* no. 2. This woman had pages and pages of court documents describing her husband's violent acts against her and their children. But this *agunah* was reluctant to accept the *p'tur* as truly freeing her. She worried that it would not be accepted by her *frum* (stringently religious) community. After another year of wrangling in court, with the help of a Manhattan attorney Daniel Schwartz, who took the case pro bono, this *agunah* received her *gett*.

The third *agunah* was put on hold for the time being at her request because of complications in her case. *Agunah* no. 4 spoke and met with Morgenstern. She began to ask around about Morgenstern's procedures, and various rabbis refused to accept his *p'sak* (ruling). One well-known Brooklyn rabbi told her that there was nothing *halakhically* invalid about Morgenstern's approach but said, "We don't do that." This fourth *agunah* was pressing Morgenstern to try to get the late, then prominent Israeli Sephardic Chief Rabbi Ovadia Yosef, to sign Morgenstern's *p'sak* dissolving her marriage. Morgenstern began to talk about going to Israel to speak to Ovadia Yosef.

In the midst of all this activity, Morgenstern reported a bizarre incident—he had been attacked on a street near his home. Morgenstern was in the habit of taking a nightly stroll with his wife, but on this night the cold weather kept his wife at home. Alone on the street, Morgenstern was assaulted by a man who put his arms around his neck and choked him. Morgenstern said he fought back, perhaps breaking his assailant's finger. He saw one or two other men down the block, dressed, like his assailant, in the black coats and hats of the type worn by right-wing Orthodox men.

Morgenstern reported the incident to the police but did not give an accurate description of his attacker for fear that linking the attack to his *agunah* work would frighten his wife, who might insist that he stop working with *agunot*. Morgenstern considered this a warning but was undeterred. Other forms of harassment followed. Impossible-to-remove glue was used to paper over Morgenstern's car windows. At one synagogue people stood beside Morgenstern during prayers and hurled insults at him. But Morgenstern resolutely carried on.

By the first week of February 1997, the new *beit din* took shape, with Rackman as Rosh (Head) and Morgenstern, Haut and Klass as *dayyanim*. Morgenstern researched the facts and relevant *halakhot* for each case and then presented the case to the other rabbis for their review and signature.

We and Honey were debating whether and when to go public about the *beit din*. An international conference on Orthodox Jewish feminism, which led to the formation of JOFA (Jewish Orthodox Feminist Alliance), was coming up in February 1997 at the Grand Hyatt Hotel in Manhattan. It was only a few weeks away, and Agunah Inc. was in charge of putting together the program for a major plenary session on the *agunah* problem. Publicizing the *beit din* at the conference would be a dramatic way to create community awareness and momentum in support of this long awaited solution to the *agunah* tragedy. Hopefully the women and men attending the conference would go home and encourage their community rabbis to obtain information and explanations about the methodology of the new *beit din*. The Orthodox rabbinate would have to respond. We were convinced that our *beit din* was on firm *halakhic* ground so we would welcome debate, confident that Morgenstern's ideas would carry the day.

On the other hand, if we delayed going public, more women would have been quietly freed by the *beit din* before its existence became widely known. Perhaps some of the women might even have remarried. Susan speculated that, *b'di'eved* (after the fact), if several freed *agunot* had remarried, the cruelty of branding these pious women as adulteresses might move the rabbis to concede that the *beit din*'s approach to freeing them to remarry was *halakhically* valid. But then again, the rabbis countenanced all manner of cruelty against *agunot*. We were leaning toward announcing at the conference.

There was one additional factor that had to be weighed in the decision of when to announce. Morgenstern was indeed planning a trip to Israel to discuss his work with Rabbi Ovadia Yosef, who was known to have made courageous rulings in order to free *agunot*. We still had a few days to decide when to publicize the *beit din*. If Morgenstern got rabbinic support in Israel that would definitely tip the scales to announcing at the conference.

Early in February 1997, about two weeks before the conference, Morgenstern left for Israel. Morgenstern could not absorb the expense of the trip, nor could any of the *agunot* pay anything toward it. Agunah Inc., therefore, agreed to cover the cost. Rabbi Rackman was instrumental in getting Morgenstern appointments with the prominent Haifa Chief Rabbi She'aryashuv Cohen and Rabbi Yosef. (Yosef later made anti-gay and racist remarks about gentiles and Arabs, but he retained his stature as a *halakhic* authority and continued to be known for being helpful to *agunot*.) Morgenstern's position was that he was going to Israel to give these other rabbis the opportunity to join him in signing his *teshuvot*; he was not seeking their approval as higher authorities. We had no expectations that any of the rabbis would sign or even lend their name to the cause, but we agreed it was worth a try.

On February 7, 1997, Susan was plowing through paper work on her desk when the phone rang. It was *agunah* no. 1. She told Susan that she had heard from Morgenstern that Ovadia Yosef had signed her *teshuvah*. Susan was exhilarated when she heard this. If this was true it was a momentous event. Yosef was a highly respected rabbinic authority. Susan told *agunah* no. 1 that she was courageous, having gone ahead with the *beit din* when the value of the *teshuvah* was unclear. Susan called to inform Rivka, who was also excited to hear the news.

A few days later, on *motzei shabbat* (at the end of the Sabbath), Morgenstern called Rivka and Irwin from Israel, and they patched Susan in on their second telephone line. We learned to our surprise and dismay that Morgenstern didn't get Yosef's signature on the *teshuvot*. Morgenstern went through a blow-by-blow description of his meeting with Yosef. He said that Yosef was warm and supportive and agreed readily to three of the *teshuvot* but wanted time to think about the fourth.

Morgenstern said that in his excitement over Yosef's supportive remarks, he forgot to get Yosef's signature on the documents. He said he would try to get another appointment for the signatures. We were pessimistic about Morgenstern getting another appointment because it had been difficult to wangle the first appointment. We also wondered whether Yosef would really be willing to make a firm commitment. Supportive words in private were one thing; signing a document that would be made public was another. Readers will remember the deceased rabbi who was later alleged to have told several rabbis that the little girls in the *kiddushei ketanah* controversy were free but who failed to issue any signed document to that effect while still alive.

Indeed, Morgenstern was unable to secure another appointment with Yosef. However, Yosef appointed a deputy in New York, a Sephardic rabbi who was a principal of a yeshivah high school in the New York area, to continue to confer with Morgenstern to help *agunot*. Irwin and Susan spoke with this rabbi, who praised Morgenstern's work and his expert knowledge in the matter of *agunot*. The rabbi told Susan that he himself had written a letter to Yosef urging him to quickly attend to Morgenstern's cases but Yosef was very busy. The rabbi had been told that his letter lay unopened on Yosef's desk.

While all this rabbinic consultation was going on, the calls to the Agunah Inc. hotline continued unabated, and we were informing many women of the possibility of going to the new *beit din*. We firmly decided to announce the *beit din* at the Feminism and Orthodoxy Conference. Rivka was particularly eager to personally make the announcement about the *beit din* at the Agunah Inc. session of the conference, which she did. Then Irwin Haut and Rabbi Rackman spoke of its ground breaking work.

The Agunah Inc. session was the most dramatic segment of the conference. The halls were buzzing with talk of the *agunah* agony and the new hope that the *beit din* represented. In the weeks following the conference we referred more women to the new *beit din*. The *agunot* were incredulous when we told them they could soon be free. We explained to them the limited acceptance of the *beit din*'s decisions, but were thrilled that we could now direct the women to a *beit din* that would help them.

## *Internal Strains at the New* Beit Din

Things were happening very fast; we and Honey decided a meeting of Agunah Inc. and the *beit din* was necessary. We needed to establish uniform fees, policy on expenses, timetables for getting the *teshuvot* typed, the relationship between Agunah Inc. and the *beit din* and other procedural rules. We called Rabbi Rackman who, as head of the *beit din*, convened a meeting to iron out these issues.

Some progress was made at the meeting though there was sharp debate over one matter. We all agreed that Agunah Inc. and the *beit din* were separate organizations and could not speak for each other. There was discussion and some decisions made about keeping accurate records of testimony in the *beit din*, taping the sessions, and keeping documents on file. A uniform fee per case was agreed upon to cover Morgenstern's expenses though he volunteered that if a woman could not afford to pay, he would take care of the case gratis. Extraordinary expenses like the Israel trip would be dealt with separately.

The contentious issue that night was a case in which Morgenstern had told an *agunah* over the phone that he felt there were grounds for voiding her marriage and that based on her account, she could begin to date. The woman, surprised, had called Agunah Inc. after hearing this from Morgenstern. We and Honey told her that we understood her surprise in light of the fact that for five years she had been told that her situation was hopeless. We explained that Morgenstern had found *halakhically* valid grounds for ending marriages like hers.

At the meeting, however, Rivka took a different position. She said she was upset by the fact that Morgenstern had so quickly told the woman she could date. She felt that Morgenstern did not have enough documentation to justify this *halakhically*. Rackman commented that although Morgenstern was not wrong, it would be better to wait until the client was more familiar with the *beit din*'s approach before giving such counsel so that there would be no misunderstandings. Rivka repeated her criticism of Morgenstern.

In response, Susan recounted the story of one of our cases, Judy, an *agunah* woman whose husband had abandoned her and whose whereabouts were unknown. Barely two days after her husband had disappeared, Shloimy Eisen, who was also trying to help Judy, contacted her to tell her that Rabbi Chippes from the Israeli rabbinate was in New York and would be stopping by Shloimy's office to discuss some *agunah* cases. Rabbi Chippes traveled regularly around the world in an effort to track down fugitive Israeli men who had left their wives in Israel without a *gett*. Shloimy invited Judy to his office to meet Rabbi Chippes, thinking that Chippes might use his detective skills to help locate Judy's husband.

Chippes told Judy that he had heard from Shloimy about her children and what a fine woman she was. Chippes commented that with several young children, Judy would probably not be in a rush to remarry, what with all the difficulties that arise in introducing a new man into the family. With marriage in the near future unlikely, Chippes felt that Judy's need for a *gett* was not urgent.

Chippes then advised Judy that, even without a *gett*, she could date, go for dinner, to shows, museums and the like with men, because all this was very public without any possibility of improper intimate relations. Susan pointed out to Rivka that Chippes, a functionary of Israel's *Haredi* dominated rabbinic court system, had given Judy the same advice that Morgenstern had given. Chippes told Judy that she could date in public less than two days after her husband had left and despite the fact that Chippes did not believe she could be freed from her marriage. By contrast, when Morgenstern advised the *agunah* on the phone that she could date, he was convinced from what she had told him that there were *halakhic* grounds for ending her marriage. Rivka didn't comment on the comparison of the two cases and didn't retract her criticism of the way Morgenstern had handled the case.

The meeting drew to a close, having resolved the agenda items of standardizing fees and procedures and clarifying that the *beit din* and Agunah Inc. were separate organizations working in tandem. Years later, Rivka told Susan that she and Irwin had decided after the meeting that they would not continue to work with Morgenstern and Rackman. In the summer of 1997, shortly after the meeting, Irwin resigned from the *beit din*.

Susan and Honey had a different perspective on the meeting. They thought that Morgenstern was audacious but knowledgeable and sincere in his commitment to help *agunot*. His dating advice to the *agunah* was, no doubt, unconventional, but in accordance with the advice that Chippes, a *Haredi* rabbi, had given and within the bounds of *halakhah* in Rackman's opinion.

## *Another Rabbi Discovered Nullifying Marriages*

Shortly after the contentious meeting, it came to our attention that Rabbi Mordechai Tendler, a grandson of Rabbi Moshe Feinstein, had been nullifying marriages quietly for years. We called Tendler, and he confirmed that he indeed had been freeing *agunot* for a number of years though on more limited grounds than Rabbi Morgenstern, mostly by finding technical errors (*ta'ut*) in the wedding ceremony, such as invalid witnesses or a problem with the wedding ring, which means that the marriage was never effectuated *halakhically*. It was void *ab initio*, from the start.

We told Tendler that we were excited to hear about his work but also distressed by the fact that he had kept this a secret. Over the years there were many women we might have referred to him had we known of his activity.

Tendler responded that we had to take account of the powerful, entrenched forces that would try to put a stop to his efforts if he were more public. He told us that if other rabbis in his family voiced open opposition to his work, he would stop despite the fact that he firmly believed that what he was doing was *halakhically* correct. However, as the reader will soon learn, something entirely different, unfortunately, put an end to Tendler's work with *agunot*.

Rivka and Irwin had a face-to-face meeting with Tendler. Tendler told them that he had released over 30 women and was considering voiding the marriage of a woman who already had a *gett* but wanted to marry a *kohen*, a member of the Jewish priestly caste. A *kohen* is not permitted to marry a divorcee, but if a woman's marriage is declared void *ab initio*, technically she was never married and she can therefore marry a *kohen*.

Tendler had also said to Rivka and Irwin that Modern Orthodox rabbis are reactionary compared to right-wing rabbis like him, who could be more innovative. Tendler, who had served as his grandfather Rabbi Moshe Feinstein's secretary, told Rivka and Irwin that Feinstein freed many more women than is publicly known and that this fact is not reflected in Feinstein's published *teshuvot*. Morgenstern had told us the same thing.

We later learned from a woman whom we sent to Tendler that around the same time that he freed her, a second woman was also freed. The second woman already had a *gett* but she too wanted to marry a *kohen*. Tendler voided her first marriage, that had already been terminated by a *gett*. About a year later Susan heard a similar story from a woman in the Midwest who told her that the Lubavitcher Rebbe, leader of the Lubavitch Chasidic community centered in Crown Heights, Brooklyn, had voided her marriage which allowed her to marry a *kohen*. The woman said that right after her marriage, the Rebbe had her new husband called up to the Torah for the *kohen aliyah*, the section of the Torah reading reserved for a *kohen*, so that everyone would see that he was still a *kohen* in good standing after marrying her.

After learning about Tendler, we and Honey had to make a decision: whether to refer women to the Rackman-Morgenstern *beit din* or to Tendler, whose right-wing status might make his rulings more widely accepted. After a brief deliberation, the right policy was clear. The best interests of the client came first, and that meant getting the most widely accepted *p'tur* even at the risk of making the Rackman-Morgenstern's *beit din* seem like it was second best. Agunah Inc. would refer women who met Tendler's more limited technical *ta'ut* criteria to him, and those who did not to the Rackman-Morgenstern *beit din*. Despite Tendler's narrower criteria for releasing women from their marriages, the fact that another prominent rabbi was freeing *agunot* meant that the new *beit din* was not a lone maverick.

Rivka later referred an *agunah* to Tendler. After researching her case, he freed her. She was a young woman who had a job in the Orthodox world. She told Rivka that nobody doubted or challenged her new single status, and she was able to move on with her life. Unfortunately, the ray of hope for *agunot* that Tendler represented went dark in 2005 when he was accused of sexual improprieties with congregants and *agunot*. Reports of several women coming forward with their stories appeared in Jewish and general media. This was a deeply discouraging blow because someone we viewed as a rescuer now stood accused of being a predator. To our knowledge, no legal action was ever taken against Tendler, but he was expelled from the RCA and lost his synagogue pulpit.

Not long after we spoke to Tendler, in late 1997, Rivka resigned from Agunah Inc. She became a member of the GET organization and an outspoken critic of the Rackman-Morgenstern *beit din*. Honey and Susan remained as directors and reincorporated Agunah Inc. as Agunah International.

As the months wore on, dozens more women appealed to the Rackman-Morgenstern *beit din* for help. By the end of the first year, more than 100 women had applied. Criticism of the *beit din* flew fast and furious, including a negative letter from Ovadia Yosef, despite the supportive praise that Yosef's colleague in New York had lavished on Morgenstern. One rabbi wrote that the *beit din*'s annulments were as worthless as the paper that comes with Bazooka bubble gum. The Agudat HaRabbanim of the U.S. and Canada, the National Council of Young Israel and the Rabbinical Council of America all issued statements questioning the legitimacy of the *beit din*. Prominent rabbis in Morgenstern's Kew Gardens community issued a statement censuring him. Though Rabbi Rackman penned countless articles explaining and defending the *halakhic* foundations of the new *beit din*, the criticism was unrelenting.

Notwithstanding the tsunami of criticism, women kept voting with their feet, coming to the *beit din* despite the fact that they knew that most of the Orthodox rabbinate had lined up against it. The Israeli newspaper *Yediot Acharonot* headlined the "storm" in the American Orthodox community over the *beit din* and characterized Rackman as standing up against the Orthodox establishment.

## A Day in the Rackman-Morgenstern Beit Din

The official name of the new *beit din* was the Beit Din L'Ba'ayot Agunot (The Rabbinical Court for Agunah Problems), but it was always referred to as the Rackman or Morgenstern *beit din*. The facts in the cases that Agunah Int'l referred to *beit din* were painful to hear—men who abandoned or battered their wives, who infected their wives with sexually transmitted diseases, who committed crimes and yet continued to act as their wives' jailers by withholding the *gett*. Honey and Susan, joined by new colleagues the late Henni Goldstein and Estelle Freilich, continued to field phone calls from five to seven *agunot* per week, directing many of them to the new *beit din* so Morgenstern could review their cases.

During most of 1997 and 1998 the *beit din* met every three weeks in the conference room of Bar Ilan University's 5th Avenue, Manhattan office. Rackman was Chancellor of Bar Ilan and still active there. Two or three cases were scheduled for each session, with Morgenstern having researched and recorded the case history of each *agunah* before the *beit din* convened. Another rabbi from Queens had by now joined the *beit din*, and a rabbi from Canada frequently joined the deliberations through a telephone hookup.

The *agunah*, almost always accompanied by parents, siblings, or friends, would recount her story to the assembled rabbis and Agunah Int'l directors. One *agunah*, in her 60s, described leaving her violent husband forty years earlier. Young, civilly divorced but unable to obtain a *gett*, she left the Jewish community, married a non-Jew and had children. Still, she longed for religious severance from her first husband. Miriam, only 16 when she married in Iran, described decades of being beaten and abused by her husband, 20 years her senior. On their wedding night, her husband claimed that he had been cheated, that she was not a virgin; her life had been a living hell ever since.

Kayla, her head covered by a scarf and her arms by long sleeves, told of discovering that her husband was a drug addict. She was terrified as he became increasingly abusive to her and their children. She had turned to several rabbis in her community, but they ignored her. One rabbi even covered up for her husband when Kayla reported the domestic violence to the police. Her husband had recently made a large donation to that rabbi's synagogue. Another *agunah* had proof of her husband's homosexual activity, and she feared infection with AIDS. When her husband refused to give her a *gett*, her rabbi pressured her to give up her share of the marital assets, which would leave her penniless. The rabbi told her to think of herself as a Holocaust survivor, stripped of everything she owned, but still alive.

The *beit din* rabbis and Agunah Int'l directors listened with a mixture of sympathy and shock. No matter how many times they heard such stories, the pain of the *agunot* moved them while the behavior of the rabbis the *agunot* had reached out to upset them. After due deliberation, the rabbis freed the woman through various *halakhic* means. Rabbi Morgenstern favored issuing a *gett zikkui* in addition to straightforward voiding of the marriage.

A *gett zikkui* is based on the rabbinic concept of *zakhin le'adam shelo b'fanav*—one can do something for another person's benefit (*zikkui*) even without their consent. A simple example of this concept playing out in modern times is that banks do not require the signature of an account owner in order to receive a deposit into that account. Anyone who has the account number can make a deposit, on the presumption that since a deposit is beneficial to the account owner, the owner would approve.

A *gett zikkui* is typically issued in cases where a woman refuses to accept a *gett* but is living with another man. In such a case, issuing a *gett zikkui* is viewed as beneficial (*zikkui*) to the wife. Despite the fact that the wife's consent to accept the *gett* is required, the *gett zikkui* is deposited for the recalcitrant wife at the *beit din* on the grounds that it is to her benefit to be divorced so that she will no longer be committing adultery. After the *gett* is deposited, the husband is free to remarry. It is hoped that the wife will pick up the *gett zikkui* when she comes to her senses and realizes that accepting the *gett* is the right thing to do.

Following that line of thought, Morgenstern held that one can issue a *gett zikkui* for the benefit of a recalcitrant husband. The *gett zikkui* benefits the husband by "doing the right thing" in his name so that he is no longer transgressing by defying rabbis who have ordered that the *gett* be given.

In addition to relying on the *gett zikkui*, Morgenstern would declare that the *gett* he had prepared was revoked and would then deliver the *gett* to the *agunah* in a way that raised doubts about whether the *gett* was properly delivered. Morgenstern felt that the revocation and questionable delivery brought into play *halakhic* points that might reinforce the grounds for annulment. The rabbis of the Talmud were concerned about leaving a woman's marital status ambiguous. They, therefore, considered *gett* revocation and questionable delivery, which put the validity of the divorce in doubt, as possible justification for rabbis to terminate a marriage in order to end any doubt that the marriage was over and the woman was free to remarry.

For each *gett*, everyone at the *beit din* would troop downstairs to the sidewalk, whereupon having declared the *gett* he had prepared revoked, Morgenstern would "deliver" the *gett* by tossing it onto the sidewalk so that it landed closer to him than to the *agunah*, creating the desired ambiguity about effective delivery. Many a curious pedestrian passed by the Bar Ilan building eyeing the group and wondering what was going on as Morgenstern tossed the *gett* on the pavement at a distance from the *agunah*, and she then stooped to pick it up, rising to see all beaming with happiness and saying, "You are free now. Mazal Tov! [Best of Luck!]"

## *The* Beit Din *and the Second Feminism and Orthodoxy Conference*

The *beit din* had been functioning for more than a year when the second International Conference on Feminism and Orthodoxy was held in February 1998. Honey and Susan were again responsible for planning the *agunah* session. Honey, Rabbi Rackman and Rabbi Shlomo Riskin were scheduled to speak. Riskin is a well-known American born rabbi who is Chief Rabbi of the Israeli city of Efrat. Rackman planned to elaborate on the *halakhic* underpinnings of the *beit din*. In the interest of open debate, Honey and Susan had called several rabbis who were openly critical of the *beit din* to speak, but they declined to appear. At the last minute, Rabbi Saul Berman agreed to join the panel.

Honey opened the session with a moving statement about the agony of *agunot* and the imperative for a systemic *halakhic* solution. Rabbi Rackman discussed expanding the parameters of *kiddushei ta'ut*, a marriage that is declared void *ab initio* because the bride was unaware at the time of the wedding of key information that would have deterred her from marrying. Rackman called for reconsidering the Talmud's *tav l'metav tandu* assumption that women are so desperate to marry that they will consent to marry almost anyone, even a violent abuser. The *tav l'metav* assumption undermines a woman's ability to testify that she would not have knowingly consented to marrying a seriously defective man because *tav l'metav* postulates that brides, as a rule, would agree to marry almost any man rather than remain single. Rackman went on to say that in our times, when physical coercion of a recalcitrant husband to give a *gett*, as described by the Talmud, is impossible, rabbis should invalidate the marriage. Loud applause from the audience punctuated Rackman's speech.

Riskin stated most energetically that the *agunah* problem was urgent and a disgrace for the *halakhic* community. However, he objected to Rackman's and Morgenstern's contention that all contemporary marriages might be binding only *d'rabbanan* not *d'oraita* (under rabbinic law, not biblical law), and therefore, more easily invalidated. Riskin then explicitly stated that when a recalcitrant husband does not yield to *beit din* pressure, a *beit din* should be empowered to end the marriage. Exactly how that would come about was left unclear.

Riskin seemed to be saying that there should be a special, central *beit din* in Jerusalem with branches around the world. He implied that the recently founded *beit din l'agunot* that was set up by the Israeli rabbinate in Jerusalem might fill that role. But in New York, we had already heard reports of serious problems with that *beit din*, including corruption. Riskin himself said that the Jerusalem *beit din* was only dealing with tens of cases per year, too few to deal with the large numbers of *agunot* in Israel alone. The word among activists in Jerusalem was that this *beit din*'s rulings caused *agunot* rather than freeing them. Furthermore, it was unrealistic to think that a *beit din* in Jerusalem would be able, any time soon, to exert jurisdiction over men withholding a *gett* in the United States. In sum, Riskin passionately decried the failure of rabbis to solve the *agunah* problem but did not outline any practical steps for improving the situation.

Next on the JOFA program was Rabbi Saul Berman, then the head of EDAH, a Modern Orthodox think tank, no longer in existence. In the opening moments of his speech, Berman candidly described himself as a critic of the new *beit din* though he praised Rackman and Agunah Int'l for their courage. He then called for supporting the Rackman-Morgenstern *beit din* "with *sechel* (wisdom) and the resources necessary to make sure its fact-finding is absolutely clear."

The main thrust of Berman's talk was that, in fact, for the Modern Orthodox community the problem of *agunot* had been largely solved by prenuptial agreements the New York State Gett Laws and synagogue sanctions imposed on recalcitrant husbands. To prove his point that the *agunot* were not a major problem for the Modern Orthodox community, Berman asked the audience of 2000 people how many of them, mostly members of Modern Orthodox congregations, knew an *agunah*. Fully one-third to one-half of the audience raised their hands. When so many hands went up, Berman seemed taken aback and flustered for a few moments, but he did not retract his statement that the *agunah* problem had been largely solved in Modern Orthodoxy.

Berman's position vis-à-vis the Rackman-Morgenstern *beit din* was unclear for while he had identified himself as a critic of the *beit din* at the beginning of his remarks, he had also called for supporting the *beit din*. In the months following the conference, however, Berman openly expressed his opposition to the Rackman *beit din*, saying it was very painful for him to take this public position against Rackman.

## *Battling for the* Beit Din's *Survival*

Criticism of the new *beit din* intensified. It seemed like the session about the *beit din* at the Second Feminism and Orthodoxy Conference triggered a new wave of condemnation. The Beth Din of America (BDA) issued a lengthy letter, signed by Rabbis Michael Broyde, Mordechai Willig and Yona Reiss, arguing that, contrary to Rackman, abandonment, cruelty or addiction discovered after the marriage "cannot possibly be grounds to annul a marriage." Broyde was the administrator of the BDA at that time though he was later ousted from the BDA for questionable conduct. The Agudath Israel of America (Aguda) and the National Council of Young Israel declared that the Rackman-Morgenstern *beit din* was outside the bounds of *halakhah* and warned that it would lead to the birth of *mamzerim*, bastards. An Aguda spokesman said that women who remarry after being freed by Rackman commit "a terrible sin." Again there were calls for Rackman and Morgenstern to publicly explain their *halakhic* arguments.

Honey and Susan felt that the ongoing delegitimization of the Rackman-Morgenstern *beit din* made it imperative that the *beit din*'s *halakhic* underpinnings be published in a formal document making the case for the *halakhic* validity of the *beit din*'s decisions.

For several months after the Second Feminism and Orthodoxy Conference, Susan and Honey tried to recruit a rabbi to write up *halakhic* sources supporting the *beit din*'s approach. One Israeli rabbi said he would do the work but would not put his name on the document. Rabbi Saul Berman said more research and publication of relevant *halakhic* sources were necessary but declined to assist in such research and turned down a request to suggest either young or seasoned rabbinic scholars to help in this endeavor. In the meantime, critics kept charging that the *beit din* hadn't published its *halakhic* sources though Rackman had elaborated them in numerous speeches and articles.

In the midst of this storm of criticism, Rabbi Rackman asked Susan to write up a short summary of the *beit din*'s procedures. As Susan wrote, her short summary evolved into the most comprehensive and annotated statement yet of the *beit din*'s *halakhic* principles and procedures. Rackman added a few lines of text and suggested some "bullet" points and wanted the document published as a two-page ad in *The Jewish Week*. Susan reworked the piece into its final form, which was published on August 28, 1998, as a centerfold ad in *The Jewish Week*, entitled "Principles and Procedures for Freeing Agunot." Finally a document (dubbed the "Principles") had been published that encapsulated the systemic *halakhic* solutions that Agunah Int'l had worked toward for so long.

The "Principles" held that *batei din* can free *agunot* on the basis of *kiddushei ta'ut* (*ta'ut* for short), a *halakhic* concept, which means that the betrothal was in error—a fundamental mistake or misperception existed at the time of the wedding. A finding of *ta'ut* by a *beit din* means the couple, though they had lived together, were never *halakhically* married and, therefore, there is no need for a *gett*. In such a situation, a *beit din* can issue a *p'tur*, a release document, which declares that a woman is single and free to remarry.

The "Principles" defined three categories of *ta'ut*, errors, that void the marriage without the need for a *gett*. All of them, *Ta'ut* I, II, and III revolve around demonstrating that the bride was misled at the time of the wedding and that, therefore, her consent to marry was never binding.

*Ta'ut* I is the voiding of the marriage on the grounds that a salient defect in one party, in this case the groom, was not disclosed at the time of the wedding. There is established precedent in rabbinic literature for declaring a marriage void *ab initio* when after marrying, a bride learns that her groom was, at the time of the marriage, a homosexual, impotent, insane, epileptic or an apostate. The rabbis declare that these defects are so serious that one can assume that had they been known to the bride, she would not have consented to the marriage. The "Principles" expanded this notion of what amounts to a serious defect, and held that domestic violence, adultery, abandonment, criminal activity, substance abuse and sadism were deviant behaviors that were rooted in the groom's personality at the time of the marriage but were unknown to the bride. These defects were deemed categorically unacceptable in marriage so that a wife may legitimately testify that she was misled about her groom's true nature and never would have married him had she known the truth.

*Ta'ut* II and III maintained that brides are unaware that the wedding ceremony grants *kinyan*, legal title, of their sexuality to their husbands and that this ownership endures no matter how abusive the husband may be. Rabbis cannot free her from this ownership. *Ta'ut* II and III hold that the marriage transaction is void *ab initio* because the bride had no intention of consenting to deliver herself into such a form of subjugation. *Ta'ut* II and III were more comprehensive than *Ta'ut* I since they did not require that the husband have a disorder that pre-existed the marriage. Even without proving pre-existence, *Ta'ut* II and III postulated that, as a rule, a woman would not knowingly agree to a marriage that is a form of bondage to an abusive, menacing spouse.

With the publication of the *halakhic* underpinnings of the Rackman-

Morgenstern *beit din* in the "Principles," critics shifted their attacks from saying that the *beit din* hadn't published its *halakhic* sources to saying that the *beit din* misinterpreted *halakhah*. They accused the *beit din* of defining *halakhic* marriage out of existence as the "Principles" might allow any *agunah* who was a victim of domestic violence to attain her freedom. To the *beit din*'s critics, declaring that domestic violence in and of itself was grounds for invalidating a marriage undermined the legal structure of Jewish marriage.

David Zweibel, general counsel of the Agudath Israel of America, quipped that Agunah Int'l should change its name to "Abolish Jewish Marriage Inc." Other critics argued that there are women who agree to marry violent men and that, therefore, an *agunah*'s testimony that she would have rejected her groom had she known he was violent is questionable. Rackman and Susan teamed up to write a rebuttal in *The Jewish Week*. The battle raged on and on, even spilling into the pages of *The New York Times*. Lay people were supportive and excited at the prospect of the Rackman-Morgenstern *beit din* finally bringing justice to *agunot*. But it was critical to attain greater rabbinic acceptance so that there would be more and more communities where newly freed women could remarry and raise families in an Orthodox environment.

## *Morgenstern Starts His Own* Beit Din

Not long after the publication of the "Principles," a British journalist questioned Morgenstern about it. In response, Morgenstern declared that he "doesn't agree with everything Susan Aranoff wrote." Several months later, Morgenstern wrote a letter to the editor of *The Jewish Week* asserting emphatically that the "Principles" ad "does not represent the principles and procedures that we (the *beit din*) use." Following the letter, Morgenstern broke away from Rackman and set up his own *beit din*.

When asked about why other rabbis opposed his *beit din*, Morgenstern would reply that those rabbis were worried about losing the fat fees they earned for adjudicating *gett* cases. He remarked that the rabbis' refusal to free *agunot* wouldn't stop these women from having sex, touching on an issue that was never publicly mentioned in the reserved Orthodox community though the rabbinic literature seems well aware of this eventuality. Morgenstern's rapid annulment of 20 marriages during a two-day session in Jerusalem in July 1998 caused a furor, leading Israel's chief rabbinate to denounce him. Likewise, Morgenstern evoked a denunciation from then British Chief Rabbi Jonathan Sacks when he performed annulments for Israeli women who met with him in London in 1999 and then officiated in London at the marriage of one of the women. But Morgenstern still had his champions. The Orthodox Israeli author and journalist Naomi Ragen called him "brilliant and heroic."

Morgenstern took more flak when word got out that years ago he had withheld a *gett* from his first wife for seven years. When challenged about this, Morgenstern said that he had come to realize what a terrible thing he had done and was now, through his work with *agunot*, trying to do *teshuvah*, to repent for that misdeed. (Susan noted the coincidence that the Hebrew word for the responsa Morgenstern was writing to free *agunot* is the same as the word for repentance—*teshuvah*.) Some of the rabbis Morgenstern worked with also aroused some notoriety. One of these was Rabbi Moshe (Marvin) Antelman, who had spoken at one of our conferences, and was head of a *beit din* that had freed Israeli *agunot*. Antelman had caused a stir with a bizarre invention of bullets containing pork, as a method of deterring Muslim terrorists who would fear being barred from the afterlife because of the forbidden bits of pig that might remain in their flesh.

Despite all the notoriety and attacks on Morgenstern, Susan and Honey were sorry that his role in the Rackman-Morgenstern *beit din* did not end on a better note. Morgenstern had been a trailblazer and took on the Orthodox rabbinate for their failure to help *agunot*. He had produced prodigious *halakhic* sources in support of his *gett zikkui* and other approaches to freeing *agunot*. Susan and Honey wrote a letter to *The Jewish Week* praising his dedication to the cause of *agunot*.

Rabbi Asher Murciano of Queens, a member of the Rackman-Morgenstern *beit din*, decided to continue serving with Rackman. Rabbi Eugene Cohen completed the panel of three rabbis necessary for a *beit din*. Rabbi Sidney Green also served for a while but left the *beit din* when he moved out of New York City. Estelle Freilich contacted the late Rabbi Haim Henry Toledano, who was a member of her synagogue. After observing the *beit din*, Rabbi Toledano decided to join. An outstanding scholar, Toledano was a valuable addition to the *beit din*. As it turned out, Murciano and Toledano, both born in Morocco, had been friends and colleagues for decades. As attacks on the *halakhic* legitimacy of the Rackman *beit din* continued, Toledano wrote an eloquent *teshuvah*, posted on Agunah Int'l's website, laying out the *halakhic* sources and reasoning of the *beit din*. The new *beit din* was renamed the Beit Din L'Inyenei Agunot and convened approximately once a month in the conference room of the law firm of Gottlieb, Rackman and Reisman where Rabbi Rackman's son Michael, Honey's husband, was a partner. As before, two or three cases were scheduled for each session.

## *The New Rackman* Beit Din *Labors On*

Prior to each *beit din* session, the case histories were researched by Agunah Int'l. When possible, Agunah Int'l contacted the recalcitrant husband to get his side of the story and invited him to appear at the *beit din*. Without exception, the husbands refused to appear, declared they would never give the *gett* or would do so only if the *agunah* capitulated to their demands. These men spewed foul language and threatened Agunah Int'l and the *beit din*.

On the day of a *beit din* session, the *agunot* waited their turn in the law firm's reception area, where Honey, Estelle or Susan would give them a quick description of what to expect once they entered the conference room to plead their case for release. Once the *agunah* entered and was seated in the conference room, along with the usual coterie of relatives or friends, Estelle would begin taping the session, recording the name of the case and the names of those rabbis and Agunah Int'l directors present. Estelle or Susan would then read the case history aloud and distribute supporting documents after telling the *agunah* that she could interrupt with clarifications or corrections and that the rabbis would then ask her questions.

Hearing the narrative of their own ordeal read aloud was traumatic for the *agunot*. The rabbis and directors of Agunah Int'l asked the necessary questions with as much sensitivity as possible. The questions dealt with the most personal and intimate matters and inevitably opened up old wounds.

Often the *agunot* told not only of the pain their husbands had inflicted on them and their children, but also of the toll the suffering had taken on their parents. One Israeli *agunah* recounted that her ailing father's one prayer had been to see her free before he died. His wish was not granted, and her mother was now holding the same vigil. The *agunah* expressed her fear that, as with her father, the grief her mother was suffering would drive her to an early grave.

After all the questions had been asked and answered, the *agunah* would leave the room so that her case could be discussed and adjudicated. Honey, Susan and Estelle participated in the discussion of the case, pointing out key aspects of the case narrative, adding relevant insights from domestic violence research, as well as citing *halakhic* bases that supported the *agunah*'s pleas for freedom. In every case it was decided that there were *halakhic* grounds for freeing the *agunah*. Critics faulted the *beit din* for this 100 percent record of freeing *agunot* as if this record was prima facie evidence against the validity of the *beit din*'s decisions. But each and every *agunah* that turned to the *beit din* was chained to a man whose intolerable conduct throughout the marriage warranted terminating the marriage.

In a handful of cases the rabbis decided that they needed more information, and the decision was delayed. Once the decision was reached, Rabbi Toledano would take out one of two forms for the *p'tur*, the document releasing the *agunah* from her marriage. One *p'tur* was used when the reason for voiding the marriage was *kiddushei ta'ut I*, a marriage created based on a mistake in that the groom had a serious concealed defect at the time of the marriage or because there had been technical *halakhic* errors made in the marriage ceremony, such as invalid witnesses.

The second *p'tur*, an annulment *meekamah te'amim* (based on a variety of grounds), was used when the grounds for invalidating the marriage were not only *Ta'ut I*, an unknown pre-existing defect in the groom, but also *Ta'ut II* and *III*, intolerable post-marital conduct by the husband such that a *beit din* can assume the bride had no intention of agreeing to a *kinyan* marriage which chained her to her husband despite his unspeakable conduct. In one such case, the wife-beating husband and his brother had criminal records and were being sought by police for gunning down someone in broad daylight on the streets of Manhattan. The *agunah* feared for her life. Some time after this *beit din* session, the TV series *Law and Order* ran an episode about an *agunah* chained to a gun-toting fugitive criminal, a story line probably picked up from the news reports and police records about this case.

After Toledano filled in the names and dates, the *p'tur* was passed around for each rabbi to sign. The directors of Agunah Int'l did not sign the *p'tur*. Estelle, Honey or Susan would go out to tell the *agunah* the good news. Many *agunot* asked to return to the conference room to thank the rabbis for their compassion, all the while knowing that the rabbis in their own communities, who had left them in chains, might not acknowledge the annulment as valid.

## *The Attacks Turn Uglier*

The Orthodox rabbinic establishment heaped criticism on Rackman, but he was undeterred. He declared that the *agunah* issue was his "last battle." Despite the Orthodox rabbinate's unremitting criticism of the *beit din*, women kept appealing to the *beit din* for relief. The rabbinic opposition to the Rackman *beit din* took an ugly turn when it became apparent that Rackman would not desist. Instead of directing their attacks against Rackman's interpretation of *halakhah*, the rabbis shifted to ad hominem attacks against him.

Orthodox rabbis barred Rackman from speaking at their synagogues though they refrained from publicizing this policy. On one evening, Rabbi Michael Broyde, at that point still the administrator of the BDA and a staunch critic of the Rackman *beit din*, was speaking at Rabbi Haskel Lookstein's Manhattan Congregation Kehillath Jeshurun (KJ) about the *agunah* problem. Rackman requested an opportunity to participate to present his position but was turned down. Susan had written a pamphlet responding to the BDA's criticisms of the Rackman *beit din*, and Rackman asked her to distribute it outside KJ after the program. Estelle accompanied Susan, and each of them covered one of the exits from the synagogue offering the pamphlet to people exiting.

Most people rushed by without taking the pamphlet. Then Susan got the idea of saying, "Rabbi Rackman asked me to distribute this." At the mention of the respected Rabbi Rackman's name, people stopped and took the pamphlet. Suddenly an officer of the synagogue confronted Susan, angrily asking her why she was handing out literature. Susan replied that Rabbi Rackman was barred from speaking at KJ and wanted people to know his response to Rabbi Broyde's criticisms. The man became enraged and called Susan a liar, insisting that it wasn't possible that Rackman was barred from speaking at KJ. At that very moment Lookstein came out of the synagogue. Susan quickly suggested that they ask Lookstein to settle the argument. Lookstein, looking uncomfortable, confirmed what Susan had said and added in Hebrew "*Zeh lo lefi k'vodo*." It wouldn't be the honorable, respectful thing to let Rabbi Rackman speak. A look of shock and disbelief came over the man's face, and he turned on his heel and dashed away.

A whispering campaign began that Rackman, entering his 10th decade, was no longer in full possession of his faculties. Another version was that he had fallen under the undue influence of his daughter-in-law Honey. All of this was false. Rackman was as sharp as ever and had advocated similar bold *halakhic* solutions based on *ta'ut* as far back as the 1950s.

A further disappointment was the failure of the Jewish Orthodox Feminist Alliance (JOFA) to issue a statement of support for the Rackman *beit din*. Susan and Honey, both board members of JOFA, had spoken to other board members and felt that many of them might have voted for a statement of support, but the question was never brought up for a vote. JOFA became reticent about having Susan speak at their conferences. One board member told Susan that she should not have written the *beit din*'s "Principles." "A man should have written it," she said.

All this indicated to Susan and Honey that the JOFA leadership was uneasy regarding the Rackman *beit din* and Agunah Int'l. Perhaps JOFA's leadership felt their organization was not qualified to take a stand in the *halakhic* disputes surrounding the Rackman *beit din*'s rulings. Perhaps they felt that an endorsement by the fledgling JOFA would do little to help Rackman but could create damaging controversy around JOFA, which was still in the early stages of establishing itself and pursuing its own broader mission within the Orthodox community.

Support from JOFA would not have carried the day for the Rackman *beit din*, but in the absence of such support, Susan and Honey often heard "Look, not even the Orthodox feminists at JOFA support the *beit din*." Over time, Susan found herself welcome again as a speaker at JOFA conferences, but JOFA never issued a statement of support for the Rackman *beit din*.

In 2004, Professor Aviad Hacohen of Bar Ilan University in Israel, where Rackman was chancellor, produced a volume which collected and analyzed *halakhic* sources for solutions to the *agunah* problem. Blu Greenberg edited the English version of Hacohen's book, entitled *The Tears of the Oppressed*. Rabbi Toledano worked with Greenberg on editing the manuscript. In a brief afterword in the book, Rabbi Rackman made a poignant appeal, calling on those who advocate *halakhic* stringency with regard to *agunot* to choose leniency instead. Rackman quoted Rabbi Binyamin Aaron Skolnik (Poland, 17th century), who wrote that while stringent rulings are appropriate regarding other matters in which rabbis have doubts "...in matters of *iggun* ... I follow a well-beaten path of ancient and modern shepherds who searched with all their might for ways and byways to be lenient in the matter of an *agunah* wife."

In October 2004, a reception was held in New York to mark the publication of *The Tears of the Oppressed*. In December 2004, the book was reviewed in the journal *Edah* (volume 4:2—Kislev 5765) by Rabbi Michael Broyde, who vigorously attacked *Tears* as "an unsuccessful defense of the Rackman *beit din*." *Edah* published responses from Hacohen, Toledano, Susan and Susan Weiss. The *Tears* volume was a valuable collection of *halakhic* sources, but the key sources supporting the Rackman *beit din* were well-known and had been cited in the "Principles" and by members of the *beit din* and dismissed by the Orthodox rabbinic establishment. *Tears* had no discernible impact on the *agunah* situation nor on the embattled status of the Rackman *beit din*.

About five years later, Professor Bernard Jackson, a scholar on the faculty of the University of Manchester, England, who had written extensively on Jewish law, began publishing an exhaustive collection of *halakhic* sources relevant to freeing *agunot*. His truly encyclopedic effort received the usual reception from the Orthodox rabbinic establishment—criticism, rejection and then silence.

## *Time Runs Out for the Rackman* Beit Din

Despite the unremitting attacks, women continued to stream to the *beit din*. Agunah Int'l always explained that the Rackman *beit din p'tur* was not accepted by the vast majority of Orthodox rabbis, but the women sought closure, release from their tormentor husbands even if other rabbis rejected this solution.

Eventually the Orthodox rabbinic establishment began to ignore the Rackman *Beit Din*. It seemed that they had decided that time would accomplish what they could not, the disappearance of the *beit din*. After all, Rackman was past 90. None of the other *beit din* rabbis were young, so time was on the side of the Orthodox rabbinate. In 2008 Rabbi Rackman passed away at the age of 98 after a gradual decline in health. Rabbi Cohen, in his 90s and Rabbis Toledano and Murciano, also up in years, could not bear the burden of leading the *beit din*.

The Rackman and Morgenstern *batei din* had offered *agunot* a ray of hope. Hundreds of women had knocked on the *batei din*'s doors and been freed. Deprived of Rackman's prestige and stature in the Modern Orthodox world, the *beit din* would be even more marginalized, so it ceased operating. Calls and emails continued to come in, but we had to inform the *agunot* that the relief that the Rackman *beit din* had provided was no longer available.

The Rackman *beit din* has disappeared from the scene, but its memory lives on. At the 2013 Tikvah/JOFA Agunah Summit held at New York University, the Rackman *beit din* was invoked as a prototype for a new *beit din* to address the *agunah* disaster. At the Summit, Rabbi David Bigman of Israel called for the establishment of a *beit din* similar to Rackman's. He suggested that easier cases like those involving domestic violence be tackled first. Bigman's suggestion was seconded by Rabbi Asher Lopatin of New York's Chovevei Tora Yeshiva, who passionately called for a "supercharged" Rackman *beit din*.

From the floor of the Summit conference, Susan praised the calls for a new Rackman-like *beit din*. She noted that the overwhelming majority, perhaps over 90 percent, of *agunah* cases involve domestic violence but questioned Bigman's characterizing these cases as the "easier ones" in light of the fact that the Orthodox rabbinate has consistently refused to free such women, and the BDA explicitly declared that cruelty after marriage cannot possibly be grounds for annulling a marriage. Susan urged the rabbis not to be deterred by the fact that they are in the minority. Even if only 15 percent of the Orthodox community accepts the new *beit din*, that would be enough of a community for freed *agunot* to find spouses and bring up a family. For *agunot* marriage to a member of the 15 percent is infinitely better than the current absolute bar to their remarriage.

A few months after the Agunah Summit, Rabbi Simcha Krauss of Israel, formerly of Queens, New York, announced that he was in the process of setting up a new international *beit din* that was committed to finding a systemic solution to the *agunah* problem and would leave "no door unopened" in the quest to free *agunot*. The announcement caused a flurry of coverage in Jewish newspapers just as the announcement of the Rackman *beit din* had. Krauss said that he had consulted with and had the support of the widely respected Israeli *Haredi* Rabbi Zalman Nechemiah Goldberg. The initial excitement about Krauss's plans subsided as various dates for his *beit din*'s inauguration passed. But the new *beit din* is moving forward and may yet revive and bring to fruition the hopes first ignited by the Rackman *beit din*.

# Conclusion

We have traveled a very long, difficult road, diverged at a crossroad, and converged again, but after thirty years, we have yet to reach our destination, the end of the *agunah* plague. Along the way we met heroic people—brave *agunot*, supporters who stood by them and called for justice but also rogues, some of whom exploited this tragedy for personal benefit. We have been disappointed that more of the Orthodox community did not join us on this journey but rather stood on the sidelines, sometimes cheering us on but often losing interest and leaving us rather alone in the field.

The *agunot* we worked with were strong and courageous figures, fighting for their freedom and to protect their children from the injustices meted out by their husbands and *batei din*. Many *agunot* bore the additional burden of shielding elderly or frail parents. The *agunot*'s commitment to Orthodox Judaism was put to the test, for it was their piety that prevented them from simply walking away after their civil divorce and beginning a new life without a *gett*. Before turning to Agunah Inc. for help, many *agunot* fought alone as their rabbis and communities did little to help them. For some *agunot*, reaching out to Agunah Inc. for help was in itself an act of bravery because their rabbis had admonished them not to contact us. These women were abused and isolated by both their husbands and their rabbis, but they mustered the strength and courage to fight the abuse.

This book has recounted the disturbing record of the Orthodox rabbinate with regard to *agunot*—denying the problem, serving as recalcitrant husbands' agents for extortion, covering up pedophilia, awarding unsupervised visitation to unfit fathers, sending wives back to abusive husbands, overselling the protection provided by prenuptial agreements and civil laws against *gett* abuse, issuing *heterim*—waivers, allowing men to remarry without giving their wives a *gett*—and failing to use remedies available within Jewish law to free *agunot*.

Alongside the rabbis is the rogues' gallery of lay people who backed recalcitrant husbands in their efforts to torment and extort their wives. Family and friends of the recalcitrants often supported their refusal to give the *gett*. Relatives spit upon and threatened us. Thugs punched and pushed us and other demonstrators. There were those who stealthily posted placards in our neighborhood declaring that we were worthy of a death sentence and should be killed on sight, and our phones often rang late at night with callers threatening retribution. There were the angry and vociferous men who, styling themselves as a fathers' rights group, advocated for men's rights to use the *gett* as a bargaining chip, to betroth their minor daughters and take concubines or second wives to satisfy their sexual desires while they withheld a *gett* from their wives.

Yet there were rabbis who acted honorably and courageously and deserve to be praised: Rabbi Moshe Morgenstern, who spearheaded the first *beit din* in New York devoted to applying all available *halakhic* solutions to help *agunot*; Rabbi Emanuel Rackman and his colleagues on his groundbreaking *beit din*— Rabbis Eugene Cohen, Haim Henry Toledano, Asher Murciano, and Sidney Green; Rabbi Irwin Haut, Esquire, who counseled numerous *agunot* and wrote extensively on the issue; Rabbi Sholom Klass, who joined Rackman, Morgenstern and Haut in freeing the first three *agunot* who came to Morgenstern's *beit din* and who used the pages of his newspaper *The Jewish Press* to advocate for *agunot* as did his daughter Naomi Mauer; Rabbi Louis Bernstein, and Rabbi Yitzchak Sladowsky, both of whom publicly admitted that they had been wrong and remiss in their attitude toward and efforts to help *agunot* and fulfilled a pledge to do more; Rabbi Simcha Krauss, who defended the 1992 New York State Gett Law designed to help *agunot* and took it upon himself in 2014 to establish an international *beit din* to help *agunot*; Rabbi Gedalia Dov Schwartz, who is quietly and compassionately applying *halakhah* to free *agunot* despite their husbands' refusal to issue a *gett*; Rabbi Moshe Antelman, who advocated and used groundbreaking *halakhic* approaches for freeing *agunot;* the unnamed rabbi who advised an *agunah* to get an order of protection rather than rely on the *beit din* to protect her and a few rabbis who attended and helped organize demonstrations in support of *agunot* in their communities.

Family members of *agunot* were also a critical part of the struggle. Mothers and fathers, sisters and brothers, grandparents, aunts and uncles, all provided emotional and financial support to *agunot*. In numerous cases they tirelessly devoted themselves to organizing demonstrations and other pressure tactics to secure the *gett*.

There were sympathetic members of the community who played pivotal roles in freeing *agunot*. There was Izzy, who posted leaflets exposing the fact that Rabbi Fox was supporting his son's withholding of the *gett*. Numerous rabbis that were approached for help in this case feared Rabbi Fox, but Izzy was undaunted and even waited outside the "Beit Din That Couldn't" in frigid winter weather until he was assured that Fox's son had given the *gett*. There was the philanthropist who used her influence to threaten the job of a rabbi who was supporting a recalcitrant husband and who generously funded a costly centerfold ad in *The Jewish Week* to raise the consciousness of the community regarding the *agunah* scourge. In the case of the "Recalcitrant Rabbi," the *zabla beit din*, which included two revered rabbis, betrayed the *agunah* and reduced her and her children to abject poverty, but the wife of one of those revered rabbis intervened in the proceedings and demanded that the rabbis not accede to depriving the *agunah* of the last few dollars that remained in her possession. Nor should we forget the quietly sympathetic *rebbetzin* who promised to urge her frail, ill husband to do what he could to secure a *gett*. And, of course, there were the friends and sympathetic strangers who turned up to picket the recalcitrant husbands.

Among public figures, Judge William Rigler of the New York State Supreme Court deserves praise for making law with his *Schwartz v. Schwartz* decision that formed the basis for the 1992 New York State Gett Law II, which potentially offers assistance to some *agunot*. The recently disgraced New York politician Sheldon Silver and COLPA deserve credit for coordinating a successful effort to push Gett Law II through the Albany legislature onto the desk of New York Gov. Mario Cuomo, who signed it into law.

Divorce has painful consequences for all, especially children. Where there is hope of rescuing a marriage, counseling and, perhaps, a waiting period are in order, but an abusive spouse should not be able to keep the other imprisoned in a marriage that is clearly beyond repair. Where there is abuse, the wife must be freed.

The friction, the opportunities for revenge and extortion surrounding the *gett* exacerbate the tension surrounding troubled marriages and bitter divorces. The *gett* becomes a weapon in the hands of men already disposed toward domestic violence. In so many cases, *agunot* told us that their abusive husbands threatened them with some version of, "You will never leave me because I will never give you a *gett*. You will be alone for the rest of your life." In many cases, this threat to withhold the *gett* caused women to stay longer in abusive marriages to the detriment of their physical and emotional health and that of their children. When those marriages that must end finally do, the angry struggle over the *gett* raises the already high degree of hostility to levels deeply damaging to the spouses as well as their children.

The damage done by the *gett* scandal is not only the human suffering of the *agunot* and their children and families recounted in this book. The damage to and weakening of the Jewish community extends far beyond that. Some *agunot*, whose stories we will never know, withdraw from the struggle and are lost entirely to the Jewish community. The injustices done to *agunot* drive others away from Judaism. In Israel, where only Orthodox marriage and divorce are available, data show that thousands of couples opt for a domestic partnership or a civil ceremony abroad to avoid marrying under the Israeli rabbinate's auspices. Valuable Jewish communal resources—money and time—are diverted from the poor and infirm and from underfunded educational and cultural institutions to bribing husbands and financing *agunah* advocacy and dysfunctional *batei din*.

As for outsiders, the scandal and injustice of *agunah* abuse is there for all to see in divorce courts where judges hear Orthodox women plead for justice and seek redress under civil law, in criminal courts as in the Zitrenbaum case and the arrest of Mendel Epstein and his collaborators, in the streets where demonstrations take place against recalcitrant husbands, on billboards, the internet, radio and television and in newspapers which recount the plight of *agunot*. Judaism's moral fabric and reputation is damaged by this festering disgrace.

Regrettably, after more than thirty years of jousting with *batei din* and fighting for reform, we must still say to women, loud and clear, "Stay away from Orthodox *batei din*." The all-male system, staffed by rabbis whose mindset is conditioned by the patriarchal bent of Orthodox family law and who fear criticism for courageous *halakhic* rulings, cannot yield justice for women and children. Rabbis admit that the treatment of *agunot* is cruel and immoral but say that they are constrained from helping these women by the dictates of Judaism's God-given laws of marriage and divorce. In light of this, civil legislators and courts must reconsider whether the financial, custody and visitation rulings of rabbinical courts should be given any weight in civil court.

The power of religion for both bad and good comes through in the stories we have told. The bad is obvious: the suffering inflicted on women and children in the name of upholding religious law. The good is harder to discern. But it is embodied in the tremendous strength and spirit that the *agunot* marshaled to challenge the system and in their refusal to abandon the tradition that they loved and honored despite the rabbinic malfeasance they encountered. True, it was the piety of the *agunot* and their obedience to *halakhah* that kept them in chains. But these women would not allow the malfeasance of the rabbis to deprive them of the beauties of the Orthodox way of life that they loved: the sacred and uplifting Sabbath, the joy and spiritual message of the holidays, the close family ties, the prizing of compassion, justice, charity, learning and modest ways, the schools that passed on to their children this tradition that they treasured. These women held tight to what they cherished, spoke truth to the powers that be and demanded justice though their demands fell on closed ears, for the most part. The courage and resourcefulness of the *agunot* and their families is a powerful counterpoint to the passivity and culpability of the rabbis in the face of injustice. This sorry record of rabbis and *batei din*, this perpetration of injustice in the name of religion is a cautionary tale against legitimizing clerical courts of any religion through official recognition or enforcement by civil authorities.

We have done all that we can in this three-decades-long struggle. When we began, we thought that raising the rabbis' awareness of the dimensions and severity of the *agunah* problem would spur them into action. When we realized that this was hopeless, we thought that mobilizing community pressure on the rabbis would bring change. That too, we discovered, was a misconception. We did succeed in putting *agunah* on the Orthodox community's agenda. We believe our *agunah* advocacy deserves credit for the adoption of religious prenuptial agreements to protect women. Though of limited value, these prenuptials are better than nothing. The marketing of these prenuptials as a comprehensive solution, however, deludes the community into thinking that *agunah* problem is solved, which, sadly, is untrue.

The establishment of the Rackman *beit din*, which offered a comprehensive systemic solution that would finally put an end to the *agunah* tragedy, was an outgrowth of our labors. Unfortunately, the Orthodox rabbinate and community failed to rally in support of Rackman. Susan and Estelle Freilich have been working quietly with Rabbi Gedalia Dov Schwartz, who has applied *halakhic* remedies to free numerous *agunot*. His approach must be more widely publicized and institutionalized in order to reach the countless *agunot* seeking relief. But with publicity comes the threat of condemnation that could smother his work though he staunchly believes that his rulings are firmly rooted in *halakhah*. Because of our reluctance to publicize Schwartz's work until now, we fear that many *agunot* who might have been freed by him remained trapped. Therefore, after 30 years, we must acknowledge that the changes we have seen are far too little and far too late. Another generation of Orthodox Jewish women are at risk of becoming *agunot*.

There are, however, some glimmers of hope. Though the Rackman *beit din* failed to gain traction, it may have paved the way for the success of the new *beit din* established by Rabbi Simcha Krauss. Has the shame of the *agunah* disgrace at long last emboldened Rabbi Krauss and his associates to implement a real systemic solution, or will the new *beit din* be overly cautious out of fear of attack from right-wing Orthodoxy? Perhaps Rabbi Schwartz will join forces with Krauss.

Other glimmers of hope: In 2014, it was reported that a panel of three rabbis in Israel voided the marriage of a woman whose husband had abandoned her after only two days. The rabbis declared that his quick abandonment of his wife indicated that he was never truly committed to the marriage. This was a breakthrough ruling; in similar cases over the centuries, rabbis have maintained that the only solution is to search for the missing husband and induce him to give a *gett*, a quest which could take years or fail completely. Also in 2014, it was reported that a rabbinical court in Safed, Israel, freed a 34-year-old woman who had been an *agunah* for seven years since the time her husband had lapsed into a coma. According to newspaper accounts, the rabbis reasoned that it was a *zikkui*, a benefit, to the husband to free his wife under the circumstances. The *beit din* could, therefore, step in and issue a *gett* for the benefit of the incapacitated husband. This ruling, if true, is major progress in that prior to this, women whose husbands became incapacitated were generally considered doomed to be *agunot* until their husbands' death freed them or a wondrous recovery occurred. The *gett zikkui* was used and strongly advocated as a systemic solution by Rabbis Moshe Morgenstern and Marvin Antelman; it is encouraging to see this approach gaining needed support.

Perhaps our work and the work of so many other dedicated *agunah* activists is finally gaining enough momentum to bring about meaningful change. If so, it is a tribute to the courage of *agunot* and to late and beloved colleagues Rivka Haut, Honey Rackman and Henni Goldstein, none of whom lived to see this book completed, to the many other *agunah* activists, all of whom worked with such dedication to right this wrong, and to Rabbis Emanuel Rackman and Moshe Morgenstern who bravely led the way. If a systemic solution to the *agunah* problem is at hand, this book will be a history of a hard-won victory for justice against cruelty to women in the name of religion.

If, on the other hand, the *agunah* calamity drags on, if Rabbi Krauss's efforts suffer the same fate as the Rackman *beit din*, we hope that the pages of this book will carry on the struggle that we began. The Midrash retold in the Preface of this book describes how the cry of one lone, anguished woman of Sodom was sufficient to bring God down from the heavens to do justice. So too, perhaps, may the collective voices of the *agunot* in this book and the thousands of *agunot* they represent eventually move the Orthodox rabbinate and community to emulate God and bring justice to these women. In the meantime, pious *agunot* pay the high price of loneliness and childlessness.

# Glossary

(Y) indicates that the word is Yiddish. All other non-English entries are Hebrew or Aramaic.

**Aginut**—The state of being an *agunah*.

**Aguda**—See **Agudath Israel of America**.

**Agudath Israel of America**—A *Haredi* Jewish communal organization in the United States.

**Agunah** *pl.* **Agunot**—Literally, "an anchored or chained woman." A woman tied to a dead marriage because her husband is missing, unwilling, incapacitated or otherwise unable to release her by granting a *gett*.

**Aliyah** *pl.* **Aliyot**—Literally, "an ascension, going up." The honor of being called up to the *bimah* (reading platform) in a synagogue to utter blessings over the reading of a segment of the Torah.

**Arkaot**—Non-Jewish courts.

**Bais Medrash** (Y)—Beit Midrash in Hebrew. A study hall in a synagogue or yeshiva. Usually a simply furnished room with study tables and shelves of Talmud volumes and other rabbinic texts.

**BDA**—See **Beth Din of America**.

**Beit Din** *pl.* **Batei Din**—Literally, "a house of judgment." A rabbinical court is typically comprised of male judges that can, theoretically, include one layperson, three judges in divorce matters. The number of judges may exceed three but should always have an odd number of judges to avoid tie votes.

**Beth Din of America**—The rabbinical court associated with the Modern Orthodox community though individuals from any segment of the Jewish community may put matters before it. In recent years some of its rabbis might be categorized as being to the right of Modern Orthodoxy. Located in Manhattan.

**Borer** *pl.* **Borerim**—Literally, "an arbitrator." A rabbinic court judge serving on an ad hoc judicial panel known as *zabla*. (See below)

**Brachah**—A blessing.

**BT**—Babylonian Talmud.

**Choson** (Y)—The groom. See **Tish** for **Choson's Tish**

**Chuppah**—The wedding canopy.

**Chutzpa** (Y)—Audacity, gumption.

**COLPA**—The National Jewish Commission on Law and Public Affairs, a group of lawyers, social scientists, academics and others committed to advocating in the legal arena for the rights and interests of individual Jews and the Jewish community.

**Daven; Davening** (Y)—To pray; praying or the prayer service.

**Din Torah**—Literally, the law of the Torah. Used to refer to a *beit din* hearing(s) during which each litigant presents their side of a dispute and in which the rabbinic judges deliberate and render a decision.

**Dinei Mamonos** (Y) Dinei Mamanot in Hebrew—Halakhic laws or litigation concerning monetary matters.

**Erusin**—Betrothal. More than becoming engaged. A woman requires a *gett* to be free from betrothal even if the couple has not yet co-habitated.

**Ezras Torah**—Founded in 1915 by Orthodox rabbis with original name of Torah Relief Society, it originally provided aid to European Jews through town rabbis and yeshivas during the turbulent years of World War I. It now focuses its assistance on *Haredi* Jews in Israel.

**The Forward**—Full name *The Jewish Daily Forward*. A left-leaning newspapers founded in 1897 as a Yiddish-language daily. The English language weekly version was launched in 1990 as Yiddish readership dwindled. There is still a Yiddish language weekly, but the English edition, which written and edited independent of the Yiddish edition, is far more prominent.

**Frum**—Strictly complying with religious law.

**GET Organization**—A Brooklyn based *agunah* advocacy organization founded in the early 1980s whose name stands for Getting Equal Treatment.

**Gett** *pl.* **Gittin** –A bill of divorce—literally, "a bill of manumission"—delivered by husband to wife. A wife may petition a *beit din* to obligate her husband or pressure him to divorce her, but she cannot issue a bill of divorce to her husband. (He releases her from her bondage to him. He is not bound to her in the first instance.) Rabbinic law stipulates that the husband must willingly grant the *gett*. Until a rabbinic decree in the tenth century a wife could be divorced against her will. After that, her agreement was required for a *gett* to be effective.

**Gett Zikkui**—A rare "constructive" *gett* issued A *gett* issued or accepted by a *beit din* when one party is unwilling to cooperate but circumstances in the case make it meritorious for the *gett* to be effectuated because some sinful conduct will be eliminated as a result.

**Halakhah** *pl.* **Halakhot**—Jewish law.

**Haredi**—Literally, "fearful" or "God-fearing." The most conservative stream of Judaism. Its members are sometimes labeled as ultra-Orthodox.

**Hatzalah**—Literally, "rescue." The name of an Orthodox EMT squad, well known in the Orthodox community for its services.

**Hazmanah** *pl.* **Hazmanot**—A summons to appear before a *beit din*.

**Heter Iska**—A way to structure a loan as a profit sharing partnership so as to avoid transgressing Jewish laws against charging interest.

**Heter Me'ah Rabbanim**—literally, "permission from 100 rabbis." A document certifying that a large number of rabbis agree with a *beit din*'s decision to permit a man to remarry even though his wife refuses or is unable to accept a *gett*.

**Inui HaDin**—Administering Jewish law in a cruel way. An undue delay in issuing a verdict is considered a form of *innui hadin*.

***The Jewish Press***—A New York–based weekly geared to Orthodox readers.

***The Jewish Week***—Full name *The New York Jewish Week*. A weekly newspaper with a readership that includes Jews from across the spectrum from unaffiliated to Modern Orthodox, but few *Haredim*.

**Kalla** (Y)—The bride. See **Tish** for **Kalla's Tish**.

**Kashrut**—The state of being kosher.

**Ketubah** *pl.* **Ketubot**—A Jewish prenuptial agreement which stipulates the groom's obligations to the bride during the marriage and if the marriage ends by divorce or his predeceasing her.

**Ketubot, Tractate**—A tractate in the Babylonian Talmud dealing with the laws of the *Ketubah* and the duties of husbands and wives toward each other.

**Kiddushei Ketanah**—The betrothal of minor daughters.

**Kiddushin**—Literally, "the act of setting aside." The transaction of a groom betrothing his bride, most commonly effectuated under the wedding canopy when the bride accepts a ring from the groom who then utters "You are betrothed unto me with this ring according to the laws of Moses and Israel." According to *halakhah*, this transaction is a binding *kinyan*, acquisition, and from this point on the woman needs a *gett* in order to exit the relationship even though the couple has not co-habited.

**Kiddushin, Tractate**—A tractate in the Babylonian Talmud dealing with the laws of betrothal.

**Kinyan**—The act of establishing ownership of or legal title to something.

**Knesset**—The Israeli government's unicameral parliament or legislative body.

**Kohen**—A male Jew who is a descendant of the priestly caste which is traced back to the biblical Aaron, the first High Priest. A *kohen* is forbidden to marry a divorcee.

**Lubavitch**—A Chasidic sect with headquarters in Brooklyn, New York. Also known as Habad or Chabad, this movement has adherents all over the world.

**Mamzer** *pl.* **Mamzerim**—A person born from a forbidden relationship.

**Mechitzah**—Literally, "a separation or barrier." The physical barrier that separates the men's and women's sections in an Orthodox synagogue. The *mechitzah* may be made of almost any material. Rabbis differ as to how high the *mechitzah* must be to be "kosher."

**Mesadder Ha'Gett/Gittin**—One who officiates at a *gett* proceeding. Arranging a *gett* is considered to require highly specialized and expert knowledge. Not all Orthodox rabbis have the required training.

**Mesadder Kiddushin**—One who officiates at a marriage, at Orthodox weddings, almost always a rabbi.

**Mesarev**—Literally, "a refuser." One who is contempt of a *beit din*'s order/decision (*p'sak*) or subpoena (*hazmanah*) to appear before the *beit din*.

**Mi Shebeirach**—A prayer for healing and good health uttered during the Torah service.

**Midrash** *pl.* **Midrashim**—Body of homiletic stories told by rabbinic sages to explain passages in the bible.

**Mikva** (Y)—A Jewish ritual bath for purifying oneself from ritual impurity. Women must immerse in the Mikva one week after their menstrual cycle ends in order to resume sexual relations which are interrupted once menstruation begins.

**Mincha** (Y)—See *minchah*.

**Minchah**—Afternoon prayers.

**Minyan**—A quorum of ten men which Orthodox Judaism requires in order to have a full prayer service.

**Mishneh Torah**—A code of Jewish law (*halakhah*) authored by Maimonides, compiled between 1170 and 1180.

**Mitzvah**—An action mandated or forbidden by God's command. Also a moral deed or act of kindness performed as a religious duty.

**Modern Orthodox**—A stream of Orthodox Judaism which maintains that a religious observant individual can be open to and benefit from participation in the secular modern world. Modern Orthodox Jews almost all aspire to high level secular education whereas *Haredi* Jews tend to view such education as a danger to their faith and as wasting time that should be spent studying holy texts. Many *Haredim*, however, do permit higher education necessary for employment to support one's family.

**Moredet** *pl.* **Mordot**—Literally, "a rebellious woman." A woman who defies her husband, especially one who refuses to have sexual relations with her husband though she has no serious complaint against him.

**Nissuin**—Marriage, the second stage of the wedding ceremony, performed under the marriage canopy following *kiddushin* and the reading aloud of the *ketubah*.

**The Orthodox Union**—Also known as the OU; full name, Union of Orthodox Jewish Congregations of America. It is best known for its supervision of the production of kosher food. It also supports a network of synagogues, youth programs, Jewish and Religious Zionist advocacy, programs for the disabled and religious studies programs.

**Payes** (Y)—See **Payot**.

**Payot**—Sidelocks or sidecurls worn by Orthodox men in compliance with the Torah injunction against shaving the corners of one's head.

**Posek**—*Halakhic* decisor.

**P'sak**—See **P'sak Din**.

**P'sak Din** *pl.* **Piskei Din**—The verdict or ruling issued by a *beit din* or rabbi.

**P'tur**—Release; a document that confirms that a woman has received a *gett* or has been otherwise released by rabbis from her marriage and is free to remarry.

**Rabbinical Alliance**—Full name, Rabbinical Alliance of America. Hebrew, Igud HaRabonim. A rabbinical association of Orthodox rabbis, founded in 1942. It established its own *beit din* at that time. Two rabbis associated with the Igud that are mentioned in this book are the late Rabbi Samuel A. Turk and Rabbi Hershel Kurzrock.

**Rabbinical Council of America**—A membership organization for Orthodox rabbis, generally viewed as Modern Orthodox though leaning more to the right over time.

**RCA**—See **Rabbinical Council of America**.

**Rebbetzin** (Y)—A rabbi's wife.

**Refuah Shlemah**—Literally, "a full recovery from an illness." Phrase used to express the wish that an ill person be granted a full recovery.

**Rosh Beit Din**—Literally, "the 'head' of the *beit din*." The senior designated leader of a *beit din*.

**Rosh Chodesh**—Literally, "the 'head' of the month." The day marking the beginning of a new lunar month of the Jewish calendar, marked by the first day and hour that the new crescent can be observed by the naked eye.

**Rosh Yeshiva**—Literally, "the 'head' of the Yeshiva." The dean of a Talmudic academy, a rabbi known for his high level of scholarship and mastery of Jewish religious texts.

**Sanhedrin, Tractate**—A tractate in the Babylonian Talmud dealing with criminal and civil court proceedings and laws.

**Satmar**—A Chasidic sect with communities in Brooklyn and in other areas of the New York metropolitan area. The name Satmar derives from the city of Szatmarnemeti, Transylvania, where Rabbi Joel Teitelbaum founded the sect.

**Sefer**—Literally, "a book." Usually designating a volume of a religious text, such as the Talmud, a law code, or some rabbinic commentary.

**Seruv** *pl.* **Seruvim**—A contempt of court citation issued by a *beit din* when a party refuses to appear before the *beit din* or comply with an order issued by the *beit din*.

**Shabbat, Shabbes** (Y)—The Sabbath.

**Shadchan**—A matchmaker who assists in arranging marriages.

**Shaliach**—An agent who may deliver or receive a get for the parties or perform other acts for the person who conveyed agency to him.

**Shalom Bayis (Bayit)**—Literally, "peace in the home." Domestic harmony.

**Shanda** (Y)—A disgrace, scandal, shameful act or situation.

**Sheitel** (Y)—A wig worn by some Orthodox women in compliance with the Jewish law requiring married women to cover their hair because of modesty, *tsniut*.

**Shidduch**—An arranged match between Jewish singles for the purpose of marriage.

**Shomrim**—Literally, "guardians or watchers." The name taken by volunteer civilian security patrols in various Orthodox neighborhoods.

**Shtar Berurin**—A binding arbitration agreement accepting the jurisdiction of a Beit Din, signed by parties when they put a matter before a rabbinical court for adjudication.

**Shtiebel** (Y) *pl.* **Shtieblach**—Literally, "a little house or room." A place used for Jewish communal prayer, smaller and less formal than a large synagogue, often in a private home owned by a rabbi with a following that seeks out the closer contact with the rabbi and congregants available in this smaller setting.

**Shul** (Y)—Synagogue.

**Siddur** *pl.* **Siddurim**—A prayer book.

**Simchas** (Y)—Joyous celebration of events such as a wedding, birth of a baby, bar and bat mitvah.

**Sofer**—A scribe.

**Takkanah**—A *halakhic* enactment which revises or amends an ordinance that no longer satisfies the requirements of the times or circumstances.

**Ta'ut**—A mistake.

**Tefillah** *pl.* **Tefillot**—Prayer or prayer service.

**Tehillim**—Psalms, often read during times of distress or, the opposite, times of great thanksgiving.

**Tichel** (Y)—A headscarf worn by Orthodox women in compliance with the Jewish law requiring married women to cover their hair because of modesty, *tsniut*.

**Tish** (Y)—Literally, "a table." At an Orthodox wedding, the **Choson's Tish** is a male-only gathering before the marriage ceremony at which the groom, usually flanked by his father and father-in-law, accepts all the obligations outlined in the *ketubah* under the supervision of the rabbis present. Two witnesses sign the *ketubah* attesting that they witnessed the groom accepting these obligations. Aside from this legal business, the Choson's Tish is characterized by generous serving of food, levity and good wishes. The groom may attempt to deliver a learned discourse about Jewish law, but traditionally the guests interrupt him, signaling that the occasion should be light-hearted and joyous rather than serious intellectual exchange. In recent times Modern Orthodox brides have held an all female **Kalla's Tish** where the bride gathers with her mother and mother-in-law and friends for similar proceedings, with the exception that there is no *ketubah* to be signed.

**To'en** *pl.* **Toanim**—A pleader or lawyer who practices in a *beit din*.

**Tosafot**—Medieval commentaries on the Talmud.

**Tosefet Ketubah**—Literally, "an addition to the *ketubah*." A clause, added to the standard *ketubah*, in which the husband commits to higher financial obligations to the wife.

**Tsnius** (Y)—See **Tsniut**.

**Tsniut**—Jewish code of modesty regarding mode of dress, but also modesty and humility of character.

**Yeshiva University**—Modern Orthodox institution which encompasses Jewish scholarship and secular higher education. Though the university includes Stern College for Women, a medical school, a law school and graduate faculties, in the Jewish community the term Yeshiva University brings to mind the all-male undergraduate Yeshiva College and REITS rabbinical seminary and its rabbinic faculty.

**Yeshivah** *pl.* **Yeshivahs** or **Yeshivot**—Talmudic academy of higher learning. Also used to designate an Orthodox parochial elementary or high school for youngsters, sometimes gender segregated, sometimes co-ed.

**Yevamot, Tractate**—A tractate in the Babylonian Talmud dealing with levirate marriage, the mandated marriage of a childless widow to her brother-in-law.

**Yiddish**—A High German language of Ashkenazi Jews which includes words in Hebrew, Aramaic and local languages depending on the location of the Jewish community.

**Young Israel**—Full name National Council of Young Israel. An Orthodox, synagogue-based organization in the United States with a network of affiliated "Young Israel" synagogues.

**Zabla**—An acronym of *Zeh Borer Lo Echad*, literally, "each picks one for himself." An ad hoc *beit din* set up by each side in the dispute picking one judge and then these two judges agreeing on the third judge to complete the three man panel that will decide the matter.

# Pseudonyms

### *Rabbis and Batei Din*

| | | | |
|---|---|---|---|
| Beer | Fox | Nissan | Spicer |
| Bitterman | Goldman | Ploni | Volin |
| Chippes | Hamber | Roth | Wasserman |
| Daitch | Kaplan | Shalosh | Weinstein |
| Eisen, Shloimy | Leventhal | Shvach | Wolff |

Chasidei Morozov Beit Din

| *Agunot* | *Husband* | *Agunot* | *Husband* | *Agunot* | *Husband* |
|---|---|---|---|---|---|
| Deborah | Rabbi Wax | Lena | Rafi | Ruth | Dovid |
| Dina | Judah | Linda | | Sarah | Tulie |
| Esther | | Melanie | | Sharon | Ira |
| Eva | Aaron | Michal | | Shulie | Meir |
| Fay | | Miriam | | Tirza | Asher |
| Frayda | | Molly | Yoram | Tova | |
| Ilana | | Naomi | | | Barry |
| Joan | | Nechama | | | |
| Kayla | | Rita | | | |
| Leah | Moti | Roberta | | | |

### *Other Characters*

| | | |
|---|---|---|
| Faigie | Kablanoff | Rebbetzin Schlissel |
| Gail | Leon | Rebbetzin Shvach |
| Izzy | Rebbetzin Fox | Wax, Mendy |

# Bibliography

## English Language Sources

Antelman, Moshe Shlomo. *The Great Aguna Debate*. Providence, RI: Zahavia, 1997.
Aranoff, Susan. "AGUNAH Inc. Replies to the Beth Din of America." Unpublished, undated.
———. "Principles and Procedures for Freeing Agunot." www.agunahinternational.com.
———. "Two Views of Marriage—Two Views of Women: Reconsidering *Tav Lemetav Tandu Milemetav Armelu*." *Nashim: A Journal of Jewish Women's Studies and Gender Issues* No. 3 (Spring/Summer 5760/2000): 199–227.
———, Michael Broyde, Aviad Hacohen, Daniel Sperber, Haim Toledano, and Susan Weiss. "Continued Discussion of *Agunah, Kiddushei Ta'ut* and *Tears of the Oppressed*." *The Edah Journal* Volume 5:1 (2005-Tammuz 5765).
Broyde, Michael. "Review Essay of *The Tears of the Oppressed*." *The Edah Journal* Vol. 4:2 (Kislev 5765).
Falk, Z.W. *Jewish Matrimonial Law*. Oxford: Clarendon Press, 1966.
Hacohen, Aviad. *The Tears of the Oppressed*. Jersey City, NJ: Ktav Publishing House, 2004.
Hauptman, Judith. *Rereading the Rabbis: A Woman's Voice*. Boulder, CO: Westview Press, 1998.
Haut, Irwin. *Divorce in Jewish Law and Life*. New York: Sefer Hermon, 1983.
Haut, Rivka, and Susan Aranoff. "Religious Courts Are Treating Agunot Unfairly." *The New York Jewish Week* October 25, 2011.
Herring, Basil, and Kenneth Auman, eds. *The Prenuptial Agreement*. Northvale, NJ, and London: Jason Aronson, 1996.
Jackson, Bernard. *Agunah: The Manchester Analysis (Agunah Research Unit)*. Liverpool: Deborah Charles Publications, 2011.
Riskin, Shlomo. *Women and Jewish Divorce*. Hoboken, NJ: Ktav Publishing House. 1989.
Weiss, Susan M. "Four Methods of Civil Response to Get Recalcitrance." Unpublished.
———. "Sign at Your Own Risk: The 'RCA' Prenuptial May Prejudice the Fairness of Your Future Divorce." *Yeshiva University Cardozo Women's Law Journal* (1999).
———, and Netty C. Gross-Horowitz. *Marriage and Divorce in the Jewish State Israel's Civil War*. Waltham, MA: Brandeis University Press, 2013.

Willig, Mordechai. "The Prenuptial Agreement: Recent Developments." *The Journal of the Beth Din of America*. Vol. I No. I (Spring 2012): 12–16.

## Hebrew Language Sources

Berkovits, E. *T'nai B'Nissuin Uv'Gett*. Jerusalem: Mossad HaRav Kook, 1967.

Feinstein, Moshe. *Sefer Igrot Moshe—Even Ha'Ezer Chelek Aleph*. New York: Noble Book Press, 1961.

Freiman, A. H. *Seder Kiddushin V'Nissuin*. Jerusalem: Mossad Harav Kook, 1945.

Rambam (Moses Maimonides). *Mishneh Torah, Hilchot Ishut*. Jerusalem: Wagshul, 1981–1982 (5742).

Rashba (Shlomo ben Aderet). *Chidushei Harashba Gittin*. Jerusalem: Mossad Harav Kook, 1998–1999 (5759).

Spektor, Yitzchak Elchanan. *Ein Yitzchak Chelek Aleph*. Vilnius: 1889.

Susskind Goldberg, Monique, and Diana Villa. *Za'akat Dalot Halakhic Solutions for the Agunot of Our Times*. Jerusalem: The Schechter Institute of Jewish Studies, 2006.

# Index

Agudas Harabonim 40
Agudath Israel of America (Aguda) 94, 100, 138, 162, 208, 210
Alt, Rabbi Reuven 40, 45–49
Alter, Susan 17–21, 26, 32
Amit Women's Organization 126, 129
Antelman, Rabbi Moshe (Marvin) 123–125, 128, 130, 143, 211, 219, 223
Archbishop of Canterbury 11
*arkaot* 75
Auerbach, Rabbi Baruch 140–141
Auerbach, Rabbi Zalman 140–144
Auman, Rabbi Kenneth 138, 181
Avitzur 176–178
*Avot D'Rabbi Natan* 134

*Badecken* 10
Bais Yosef Beit Din 40, 46–48
Bar Ilan University 195, 204–205, 215
Becher, Mina 168–169
Becher, Yehuda 168–169
Beit Din Kollel Harabonim of Monsey 40, 43, 121
Bernstein, Rabbi Louis 128–130, 219
Beth Din of America (BDA) 40–42, 46, 50–51, 56–58, 63–64, 94, 142, 170–172, 180–184, 186–192, 208, 214–216
Bleich, Rabbi J.D. 139, 167–168
*borer* (*borerim*) 22–24, 81, 85, 91
Borough Park 17–18, 40, 46, 72–73, 98, 103, 112, 135
Broyde, Rabbi Michael 192, 208, 214–215
Buchanan, Pat 105

Cohen, Deborah Nussbaum 141
Cohen, Rabbi Eugene P. 211, 216, 219
Cohen, Rabbi She'aryashuv 198
COLPA 121, 138–139, 220
Cooperman, Rabbi Elimelech 141

*dayyan* (*dayyanim*) 19, 44, 53, 95, 120, 140, 143, 185–186
*din torah* 44–46, 60, 82, 85, 185
*dinei mamonos* 96

Eiferman, Deborah 122
Eisen, Shloimy 21, 22, 24–25, 28–30, 37, 152, 200, 232
Epstein, Rabbi Mendel 73, 175, 221
Epstein, Tamar 51, 72
*erusin* 55
Ezras Torah 102–103, 157

Feinstein, Rabbi Moshe 50, 58, 129, 195, 201–202
Freilich, Estelle 188, 204, 211, 222

Get Free Organization 71–72, 105, 128
GET Organization 13, 18–19, 30, 33, 122, 128, 163–164, 203
*gett al yedei zikkui* 51, 123–124, 128, 205, 211, 223
*gett* laws 169–170; New York State 42, 66, 120, 126–127, 129, 139, 161–170, 179, 207, 219–220
*gett zikkui* see *gett al yedei zikkui*
Goldberg, Rabbi Zalman Nechemiah 140, 141, 217
Goldstein, Gita 140, 141

# Index

Goldstein, Henni 204, 223
Goldstein, Israel 134–136, 138–140, 143–144
Green, Rabbi Sidney 211, 219

Hacohen, Aviad 2, 215
*halakhah* 2, 5, 7, 9, 10–11, 15, 18, 19, 24, 27–28, 49–51, 54, 57, 63, 65, 70, 73, 77, 81–83, 85, 91, 94–95, 98, 109–110, 116, 121–125, 127–128, 131–132, 134–144, 147, 149, 156, 163, 165, 167–171, 173, 175–177, 180, 188, 191–192, 194–197, 200–203, 205–206, 208–215, 219, 221–222
Haut, Rabbi Irwin 2, 18–19, 117, 195, 197, 199, 219
*hazmanah* 22, 29, 43–44, 46–47
Herbst, Rabbi Solomon 40–43, 138
*heter me'ah rabbanim* 43, 147, 149–150, 173, 218

*innui hadin* 154
*irur* 45, 47

Jackson, Prof. Bernard 215
Jewish Orthodox Feminist Alliance (JOFA) 176, 192, 197, 206–207, 214–216
*The Jewish Press* 63, 73, 125, 140–143, 165–167, 195, 219
*The Jewish Week* 188, 208, 210–211, 215, 220
Joseph, Norma 121

*ketubah* 24, 49, 52–60, 62–70, 90, 148, 174, 176, 184
Ketubot, Mishnah 52, 53
Ketubot, Tractate 52, 54
*kiddushei ketanah* 131–132, 134–135, 137–144, 199
*kiddushin* 143
Kiddushin, Tractate 133–134, 142
Klass, Rabbi Sholom 142, 165, 195, 197, 219
*kofin* 42, 174
*kohen* 62, 143, 202
Krauss, Rabbi Chaim 40–41, 43
Krauss, Rabbi Simcha 51, 128–130, 217, 219, 223

Lagnado, Lucette 34
Lakewood 102–103
Landesman, Rabbi L. 40, 43–45, 47, 120
Levin, Yehuda 71–72, 105, 125
Lewin, Nathan 169
Lieberman, Rabbi Shaul 176–177, 180

Light, Rachel 189–190
Lopatin, Rabbi Asher 216

Maimonides 49, 174–175
Malinowitz, Rabbi Chaim 40, 43, 127, 138, 143–144
*mamzer* (*mamzerim*) 9, 39, 128, 173, 208
*mamzerut* see *mamzer*
Mauer, Naomi 165, 219
*mechitzah* 34
*mesarev* 31, 157
*mesarev l'din* see *mesarev*
*minchah* 33–34, 85–86, 157–159
*minyan* 35, 157
Mishnah 52, 53, 133
*mitzvah* 13, 68, 89, 124
Monsey, New York 6, 40, 43–48, 111, 114–115, 117, 120, 127, 138, 143
*moredet* 24
Morgenstern, Rabbi Moshe 195–208, 210–211, 216, 219, 223
Murciano, Rabbi Asher 211, 216, 219

*nissuin* 55

Ontario 11, 170
ORA 191

pedophilia 1, 10, 12, 49, 50, 76–77, 218
*posek* 143
prenuptial agreements 1, 41, 52, 63, 90, 120, 124, 156, 160, 172–192, 207, 218, 222
"Principles and Procedures" ("Principles") 208–210, 215
*p'sak* 24–26, 47, 82–89, 118, 196
*p'tur* 62, 65, 154, 196, 202, 209, 213, 216

Rabbenu Gershom 123, 147
Rabbenu Tam 49, 175
Rabbinical Alliance 143
Rabbinical Council of America (RCA) 40, 41, 42, 43, 46, 48, 56, 57, 63, 94, 120, 128, 137, 142, 172, 173, 176, 177, 178, 180, 181, 182, 183, 184, 187, 188, 191, 192, 203
Rackman, Rabbi Emanuel 51, 122–123, 128, 176, 195, 197–201, 203–204, 206–208, 210–216, 219, 222–223
Rackman, Honey 112, 122, 137, 195, 206, 211, 223
Rackman Beit Din 51, 194, 196, 203–204, 207–208, 210–211, 214–217, 222–223
Ralbag, Rabbi Aryeh 40–41, 43, 48

Rapps, Dennis 121, 169
Rigler, William (New York State Supreme Court judge) 166, 168–169, 220
Riskin, Rabbi Shlomo 2, 176, 206–207
Rominek, Rabbi Eliyahu 140–141
Rubin, Avraham 2, 72–73

Sanhedrin (Tractate) 5, 22, 134
*Sanhedrin Ketanah* 143
Schwartz, Daniel 196
Schwartz, Rabbi Gedalia Dov 51, 58, 137, 142, 219, 222, 223
*seruv* 29–33, 35–37, 39–49, 84–85, 87, 90–91, 123–124, 143, 157, 158, 160
Shalom Bayis Organization 137–138
*sharia* 11, 162, 169–170
Shereshevsky, Yossi 2, 135–136, 138, 140–141, 143–144
Shloimy *see* Eisen, Shloimy
Shomrim 112
*shtar berurin* 23, 25–26, 44, 46, 81–83
Silver, Assemblyman Sheldon 138–139, 162
Sladowsky, Rabbi 121–122, 125, 219
Sodom 5, 224
*sofer* 44, 56, 59, 60–61, 64–65, 68, 149–151, 154–155
Sternbuch, Rabbi Moshe 140–141

*takkanah* 117
Talmud 3, 5, 13, 22, 49, 52–56, 58, 60, 70, 107, 123–124, 131–133, 173–174, 176, 205–206
Taussig, Rabbi Yossef 134
*ta'ut* 50–51, 196, 201, 206, 209, 213–214
Tendler, Rabbi Mordechai 50, 201–203
*Teshuvah* 140–141, 143, 183, 196, 198, 211
*to'en* 43, 47
Toledano, Rabbi Haim Henry 211, 213, 215–216, 219
*Tosafot* 133, 142
*tosefet ketubah* 90
Turk, Rabbi Samuel 122–123, 125

Weiss, Rabbi Abner 172, 177–180
Weiss, Rabbi Avi 176
Weiss, Dr. Susan 1, 192, 215
Weissmann, Rabbi Shlomo 64–66, 183, 189–191
Willig, Rabbi Mordechai 171–173, 180–181, 188, 208

*Yevamot* 133

*zabla* 22, 28, 44, 47, 79, 80–82, 145–146, 220
Zitrenbaum, Blima 2, 6, 11, 112–114, 116–117, 221
Zitrenbaum, Joseph 2, 6, 11, 112–114, 116–117, 221
Zweibel, Rabbi David 96, 138, 142, 210

www.ingramcontent.com/pod-product-compliance
Ingram Content Group UK Ltd.
Pitfield, Milton Keynes, MK11 3LW, UK
UKHW041941140426
5217IPUK00014B/605